PURITANISM AND THE WILDERNESS

PURITANISM AND THE WILDERNESS

The Intellectual Significance of
the New England Frontier
1629-1700

by
PETER N. CARROLL

NEW YORK & LONDON
COLUMBIA UNIVERSITY PRESS
1969

TO AMY

Preface

SINCE 1893, when Frederick Jackson Turner presented his frontier hypothesis, American historians have pondered the relationship between the wilderness and the American mind. Despite this widespread interest in frontier history, there have been few studies of the impact of the forest upon the first American colonists. The otherwise comprehensive analyses of the seventeenth-century mind by such intellectual historians as Perry Miller have dealt only tangentially with this problem. This void in historical scholarship is particularly surprising since throughout the seventeenth century the colonial settlements, regardless of geographical position, were largely wilderness communities. During this period, the differences between costal and interior towns were less significant than the essential similarities in their relation to their natural environment. The main thrust of this study, therefore, is to examine the role of the wilderness in the thought of one group of colonists, the settlers of New England. It will analyze both the Puritan attitude toward the forest and the influence of the wilderness upon Puritan social thought.

The nature of the topic enjoins the intellectual historian to remain methodologically flexible. Ideas do not exist in a vacuum, but are closely intertwined with social, economic, and political currents. At times, ideas generate actions, while at other times intellectual processes seem to rationalize behavior. This study attempts to analyze the complex interactions between Puritan ideas and the wilderness environment. Moreover, ideas shared by the members of a community are often reflected in the overt statements of a few leaders. For the seventeenth century, a paucity of sources complicates this problem. In this work, an attempt has been made to balance the ideas of the intellectual elites with those of lower status. Hopefully this approach will improve the scholarly comprehension of the age as a whole.

In reproducing seventeenth-century writings, the original orthography, with a few exceptions, has been followed. All abbreviations have been expanded and superscriptures have been eliminated. Where relevant, "i" has been substituted for "j," "u" for "v," "v" for "u," and "c" for "t." Since italicized words often followed convention, only those which add meaning to quotations have been retained; unless otherwise noted, all italicized words appear in the original sources. All dates refer to the seventeenth-century calendar (Old Style) in which March 26 constituted the first day of the year. For purposes of clarity, however, dates falling between January 1 and March 25 are considered part of the new year.

To the many people who assisted me in the preparation of this book, I wish to express my thanks. Let me begin by praising my wife, Amy, for the disarming sensibleness of her suggestions throughout the difficult period of writing and rewriting.

The staffs of the American Antiquarian Society, Boston Public Library, Houghton Library, Massachusetts Historical Society, Newberry Library, New York Public Library, and Northwestern University Library frequently went out of their way to help me in my research. I owe special appreciation to Majorie Carpenter of the Deering

Library at Northwestern, Winifred Collins and Malcolm Freiberg of the Massachusetts Historical Society, and Arthur Breton of the New-York Historical Society for a variety of favors.

Michael C. Batinski, George H. Daniels, and Kenneth Lockridge read various versions of the manuscript and provided numerous suggestions for its improvement. I am particularly indebted to Clarence Ver Steeg for his early and firm support of this project and for his continued encouragement during its execution. In the later stages, Bernard Gronert and Frederick Nicklaus of the Columbia University Press offered invaluable assistance, for which I am grateful.

Peter N. Carroll
Evanston, Illinois
February 23, 1969

Contents

Introduction

STUDIES of Puritan intellectual history traditionally stress the Old World origins of the New England mind. The writings of Samuel Eliot Morison, Perry Miller, and Edmund S. Morgan, to name the most influential historians of Puritanism, attest to the fecundity of this approach. As a transplanted culture, seventeenth-century New England provides a valuable and convenient example of the tenacity of a priori concepts. Religion, the benchmark of all seventeenth-century thought, obviously was transported to the New World in the minds of the first New England colonists. Moreover, the cluster of ideas which surrounded Puritan religion—the notion of the organic state, the belief in the just price, the mission to establish a city on a hill—also reflects the European basis of New England's intellectual apparatus.

But in describing the geography of the Puritan mind, these studies tend to minimize, if not neglect, the importance of the New World in restructuring and redefining Puritan ideas. Placed in a radically new environment—the raw American wilderness—Old World attitudes and concepts were forced to prove themselves anew. The novelty of the American situation impinged, at times subtly, at times brutally, at times to no apparent effect, upon the founders of New England. This dialogue between the European mind and the American environment can be analyzed in the context of Puritan attitudes and responses to the wilderness. By using the wilderness as a focal point, it is possible to assess the relative importance of the virgin forest as a conditioner of Old World thought in America.

The Puritans had developed specific views of the wilderness situation prior to their migration to Massachusetts Bay. Derived largely from Biblical metaphors, these concepts provided New Englanders with elaborate rhetorical devices with which they could judge their own experiences. Disregarding inherent contradictions, the colonists identified the New England forest with the Biblical wilderness and employed traditional Christian language to articulate their life in America. The notion of the wilderness as a refuge from worldly corruption, for example, moved the settlers of New England to stress the advantages of sanctuary in justifying their departure from the degeneracy of England. In other contexts, the Puritans interpreted the wilderness as the place of religious insight, and therefore could challenge ecclesiastical deviation both in America and in Europe. Furthermore, as the children of Israel, they translated their hardships in the New World as God's testing of his chosen people—a necessary prelude to everlasting salvation. The continued use of these metaphors illustrates the Puritans' remarkable ability to apply preconceived ideas to the experientially different world of New England.

These continuities, however, comprise only one aspect (though indeed an important one) of the Puritans' view of the New World. While the colonists interpreted the American wilderness with traditional metaphors, in effect, the physical realities of the New World challenged the symbolic wilderness of the Bible. The modifications wrought by this interaction can be examined in the realm of Puritan social theory.

Within the matrix of Puritan social thought lay two logically antithetical versions of the mission to New England. First, the founders of Massachusetts Bay intended to erect a city on a hill, a unified, organic society bound internally by Christian love. Modelled, in theory, on the medieval town, such a city would enclose the entire population within the confines of strong walls. In insisting upon social cohesion, the leaders of New England expected the commonwealth to function without reference to the areas outside the community.

Beneath the ideal of a collective society, however, lay the seeds of its destruction, the paradoxical element within Puritan social theory. In defending their migration to the New World, the colonists emphasized the importance of settling uncultivated areas. According to Genesis, they argued, the Lord had commanded the sons of Adam to subdue the earth and, they concluded with self-assurance, God undoubtedly had included the American continent in this commission. The Puritans' endorsement of the subjugation of wild lands, however, provided enterprising settlers with an effective rationalization for expanding beyond the organic community intended by the founding fathers. In time, the colonists celebrated the process of transforming the wilderness despite the evident dangers to the collective society. The resulting tension emerged to govern the Puritans' comprehension of the wilderness condition.

Throughout the seventeenth century, neither idea established hegemony over the other. Instead, both versions of the wilderness community—the cohesive and the expansive—flourished simultaneously. Despite the obvious contradictions, Puritan leaders praised both virtues and argued for both causes. While they blessed the subjugation of the forest because it fulfilled a divine commandment, the ministers urged the settlers to resist the forces of frontier expansion. This failure to resolve the paradox between cohesion and dispersal resulted in an abdication of social leadership. As the colonial authorities wavered within the balance, New England society lacked a clearly defined direction in adjusting to the wilderness in the seventeenth century. In the area of social theory, therefore, traditional solutions proved unworkable in the American environment.

The Puritans' inability to produce a suitable theory of society during the seventeenth century reveals the importance of the wilderness in the development of New England thought. Although traditional metaphors and symbols facilitated the process of adaptation in the early years of settlement, such language failed to satisfy the needs of a new society in America. By raising questions and posing challenges, the wilderness forced the Puritans to come to grips with their unique environment and altered considerably their understanding of the wilderness condition and the nature of a colonial society.

PART I

TWO WORLDS

IN March 1629, Charles I abruptly dismissed a rancorous
Parliament and embarked on an era of personal rule. For
Puritans throughout England, the royal decision signaled the
defeat of the forces of reformation. Nervous about the future
of their country, many of these disenchanted men now began
to consider the possibility of departing from their native land
to erect a godly commonwealth in America. As they projected
their hopes to the lands beyond the Atlantic Ocean, the vision
of the New World captivated their imaginations and excited
their minds. Influenced by promotional literature and inner
expectations rather than by concrete experience, the Puritan
colonizers articulated their notions of America in ambiguous
language. The wilderness continent meant different things to
different people, and Puritan views of America ranged from
a paradise to a wasteland.

Separating the vision from the reality lay the Atlantic Ocean.
This vast sea played a dual role in the formation of New
England society. It led the colonists into new realms of experience and, at the same time, sealed them off from the familiar world of the English countryside. Thus as a channel
and as a barrier the Atlantic influenced the colonial mind from
the beginning of settlement and figured prominently in the
Puritans' quest for identity in New England.

The European vision of America, nevertheless, provided
limited preparation for the initial contacts with the virgin
continent. When confronted by the wilderness, the Puritans'
ambiguous notions of the New World produced contradictory

responses. Those who expected a veritable Eden lamented the absence of milk and honey in Massachusetts; others who anticipated barren soil lauded the ability of the land to sustain agricultural undertakings. Moreover, a lack of understanding of New England geography resulted in disproportionate statements about the American situation. Only after continued contact with the wilderness did the colonists restrain their tendency to generalize from singular experiences.

Although the wilderness environment often repudiated the Old World image of America, the varied responses among Puritans to the wilderness reveals the importance of understanding the European mind as an antecedent of New England thought. The differences between Puritan views of the wilderness in England and in America illuminates both the continuities of Old World thought and the modifications wrought by the New World within the minds of the settlers of Massachusetts Bay. As they assessed the lands of New England, the Puritan colonists relied upon traditional images as well as their experiences in the wilderness.

CHAPTER I

"The Good Land"

TWO generations after the settlement of New England, Puritan historians extolled the courage of their patriarchs, the men who first established beachheads upon the virgin continent. William Hubbard, whose *General History of New England* won the endorsement of the Massachusetts General Court in 1682, recounted the single-minded commitment of John Winthrop, "that honorable and worthy gentleman," who guided the Great Migration of 1630. At "a solemn feast" shortly before his last farewell, Governor Winthrop, "finding his bowels yearn within him," broke into "a flood of tears" which "set them all a weeping." But despite the distress at losing dear friends forever, this passionate outburst failed to dampen their spirits "as to think of breaking off their purpose so far carried on."[1] Cotton Mather, writing nearly three decades after Hubbard, was similarly struck by the resolution of the founding fathers. It was, he felt, "a strange work of God" which inspired diverse men "to secede into a wilder-

[1] William Hubbard, "A General History of New-England from the Discovery to 1680," reprinted in *Collections of the Massachusetts Historical Society*, second ser., V–VI (1848), V, 125. (Hereafter cited as *Colls. M.H.S.*); *Records of the Governor and Company of the Massachusetts Bay in New England*, ed. by Nathaniel B. Shurtleff, 5 vols. (Boston, 1853–54), V, 378. (Hereafter cited as *Recs. of Mass. Bay*.)

ness, they knew not where, and suffer in that wilderness, they knew not what." [2]

The Puritans, despite this ignorance of their destination, were strikingly confident about their adventure. Assured that they were transporting the Protestant Reformation to a new citadel in America, they projected their optimism onto the unknown soil of New England. Although a paucity of sources compels the contemporary historian to rely for analysis upon the expectations of a few influential men, it is nevertheless apparent that most of the passengers who crowded aboard the ships bound for Massachusetts agreed with John Winthrop that America was "the good land." [3] To be sure, this statement meant different things to different people. Conditioned by Biblical metaphors and promotional literature, the Puritans viewed the wilderness from a variety of perspectives. For some, New England signified the New Canaan; others anticipated a barren wasteland; some regarded America as a land of spiritual darkness; and an important segment of the ministry lauded the New World as a refuge. But regardless of these paradoxical assessments, a sense of self-assurance pervaded the entire mission.

Probably the most influential theme in bulwarking Puritan optimism on the eve of migration was the idea of New England as the promised land. John Cotton, then minister

[2] Cotton Mather, *Magnalia Christi Americana; Or, The Ecclesiastical History of New-England,* 2 vols. (Hartford, 1855), I, 240 (first published in 1702).

[3] John Winthrop, "A Modell of Christian Charity," *Colls.* M.H.S., third ser., VII (1838), 48. It is possible to deduce the optimism about America among the rank-and-file migrants from their initial antipathy to the American forest. For a fuller discussion of the widespread disappointment among the settlers upon their first contact with the wilderness, see Chapter III.

[4] For a summary of the various Christian ideas about the Wilderness, see George Hunston Williams, *Wilderness and Paradise in Christian Thought* (New York, 1962).

of the Boston congregation in Lincolnshire, journeyed to Southampton to bid farewell to the Winthrop fleet and preached on the text, "Moreover I will appoint a place for my people Israell, and I will plant them, that they may dwell in a place of their owne, and move no more." [5] He assured the departing colonizers that God selects a specific country in which to plant His people. They shall have "firme and durable possession" there, and the Lord will not uproot them if they continue to propagate their religion.[6] In a similar tone, John Winthrop parried the words of the less optimistic. In answer to the objection that "many speak ill of this Countrye [New England], of the barrennesse etc. of it," Winthrop retorted, "so did the Spyes of the lande of Canaan." [7]

The origin of the paradisaical motif lay not only in Biblical exegesis, but also in the promotional tracts designed to attract settlers to New England. While similar advertisements attempted to promote other colonial endeavors during the seventeenth century, these writings excited the imagination of the Puritan colonizers.[8] In depicting the New World as the terrestrial paradise, this literature portrayed New England in iridescent colors and acclaimed the lusciousness of the land.

John Smith wrote one of the earliest of these brochures in 1616 in which he praised the fecundity of the American soil and its capacity to produce "any grain, fruits or seeds you will sow or plant." He favorably compared the soil with that of England and assured readers that "all good

[5] II Samuel 7:10. Biblical citations throughout this study refer to the King James version.

[6] John Cotton, "Gods Promise to His Plantation," in *Old South Leaflets*, III (Boston, n.d.), 4–5, 14.

[7] "General Conclusions and Particular Considerations: Early Draft" [1629], *Winthrop Papers*, 5 vols. (Boston, 1929–), II, 127.

[8] For a discussion of some of these non-Puritan promotionalists, see Robert Ralston Cawley, *The Voyagers and Elizabethan Drama* (Boston, 1938), pp. 290–91.

provisions for man's sustenance may with . . . facility be had, by a little extraordinary labor." And although Smith was sufficiently realistic to state that the plenty of New England was seasonable, he nevertheless added, "worthy is that person to starve that here cannot live, if he have sense, strength and health." The natural blessings of America, he continued, are so plentiful "that a hundred men may, in one hour or two, make their provisions for a day." John White, whose promotional undertakings were published shortly after the embarkation of the 1630 expedition, also stressed the beneficence of the American forest. Using an economic argument in favor of the colonization of New England, White described the natural abundance and variety of fish and furs, timber and vines. He also praised the salubriousness of the climate there ("No Countrey yeelds a more propitious ayre for our temper, then New-England. . . .") and suggested the availability of plenty. White brushed aside all testimony to the contrary and concluded that the soil could produce sufficient quantities of food.[9] Even more immediate than these pamphlets in bolstering the spirits of the Winthrop group were the optimistic letters sent back to England by Francis Higginson of Salem who arrived in New England in 1629. These reports, which circulated among the Puritan colonizers, extolled the beauty and plenty of New England.[10]

Although the Puritans were usually confident about the physical attributes of New England, they had serious

[9] John Smith, "A Description of New England . . ." [1616], reprinted in *Colls. M.H.S.*, third ser., VI, 112, 115–16, 121; John White, "The Planter's Plea or the grounds of plantations examined and usuall objections answered" [1630], reprinted in *Proceedings of the Massachusetts Historical Society*, LXII (1929), 384–85, 386, 388–89. (Hereafter cited as *Proc. M.H.S.*)

[10] John Winthrop to His Wife, October 9, 1629, Margaret Winthrop to Her Husband [October 13, 1629], *Winthrop Papers*, II, 157–58. For a fuller discussion of the promotional missives sent to England by the advance-guard colonists, see Chapter III.

doubts about its spiritual state. For beneath the florid plenty of the New World, the Puritan settlers saw the Devil lurking in the wilderness. In an age dominated by theological presuppositions, it was evident to them that America lacked all the blessings of Christianity. To many, the savage state of the wilderness signified Satanic power; they were convinced that America, the land of spiritual darkness, was the realm of the Antichrist. The inhabitants of that world, the Indians, were believed to be trapped in "the snare of the Divell." John White considered these people to be "men transformed into beasts," the very "bond-slaves of Sathan." [11] Because the importation of true religion into this doctrinally barren ground would threaten the Devil's kingdom, the Puritans were prepared to meet with strong Satanic opposition in America. The Devil, they felt, would muster all his power to prevent the incursion of Christianity into the wilderness. Satan would rely upon the reprobates of the world—the English episcopacy as well as the Indian—as instruments of his malice. Thus Francis Higginson urged the settlers to come quickly before Satanic efforts effectively delayed the migration by prohibiting egress from England.[12]

Instead of making the Puritans wary of entering the New World, these religious assumptions merely strengthened their desire to erect the true church in the wilderness. New England, wrote John White, "is destitute of all helpes, and meanes, by which the people might come out of the snare of Satan." This situation then led him to extol the historical transit of religion from east to west. And John Winthrop observed that the settlement of New England would be "a

[11] "Sir John Eliot's Copy of the New England Tracts" [1629], *Winthrop Papers*, II, 145; White, "Planter's Plea," 394–95.
[12] Francis Higginson, "Some brief Collections out of a letter that Mr. Higginson sent to . . . Leicester" [1629], reprinted in Alexander Young, comp., *Chronicles of the First Planters of the Colony of Massachusetts Bay* (Boston, 1846), p. 260. For a more complete discussion of the Puritans' attitude toward Satanic opposition, see Chapter IV.

service to the church of great consequens by carringe the gospell into those parts to raise a bulworke against the kingdom of antichrist." [13] Nearly every defender of colonization in the seventeenth century proclaimed the advantages of exporting Christianity to America. Regardless of doctrinal variations, such appeals reflected and highlighted the theological premises of contemporaneous society, the need to interpret all behavior in religious terms. For the Puritans, the logic of this position became a prime justification for the establishment of a colony in New England.[14]

The planting of religion in Massachusetts, however, meant more than simply importing good Christians into the wilderness; it also denoted the desire to convert the Indians from their sinful state. To be sure, other exponents of colonization frequently employed similar rhetoric to justify their settlements.[15] But there is no reason to doubt the sincerity of the promoters of New England. Recent scholarship confirms the idea that the Puritans did not regard the Indians as a race apart, but merely as man in the state of sin.[16] That was, nevertheless, an unenviable situation, and the Puritans articulated a desire to alter the spiritual orientation of the natives. Over a year before the sailing of the Winthrop fleet, Mathew Cradock, then Governor

[13] White, "Planter's Plea," 388, 377; "General Observations for the Plantation of New England" [1629], *Winthrop Papers*, II, 111.

[14] Several historians have noted that the seventeenth-century promotionalists stressed the need to advance the cause of Christianity through colonization; see, for example, Louis B. Wright, *Religion and Empire: The Alliance between Piety and Commerce in English Expansion, 1558–1625* (Chapel Hill, 1943), p. 155 and Cawley, *The Voyagers*, pp. 299–300. J. H. Parry, in *The Age of Reconnaissance* (New York, 1963), p. 232, writes, "Every colonizing company in every European country . . . claimed the spreading of the Gospel among its leading motives."

[15] See, Wright, *Religion and Empire*, pp. 5–6 and Perry Miller, "Religion and Society in the Early Literature of Virginia," *Errand Into the Wilderness* (Cambridge, [Mass.], 1956), p. 101.

[16] For the best examination of the Puritan idea of the Indian, see Alden T. Vaughan, *New England Frontier: Puritans and Indians, 1620–1675* (Boston, 1965)

of the New England Company, expressed sorrow at the low level of spiritual development among the Indians and urged the people of New England to strengthen their efforts "to bringe [the natives] out of that woeful state and condition they now are in." John White similarly exhorted the colonists to treat the Indians mercifully and supported the erection of churches among them. Although the natives appeared to be in the clutches of Satan and "live without God in this present world," their situation was not necessarily permanent, for the Puritans could raise them "unto a forme of Piety and godlinesse." John Cotton's valedictory address at Southampton also reflected this concern for the Indians' salvation and advocated the conversion of the heathen.[17]

Besides the absence of appropriate religious institutions, the American wilderness also lacked the garments of civilization. Many Puritans viewed "the good land" simply as vacant soil. This idea was reinforced by the knowledge of the plague which decimated the Indian population in New England shortly before the arrival of the Pilgrims in 1620. The sparsity of Indian inhabitants in Massachusetts not only enabled the Puritans to justify the settlement of that area, but also provided them with a rationalization for claiming title to the surrounding lands. John Cotton interpreted the Indian epidemic as a sign from God that He would have the English settle there. When the Lord chooses to transplant His people, preached Cotton, "hee makes a Countrey though not altogether void of inhabitants, yet voyd in that place where they reside." John White endorsed this view and added that men have "a cleare and sufficient warrant from the mouth of God" for "replenish-

---

[17] Mathew Cradock to John Endecott [?], February 16, 1628/29, *Recs. of Mass. Bay*, I, 384; White, "Planter's Plea," 394–95, 376; Cotton, "Gods Promise," 14–15.

ing wast and voyd Countries." [18] Thus the idea of America as a wasteland did little to diminish the Puritans' optimistic attitude toward the wilderness.

The belief that America was vacant soil also served as a convenient justification for the Puritans' claim to the Indian lands. John Cotton argued that "hee that taketh possession" of vacant lands, "and bestoweth culture and husbandry upon it," has an unimpeachable claim to that land. John Winthrop bolstered this position by citing *Genesis* 1:28 wherein the Lord gave man a general commission to "encrease and multiply and replenish the earth and subdue it." This is especially true, he added, since England is overpopulated and abundant land "lyes waste" elsewhere. Supporting these colonizing endeavors, John White appealed to God's command that men replenish and subdue the earth. This task, he maintained, binds Adam's posterity "as long as the earth yeelds empty places to be replenished." Moreover, he concluded, as a result of the Indian epidemic in New England, "there is no person left to lay claime to the soyle which they possessed." Winthrop also argued that the Indians' claim to the American wastes was extremely tenuous because "they inclose noe Land, neither have [they] any setled habytation, nor any tame Cattle to improve the Land by." The natives, he maintained, "ramble over much land without title or property." And if "the whole earthe is the Lordes garden," he asked, why should we contend for living space while other places equally "fruitfull and convenient for the use of man . . . lye waste without any improvement"? [19]

The idea of the wilderness as a wasteland which had to be cultivated and improved led logically to the notion that

[18] Cotton, "Gods Promise," 5–6; White, "Planter's Plea," 376.

[19] Cotton, "Gods Promise," 6; John Winthrop to—[1629], *Winthrop Papers*, II, 123; White, "Planter's Plea," 376, 371–72, 385–86; "Reasons To Be Considered, And Objections With Answers" [1629], *Winthrop Papers*, II, 140–41; "General Observations," 113, 115.

America, if not the New Eden, was, at least, a potential paradise. Such a view of the wilderness was the most realistic, because it implicitly anticipated a struggle in transforming the waste places into habitable grounds. In reply to the objection that New England would offer a lean subsistence, Winthrop insisted that "whatsoever we stand in need of is treasured up in the earthe by the Creator, and is to be fetched thence by the sweatt of our browes." Another version of the belief that the wilderness, if not a land of plenty, at least possessed the potentiality of abundance can be seen in proposals to exploit what natural wealth existed in New England. Among these possibilities were the husbandry of livestock, fishing, fur trading, salt manufacture, and vine planting. The implementation of such a program, it would seem, was to be no easy task. John White, in a rare moment of moderation, confessed that "there is nothing to bee expected in New-England but competency to live on at best, and that must be purchased with hard labour." Even as they huddled in the ships about to leave for Massachusetts, the settlers forecasted "manifold necessities and tribulations" in the wilderness.[20]

But instead of cooling their ardor for New England, the Puritans translated their expected hardships into blessings. White claimed that countries with "riche soile" where men could live in ease were the source of social evil. "Piety and godlinesse," he wrote, emerge in places like New England "which may yeeld sufficiency" only "with hard labour and industry." Entering upon uncultivated lands inspires frugality and invention. Such efforts provide "a naturall remedy against covetousnesse, fraud, and violence" because "every man may enjoy enough without wrong or injury to his neighbor." John Winthrop assumed a similar stance in

---

[20] "Objections Answered: First Draft" [1629], "Sir John Eliot's Copy," "The Humble Petition," April 1630, *Winthrop Papers*, II, 136, 146–47, 233; White, "Planter's Plea," 390–91.

rejecting the charge that he was brought up "amonge boockes" and would therefore suffer greatly in "a barbarous place where [there] is no learnynge and lesse cyvillytie." "It may be," reasoned Winthrop, that "God will by this meanes bringe us to repent of our former Intemperance." The same motives moved the Lord to carry "the Isralites into the wildernesse and made them forgette the fleshpotts of Egipt." [21] Winthrop, in this manner, glossed over the anticipated difficulties of settling the raw continent.

In his emphasis upon the need to be liberated from the "fleshpotts" of the world he knew best, Winthrop implicitly suggested that "the good land" was also a sanctuary. This idea of America as a refuge clarifies the haste and compulsory nature of the migration of 1630. It implies that the Winthrop fleet sailed not only *to* New England, but also *away* from old England.[22] What then had occurred at home to compel the Puritans to flee into the remote wilderness?

It must be remembered that the Puritan vision, like that of most seventeenth-century men, focussed sharply upon religion and God. Everything in this world had theological ramifications, and nothing possessed meaning aside from God. Thus the Puritans believed that political, social, and economic affairs reflected, in some way, the mind of God. When the Lord smiled upon a nation, He blessed that

[21] White, "Planter's Plea," 390–91, 373; Robert Ryece to John Winthrop, August 12, 1629, "Reasons To Be Considered," *Winthrop Papers*, II, 105–106, 144.

[22] Edmund S. Morgan suggested the significance of New England as a refuge for Governor Winthrop in *The Puritan Dilemma: The Story of John Winthrop* (Boston, 1958). It appears, however, that this idea was also extremely influential among other Puritan intellectuals. Michael Walzer places the concept within the context of intellectual alienation; see, *The Revolution of the Saints: A Study in the Origins of Radical Politics* (Cambridge, Mass., 1965), pp. 142–43.

people with political stability, social security, and economic well-being; when God frowned upon a land, He permitted these blessings to be dissipated. The Puritans articulated the sense of God's grace upon a country with the metaphor of the "Hedge," a protective wall which surrounded a people and assured them that the Lord would not forsake that nation. John Preston, a staunch defender of English Puritanism, described God's special protectiveness for His people with the metaphor of the wall. And John Cotton, viewing the Hedge as "some defence set about church or commonwealth, whether counsel, laws, or guard of military men," remarked that "the breaking of a hedge" violates this protective shell and threatens the safety of the entire nation.[23]

The nature of English society in the 1620s led many Puritans to believe that a shattering of this Hedge was imminent. Time and again the Puritans lamented the evils of the age and feared that the worst was yet to come. Early in 1622 John Winthrop wrote of "the present evill tymes" and predicted a dismal future. "The Lord looke mercifully upon this sinfull lande," he continued, "and turne us to him by some repentence, otherwise we may feare it hath seene the best dayes." Such words were repeated so frequently that "the evill of the tymes" became a cliché. In 1623 Winthrop admitted that the sins "of the whole land doe call for judgementes rather then blessinges," and he placed his hopes in the manifold mercies of the Lord. For a time, he even expressed interest in a plantation in Ireland as a means of escaping from the sinfulness of English society. But in 1624 the political wheel turned, and it appeared that England might reform itself. In that year

---

[23] John Preston, *The New Covenant, or the Saints Portion* . . . (London, 1629), p. 43; John Cotton, "A Brief Exposition Upon Ecclesiastes," reprinted in *Nichol's Series of Commentaries* (Edinburgh, 1868), II, Part II, 108, 109.

Prince Charles's efforts to marry a Spanish princess appeared futile, and the Duke of Buckingham seemed amenable to the summoning of Parliament. By 1626, however, the wheel had turned again, and the Winthrop correspondence became cluttered with regrets at "the dangers and discouragementes of these declininge tymes." [24] As the decade drew to a close, cries of anguish reverberated through the land. "Consider the present time of the Church," intoned John Preston shortly before his death in 1628, "consider how soone the times may come upon us, when we shalbe be put to it; for now things are *in praecipito;* hastening downe to the bottome of the hill." John Wilson, later pastor of the Boston church in New England, lamented the evils of the age with an equally poignant sense of frustration. "What hope is left us," he implored, but the mercy of the Lord. [25]

Wilson's faith in the Lord was not unfounded. For at this moment of peril, the Almighty God, in His infinite mercy, provided a wilderness sanctuary for His people. If the Lord would turn his face from the English and punish that nation with His wrath, He would seek to preserve His children from the impending storm. Francis Higginson bade farewell to England on this theme. According to New England tradition, Higginson foresaw the calamities with which God would chasten the mother land and composed

[24] John Winthrop to Thomas Fones, January 29, 1621[/22]; John Winthrop to John Winthrop, Jr., August 6, 1622; Forth Winthrop to John Winthrop, Jr., April 17, 1623; John Winthrop to John Winthrop, Jr., April 20, 1623; John Winthrop to His Wife, September 27, 1623; John Winthrop to John Winthrop, Jr., March 7, 1623[/24]; John Winthrop to John Winthrop, Jr., December 18, 1626; *Winthrop Papers*, I, 268, 271, 279, 281, 286, 311, 337. For a description of the social problems of the 1620s, see Carl Bridenbaugh, *Vexed and Troubled Englishmen: 1590–1642* (New York, 1968), *passim.*

[25] John Preston, *Life Eternall . . .* , fourth ed. (London, 1634), Part I, 87; John Wilson to John Winthrop, February 3, 1628 [N.S.], *Winthrop Papers*, II, 57–58.

a sermon on the text, "When you see Jerusalem compassed with armies, then flee to the mountains." [26] Preaching to a large congregation in Leicester, he warned his audience of its provoking sins and the likelihood of divine chastisement. New England, he felt, was a haven for the chosen people during the coming time of troubles. At this time, John Winthrop's thoughts were also being channeled in this direction. Writing to his wife, he criticized the evils of the time and observed that "the increasinge of our sinnes gives us so great cause to looke for some heavye Scquorge [*sic*] and Judgment to be comminge upon us." God "hath admonished, threatened, corrected, and astonished us," he continued, "yet we growe worse and worse." Referring to the setbacks to Protestantism on the European continent, the success of the forces of Counter-Reformation in France, Denmark, and Germany, Winthrop bemoaned England's failure to take heed and reform itself. This hard-heartedness, he asserted, would inevitably attract the Lord's wrath. "I am veryly perswaded," he wrote, "God will bringe some heavye Affliction upon this lande, and that speedylye." Yet despite these impending horrors, Winthrop did not conclude with despair. Optimistically he added, "If the Lord seeth it wilbe good for us, he will provide a shelter and a hidinge place for us and ours." [27]

The theme of the wilderness as a refuge became increasingly important in Winthrop's justification of the migration of 1630. Citing appropriate Biblical passages, he argued that members of the church "may be of better use

---

[26] Luke 21:20, 21. The discussion of Francis Higginson is based upon Mather, *Magnalia*, I, 361–62. Although Mather's interpretation of the refuge idea is frequently distorted, his narrative regarding Higginson is probably accurate since the *Magnalia* won the endorsement of Higginson's son, John, who at the age of thirteen accompanied his father to New England.

[27] John Winthrop to His Wife, May 15, 1629, *Winthrop Papers*, II, 91–92.

to their mother Churche heere in tyme then those whom she shall kepe in her bosome." [28] The true church, he maintained, "hath noe place lefte to flie into but the wildernesse." Stressing the catastrophes which had befallen European Protestantism elsewhere, Winthrop asserted that the Lord probably selected New England as a sanctuary for those He wished to save. English Puritans should learn from the tragedies elsewhere "to avoyde the plague when it is foreseene, and not to tarrye, as they did, till it overtake us." [29]

Winthrop's reasoning won the support of other Puritans. One correspondent, Robert Ryece, agreed that "it is juste to seeke refuge for saftye, especially where safest hope maye be founde." Echoing Winthrop's sentiments, Ryece praised the wonders of divine providence "that hathe reysed this newe plantation, for so comfortable a refuge." And citing the evils of the age, he concurred that it is better "to seeke to dye . . . in the wyldernes" than to remain besmirched in a land of sin.[30] The great William Ames, a leading English Puritan, defended the Winthrop migration along similar lines. Although he opposed the removal of communicants from church society as a violation of the sacred covenant, he asserted that under certain circumstances such departures were lawful and necessary. For example, he proceeded, "if a man cannot continue his communion, without a communication of their sinnes," or "if there be any eminent danger of being seduced," it was then appropriate for the true Christian to withdraw. Thus the need to avoid culpability for other people's crimes authorized the quest for safer lands.[31]

---

[28] Revelation 12. "General Conclusions and Particular Considerations," 125.

[29] "Reasons To Be Considered," 138–39; "General Observations," 111, 116.

[30] Robert Ryece to John Winthrop [1629], *Winthrop Papers*, II, 128–30.

[31] William Ames, *Conscience with the Power and Cases thereof . . .*

John Cotton agreed with Ames's appraisal of the situation in his farewell address to the Winthrop group. He emphasized the importance of evading calamities, "when some grievous sinnes overspread a Country." "A wise man," he suggested, who "foreseeth a plague . . . [may] hide himselfe from it." John White approached this problem from a slightly different perspective. Since his tract was obviously designed for widespread public consumption, he had to justify the departure of so many men at a time of social crisis. After dismissing the allegation that the departure would weaken England, White then denied that "this withdrawing of our selves in time of so great hazard betrayes weaknesse of heart." Unlike the founders of Plymouth Colony, the settlers of Massachusetts Bay never embraced a Separatist theology which involved the total repudiation of English society because of the religious deviations within the Church of England. The establishment of a colony in New England therefore did not absolve the Puritans from their temporal obligations to live in the world of sin. To those who might suggest that the Puritans were withdrawing from all worldly corruption, White replied that New England would not be beyond the scope of divine punishment if she too lapsed into sin. He thereby protected the Puritan refugees from the logic of their hasty retreat.[32]

The belief that America was a haven from inevitable catastrophe in England continued to influence important Puritan preachers to migrate to safer shores. To be sure, there was no unanimity among Puritans that the storm would break. Some, like James Hopkins, were reluctant to leave their homes. In a letter to Winthrop, he declared,

(London, 1643), Book V, 141. For a discussion of the relationship between Ames and the Massachusetts Bay Company, see Keith L. Sprunger, "William Ames and the Settlement of Massachusetts Bay," *New England Quarterly*, XXXIX (1966), 66–79.

[32] Cotton, "Gods Promise," 9; White, "Planter's Plea," 405.

"if our peace be continued . . . we hold our selves tied heere, and dare not breake loose till god sett us loose." But many felt that safety demanded that they depart at once. Shortly after the silencing of John Cotton by the Laudian episcopacy, an anonymous writer expressed fear that such policies would threaten the safety of the nation. These perils are greater than any "Arme of flesh," for they provoke "the Lord our Shield . . . to Depart from us." Such warnings apparently influenced Cotton, for he later claimed to have solicited the advice of "the chefe of our people," "the men of God greatly revered for their piety and saintly wisdom," before deciding to embark for New England. These men urged Cotton "to withdraw . . . from the present storme" and continue his ministry in America.[33]

Thomas Hooker, a ship-mate of Cotton's during the voyage to New England, repudiated his native land for similar reasons. In the farewell address to his English congregation, Hooker preached on the danger of God's desertion of England. He warned that the Lord was "taking down the wals" of his protection by permitting the foundation stones, magistrates and ministers, to withdraw. God was uprooting the Hedge of grace which formerly had assured England of a semblance of domestic tranquillity. With his eye on the Continent, where Protestant "Churches [are] made heaps of stones," Hooker suggested that England was surely headed for a similar fate. "All things," he remarked, "are

---

[33] James Hopkins to John Winthrop, February 25, 1632 [/33], *Winthrop Papers*, III, 106;—to [John Cotton] [c. 1633], John Cotton Mss., Prince Collection, Boston Public Library; "Mr. Cotton's letter, giving the Reasons of his and Mr. Hooker's Removal to New-England," December 3, 1634, reprinted in [Thomas Hutchinson, comp.], *A Collection of Original Papers Relative to the History of the Colony of Massachusetts-Bay* (Boston, 1769), p. 56; John Cotton, "An Apologetical Preface," in John Norton, *The Answer to . . . Appolonius . . .* [1648], ed. and tr. by Douglas Horton (Cambridge, Mass., 1958), pp. 10–11.

ripe for ruin," and "when God departs all miseries come." [34]

Other Puritan divines were equally impressed by the need to flee England before the Lord unleashed the worst of His fury. Thomas Shepard, who, with Hooker and Cotton, was destined to play a prominent role in the shaping of the New England Way, responded as they did to the English situation. In his autobiography written in the mid-1640s, Shepard alleged that the departure of Cotton and Hooker had a great impact upon him. "I saw the harts of most of the godly . . . bent that way and I did thinke I should feele many miseries if I stayd behind." But even before his decision to migrate to New England, Shepard had attacked the sinfulness of the age in which he lived. "Consider the approaching times," he wrote, "I doe beleeve the Lord at this day is coming . . . to teare and rend from you your choysest blessings, peace and plenty." Such a catharsis was necessary, he asserted, because "our age grows full, and proud, and wanton." The Lord, he maintained, would punish "this God-glutted, Christ-glutted, Gospel-glutted age" with "sore afflictions of famine, war, bloud, mortality, deaths of Gods precious servants especially." Such a catalog of horror persuaded Shepard to seek sanctuary in America. In a farewell letter to a friend, he prayed that the Lord would carry him "to that good land, and those glorious ordinances" of Christ. In this missive, he restated his loathing for England's degeneracy and expressed hope that the recipient would be "preserved from national sins, which shortly [will] bring national and most heavy plagues." [35]

[34] Thomas Hooker, *The Danger of Desertion or A Farewell Sermon of Mr. Thomas Hooker* . . . (London, 1641), pp. 4, 5, 11. Hooker apparently preached in a similar manner while in self-exile on the Continent; see, "The Examination of Mrs. Ann Hutchinson at the court at Newtown," reprinted in Thomas Hutchinson, *The History of the Colony and Province of Massachusetts-Bay*, ed. by Lawrence Shaw Mayo, 3 vols. (Cambridge, Mass., 1936), II, 385.

[35] [Thomas Shepard], "The Autobiography of Thomas Shepard," *Pub-*

Richard Mather, who later became the bulwark of the Dorchester church in New England, drafted an elaborate defense of his proposed departure from England in which he too proclaimed the dangers of remaining in a sinful land. Entitled "Arguments tending to prove the Removing from *Old England* to *New* . . . to be not onely lawful, but also necessary . . . ," the tract condemned the duplicity of English society and endorsed the desirability of flight. By remaining in corrupt places, wrote Mather, "We do endanger our selves to be corrupted." Declaring that such inertia "is a Tempting of God," Mather reminded himself that it was a Christian duty to flee from a place which proscribed God's ordinances. Like Shepard, Mather listed the provoking sins of the age and interpreted them as precursors of divine punishment. "To remove from a place where are fearful signs of Desolation," he concluded, "to a place where one may have well-grounded hope of preservation, and of Gods protection, is necessary to them that are free." And Mather had no doubt that New England was such a place.[36] A less influential Puritan, Michael Metcalfe, bade farewell to his native land with similar language. In a public letter to his parishioners, he condemned England for its sins. Urging repentance and reformation, he warned that the Almighty "is about to try his people in the furnace of affliction." [37]

But for Metcalfe, as for the other Puritans, the New

lications of the Colonial Society of Massachusetts, XXVII (1932), 375; Thomas Shepard, *The Sound Beleever. Or A Treatise of Evangelicall Conversion* (London, 1653), pp. 139–40, 251–52; Thomas Shepard, "Some Select Cases Resolved," reprinted in *Three Valuable Pieces* (Boston, 1747), p. 53.

[36] Richard Mather's essay is printed in [Increase Mather], *The Life and Death of . . . Richard Mather* (Cambridge, Mass., 1670), pp. 12–18.

[37] Michael Metcalfe "To all the true professors of Christs gospel within the city of Norwich," January 13, 1636 [/37], printed in *New England Historical and Genealogical Register*, XVI (1862), 281–83. (Hereafter cited as *N.E.H.G.R.*) Metcalfe later became schoolmaster of Dedham, Massachusetts.

England wilderness afforded a haven from that wrath. Although the Lord might uproot His Hedge and bring suffering upon England, "the good land" beyond the sea remained as a refuge for His chosen people. The men and women who migrated to New England applied a variety of attributes to that land. And although they possessed scant knowledge of America, they did not venture forth in complete ignorance; their imaginations had already filled the void.

CHAPTER II

"Sad Stormes
and Wearisom Dayes"

IF the Puritans compared old England to the "fleshpotts
of Egipt" and viewed New England as the promised
land, it was fitting that the "vast sea" between these countries would be described with similar Biblical metaphors.
For the seventeenth-century Israelites, the Atlantic Ocean
posed a formidable obstacle on the way to the New Canaan. And it was therefore probably no coincidence that
John Winthrop, in one of his last letters before leaving
England forever, referred to "the streights of the redd sea"
in acclaiming the power and mercy of the Lord.[1]

Three months later, Winthrop was certain that his appraisal of divine sovereignty was correct. "We had a longe
and troublesome passage," he wrote to his wife in the first
letter he directed to England, "but the Lord made it safe
and easye to us." To his eldest son, Winthrop praised God
for "a Comfortable passage." [2] Winthrop's account of the
voyage aboard the three hundred and fifty ton *Arbella*, the
flagship of the 1630 fleet, however, was greatly enlarged.
Despite his insistence to the contrary, Winthrop, in his

[1] John Winthrop to His Wife, March 10, 1629[/30], *Winthrop Papers*,
II, 219.
[2] John Winthrop to His Wife, July 16, 1630, John Winthrop to John
Winthrop, Jr., July 23, 1630, *Winthrop Papers*, II, 302, 304.

sea journal, betrays a great deal of discomfort and trouble in the transatlantic voyage. Upon entering the high seas, the *Arbella* encountered several severe storms, and although Winthrop denied the gravity of these ocean crises, it is evident that he protested too much. "All the time of the storm," he wrote in mid April, "few of our people were sick, . . . and there appeared no fear or dismayedness among them." Two weeks later, Winthrop depicted another tempest which "continued all the day . . . and the sea raged and tossed us exceedingly." His comment that "through God's mercy, we were very comfortable," however, is unconvincing, since shortly thereafter, the Governor maintained that "our people were so acquainted with storms as they were not sick, nor troubled, though we were much tossed forty-eight hours together." [3]

John Smith's version of the *Arbella* expedition, based upon hearsay evidence, provides a necessary corrective to Winthrop's journal. Midway between two worlds, Smith reported, the fleet met with unusually bad weather which lasted ten days. The two-hundred head of cattle aboard the ships "were so tossed and brused" that seventy died, and many of the passengers fell sick. Winthrop himself admitted that "the voyage [was] more teadious then formerly . . . in this season," but merely viewed this discomfort as a further example of divine providence, for the experience of the *Arbella's* crossing, argued Winthrop, proved that the Lord could safely transport the frailest women and children to America. Edward Johnson, a first-generation New England historian, interpreted the difficulties of the *Arbella* voyage in a different manner. The Lord, he maintained, aggravated the normal oceanic hardships so that the land they were approaching "might not

[3] John Winthrop, *Winthrop's Journal, "History of New England": 1630–1649*, ed. by James Kendall Hosmer, 2 vols. (New York, 1908), I, 33, 38, 40.

be deserted by them at first enterance, which sure it would have been by many, had not the Lord prevented by a troublesome passage." [4]

All seventeenth-century colonists, of course, confronted the hazards and uncertainties of the Atlantic crossing. Regardless of national origin or religious predisposition, the men and women who migrated to the American coasts feared the terrors of the unknown seas and appealed to divine providence for protection. But despite these analogous responses, each group of colonists reacted introspectively and viewed its own experiences as unique. Such similarities therefore did not diminish the significance of the ocean for the settlers of New England. The Atlantic voyage introduced the Puritan colonists to new wonders of divine creation and prepared them for the natural rarities of the wilderness. Moreover, the dangers of shipboard life served as a centripetal force among the Puritans and reinforced their social identity.

By initiating the settlers in a variety of new experiences, the ocean voyage preconditioned the Puritans for the novelties of the American wilderness. The passengers who huddled aboard the ships bound for Massachusetts Bay were intensely interested in the wonders of the deep which they encountered for the first time. An outgrowth of the Renaissance, this concern for marine novelty reflects an enhanced sensitivity toward natural history among men throughout Europe. And like their contemporaries elsewhere, the Puritans cluttered their sea diaries with observations of oceanic occurrences.[5] Francis Higginson, who

---

[4] John Smith, "Advertisements For the unexperienced Planters of New-England, or any where" [1631], reprinted in *Colls. M.H.S.*, third ser., III (1833), 40; John Winthrop to His Wife, July 23, 1630, *Winthrop Papers*, II, 303; Edward Johnson, *Johnson's Wonder-working Providence, 1628–1651*, ed. by J. Franklin Jameson (New York, 1910), p. 57.

[5] See, Parry, *Age of Reconnaissance*, pp. 48–52. People of divergent

sailed for New England in the spring of 1629, studded his
journal with descriptions of "grampus fishes," "bonny
fishes," porpoises, and a turtle. On June 5, he noted, "I
saw a fish very strange to me . . . wafting along the top
of the water." Called by the seamen a carvel, it seemed
"like a bubble above the water, as big as a man's fist; but
the fish itself is about the bigness of a man's thumb."
Higginson also reported seeing "a mountain of ice . . .
like to a great rock or cliff on the shore." The iceberg
"stood still, and therefore we thought it to be on ground,
and to reach the bottom of the sea." ⁶ Such descriptions
reveal a significant concern for accuracy among Puritan
diarists. Careful to note sizes and shapes, colors and names,
the travelers were enthralled by the minutiae of God's
oceanic providences. John Winthrop also expressed interest in these nautical oddities. To Higginson's catalog
of novelty, the Governor added sea fowl, driftwood, and
whales. One of the whales, he recorded, "lay just in our
ship's way" and "would not shun us; so we passed within
a stone's cast of him, as he lay spouting up water." ⁷

The wonders of the Atlantic, though experienced by
earlier Puritan colonists, continued to impress later travelers. Richard Mather, who apparently had read Higginson's sea journal, nevertheless filled his own diary with

background expressed interest in oceanic novelty; see, for example, Father
Andrew White, "A Briefe Relation of the Voyage unto Maryland . . . ,
1634," printed in *Narratives of Early Maryland: 1633–1684*, ed. by Clayton Colman Hall (New York, 1910), pp. 32–33. Eighteenth-century voyagers also devoted much space to the oddities of the Atlantic. See, Pierre
de Charlevoix, *Journal of a Voyage to North-America*, 2 vols. [London,
1761] (Ann Arbor, 1966), I, 73–77, 81–82.

⁶ Francis Higginson, "A True Relation of the last Voyage to New-England" [1629], reprinted in Young, *Chronicles*, pp. 226–29. John Josselyn,
during his voyage in 1638, also described an "Island of Ice" on which he
claimed to have seen "two or three Foxes, or Divels skipping" about. See,
"An Account of Two Voyages to New-England," *Colls. M.H.S.*, third
ser., III, 218.

⁷ Winthrop, *Journal*, I, 38–39, 41.

accounts of marine occurrences. He described in great detail the dissection of a large porpoise which he compared favorably to a hog. It was "marvellous merry sport" and "delightful recreation to our bodies," he concluded, to catch and open "this huge and strange fish." Other sights were equally noteworthy. So struck by the "incredible bigness" of a passing whale, Mather exclaimed, "I will never wonder that the body of Jonas" could fit within its belly. The frequency of such contacts with maritime wonders acclimated the Puritans to novelty itself. Nearly two weeks after first observing the mammoth whale, Mather noted, with some detachment, "this day . . . we saw multitudes of great whales; which now was grown ordinary and usual to behold." [8]

Thus the transatlantic journeys not only introduced the Puritans to the varieties of nature, but also conditioned them to that novelty, thereby diminishing the extreme shock of viewing the unknown continent toward which they were sailing. Higginson and Mather evaluated the ocean crossing in almost identical language. "Our passage," wrote Higginson, "was both pleasurable and profitable" because it enabled us to behold "the wonders of the Lord in deep waters." "Those that love their own chimney-corner, and dare not go far beyond their own town's end," he concluded, "shall never have the honor to see these wonderful works of Almighty God." [9]

Such attractions, however, did not diminish the widespread fear of the ocean crossing. Though not unique to English Puritans, this antipathy to the Atlantic neverthe-

[8] Richard Mather, "Richard Mather's *Journal*," printed in Young, *Chronicles*, pp. 459–61, 465, 469. The similarity in texts suggests that Mather probably read Francis Higginson's sea journal; see below, fns. 9 and 18.

[9] Higginson, "A True Relation," p. 237; Mather, "Journal," p. 479 similarly extolled the "pleasure and instruction in beholding the works and wonders of the Almighty in the deep."

less represents a typical response among the colonists of New England.[10] People like Margaret Winthrop and Emmanuel Downing, who expressed confidence that "the lord shall open me the way" to New England, were exceptional. More often the future colonists reacted in the fashion of Downing's wife, Lucy, who rationalized her fears of the ocean by credulously accepting the unfavorable reports from New England. Only if the Lord ultimately removed His ordinances from England would she "then hope for comfort in the hazards of the sea." [11]

John White, who aimed his promotional pamphlet at these timid souls, emphasized the facility of settling New England by sea voyages. But even he could not connive at the many hazards of the journey. William Wood, a later and more determined promoter of New England, dismissed the widespread fear of the ocean as groundless. He claimed that "all such as put to Sea, confesse it to be lesse tedious then they either feared or expected." "A ship at Sea," he assured would-be settlers, is like "a Cradle, rocked by a carefull Mothers hand, which though it be moved up and downe, yet is [never] in danger of falling." Many people, however, were unconvinced by such logic. One correspondent cited the dangers of the ocean in excusing his failure to acquire laborers for New England. Men

---

[10] Metaphors of the malevolence of the ocean flourished in Elizabethan literature; see, Robert Ralston Cawley, *Unpathed Waters: Studies in the Influence of the Voyagers on Elizabethan Literature* (Princeton, 1940), pp. 178–79. For evidence of other non-Puritan fear of the ocean, see, George Alsop to his Father, September 7 [1658], printed in "A Character of the Province of Maryland," in Hall, ed., *Narratives of Maryland*, p. 374; Marc Lescarbot, *The History of New France*, tr. by W. L. Grant, 3 vols. (Toronto, 1907–14), I, 15. Edmundo O'Gorman places Renaissance man's antipathy to the ocean within a philosophical framework; see, *The Invention of America: An inquiry into the historical nature of the New World and the meaning of its history* (Bloomington, 1961), p. 67.

[11] Emmanuel Downing to John Winthrop, December 8, 1630, Margaret Winthrop to John Winthrop, Jr. [c. May 24, 1631], Lucy Downing to John Winthrop [c. July 1636], *Winthrop Papers*, II, 324, III, 35, 279.

who are "good workmen and can get theyer living heare," he wrote, "ar fearfull to goe to seae for feare [that] they shall not live to com to your land." But, he concluded, "wear it not for the danger of the seas you mought have inough" assistance.[12]

Those people who migrated to New England did so despite such fears and subsequently attested to the dangers and difficulties of the ocean voyage. As John Norton recalled in the mid-1650s, "To be long at sea, and not meet with one storm, is unusual."[13] The descriptions of sea voyages made to New England verify Norton's statement and suggest that the oceanic experience was extremely terrifying to men who had lived their lives entirely on land. One day, noted Higginson, the wind blew "strongly, and carried us on amain with tossing waves, which did affright them that were not wonted to such sights." Less than a week later, he described another storm in which "the wind blew mightily, the rain fell vehemently, the sea roared, and the waves tossed us horribly." During this squall, Higginson admitted, "I lay close and warm in my cabin" praying to God for mercy.[14]

Other crossings were equally frightening. The *Handmaid*, according to Winthrop, "was twelve weekes at sea in such tempests, as she spent all her masts." John Hull recalled, in like manner, his own tempestuous voyage of 1635. Early in the trip, "the ship struck upon the ground or sands thirty blows, to the amazement of master and mariners." The seamen, in fear, attempted to flee in their longboats. But, as Hull saw it, God would not permit

---

[12] White, "Planter's Plea," 383, 410; William Wood, *New Englands Prospect* [1634], ed. by C. Deane (Boston, 1865), p. 56; John Wolcott to Henry Wolcott, April 15, 1639, printed in *N.E.H.G.R.*, II (1848), 373.

[13] John Norton, *Abel being Dead yet speaketh* . . . (London, 1658), p. 23. See also, Charles A. Le Guin, "Sea Life in Seventeenth-Century England," *American Neptune*, XXVII (1967), 128.

[14] Higginson, "A True Relation," pp. 221, 224, 225–26.

them to escape and, "after long beating there and much fear," the Lord "turned the ship off again into the sea." Richard Mather reported similar problems in his passage to New England. Shortly before the conclusion of the trip, Mather praised the Lord for bestowing upon His people numerous sea fowl, fresh cod, and a favorable wind. "But lest we should grow secure, and neglect the Lord through abundance of prosperity," Mather recorded in his diary the following day, "our wise and loving God was pleased . . . to exercise us with a sore storm and tempest of wind and rain." John Winthrop, Jr. later described another crossing marred by frequent storms in which the travelers were in great danger "almost every day."[15]

The terrors associated with the Atlantic passage and the frequency of crises in mid-ocean probably accelerated the process of social cohesion. Many Elizabethan seamen believed that the Lord created oceanic tempests as a means of chastising sinful people aboard the ships.[16] In a heterogeneous passenger group, such storms might lead to bitter recriminations among the voyagers, each faction blaming the other for the outbreak of fearful turbulence. But the homogeneity among the colonists bound for New England produced the opposite effect. Traveling in cramped quarters and beset by external and uncontrollable forces, the passengers drew closer together during periods of crisis. The ocean voyage was, in short, a com-

[15] John Winthrop to His Wife, November 29, 1630, John Winthrop, Jr. to Elizabeth Winthrop, October 8, 1641, *Winthrop Papers*, II, 319, IV, 342; Thomas Dudley, "Letter to the Countess of Lincoln" [1631], reprinted in Young, *Chronicles*, p. 330; John Hull, "Some Passages of God's Providences," *Transactions and Collections of the American Antiquarian Society*, III (1857), 142; Mather, "Journal," pp. 461, 468.
[16] Cawley, *Unpathed Waters*, pp. 202–203.

munal experience in which earlier loyalties and friend-
ships were forged even more strongly.

These cohesive tendencies were undoubtedly reinforced
by the Puritans' sensitivity to their isolation from England. In an age when long-distance travels were rare, the
voyage to New England was indeed a bold venture and
the immense distance between Europe and America awed
contemporary Englishmen.[17] Most of the colonists were
probably very conscious of the fact that they could reach
America only "by passing through a dreadfull and terrible
Ocean of nine hundred Leagues in length." At the conclusion of their voyages to Massachusetts, both Higginson and Mather expressed gratitude that the Lord had
ended "our long and tedious journey through the greatest sea in the world." Edward Johnson graphically depicted the sense of remoteness in his narrative of the
Endecott expedition of 1628. The hardships which
plagued that group, declared Johnson, were intensified
by "the Ditch" which separated the settlers from their
native land. A petition from the Connecticut General
Court later in the century also bemoaned the existence
of "soe vast an Ocean" which isolated New Englanders
"from our deare English brethren." [18]

Since every settler in New England had to undergo the
dangerous process of physical transplantation, the ocean
voyage became an initiation ritual, a series of experiences
which was shared by all the members of that society. In
emphasizing their singularity, the Puritan settlers disre-

[17] Robert Cawley, in *The Voyagers*, pp. 287–88, writes: "The crossing
came to be used as a symbol of distance even as we use a voyage to the
moon."

[18] Johnson, *Wonder-working Providence*, pp. 49, 45; Higginson, "A True
Relation," p. 235; Mather, "Journal," p. 476; Connecticut General Court
to King Charles II [1661], reprinted in *Public Records of the Colony of
Connecticut*, ed. by J. Hammond Trumbull, 15 vols. (Hartford, 1850–90),
I, 582. (Hereafter cited as *Pub. Recs. Conn.*)

garded the parallel experiences of other colonials. An early New England poet, Thomas Tillam, stressed the social uniqueness engendered by the Atlantic crossing. "Come my deare little flocke," he wrote upon arriving in Massachusetts, "who . . . hazarded your lives o'th raginge floods."[19] Like all rituals, the ocean voyages were not soon forgotten in New England. In 1642, after the outbreak of civil war in England, several English Puritans requested that Cotton, Hooker, and John Davenport return to their native land to assist in the erection of true religion there. Cotton, noted Winthrop, believed that he was obliged to go despite the fact that he was "very adverse to a sea voyage." Over a decade later, historian Edward Johnson extolled the providences of God "in delivering this his people in their Voyages by Sea, from many foule dangers." You are the people, he wrote of New Englanders, "who are pickt out" by the Lord "to passe this Westerne Ocean" to transport His name into the wilderness.[20]

But even more influential in shaping the Puritans' sense of self-identity was the seeming protectiveness of the Lord toward His children during their transit to the New World. To be sure, nearly all seventeenth-century men, regardless of their religious persuasion, shared the belief that God watched over His people on the high seas.[21] But for the Puritans the sense of divine protection merely strengthened their self-image as the chosen Saints. At mid-century, John Davenport preached upon the relation between religiosity and safe oceanic crossings and ad-

[19] Thomas Tillam, "Uppon the first sight of New England: June 29, 1638," printed in Harold S. Jantz, ed., "The First Century of New England Verse," *Proceedings of the American Antiquarian Society*, LIII (1943), 331.

[20] Winthrop, *Journal*, II, 71–72; Johnson, *Wonder-working Providence*, pp. 61–63, 56–57, 28.

[21] See, Wright, *Religion and Empire*, p. 5; Lescarbot, *History of New France*, II, 251.

vised his audience "To exercise faith in committing ours[elves] to God in Sea Voiages, when he calleth us thereunto." [22]

The Puritan record of safe passages through the Atlantic attested to their faith in the Lord and assured them of their special calling. "I and all mine are passed the deepes and are alive and well," reported one minister to his congregation in England, "yea mercy, mercy in the Lord inwardly [and] outwardly, in spite of Divells and stormes, [we are] as cheerfull as ever." "Wee were often put into some feare of pyrates or men of warre," declared another voyager a few years later, "but our God preserved us." Winthrop noted in his journal that one, William Hibbins, shortly after his safe return to New England, presented a public statement to the Boston church in which he described God's providences to his vessel. The Lord, said Hibbins, delivered them from such "desperate dangers" that even "the eldest seamen were amazed." A report of all "such preservations and deliverances," added Winthrop, "to such ships as have carried . . . the Lord's family between the two Englands . . . would fill a perfect volume." [23]

The protection of God for His people at sea was articulated frequently in support of New England policy. A promotional tract designed for English consumption emphasized the Lord's favor toward New England in providing "such merveilous safe Passage from first to last, to so many thousands that went thither." This series of successes, maintained the author, "hath hardly been ever

[22] John Davenport, Sermon of October 27, 1650, Davenport, Mss., Shepard Historical Society.

[23] Winthrop, *Journal*, II, 71; Master Welles to his people at Tarling in Essex, 1633, Sloane Mss., 922, fol. 90–91, Transcription in Library of Congress; "Report of Edmund Browne [to Sir Simonds D'Ewes, September 1638]," printed in *Publications of the Colonial Society of Massachusetts*, VII (1905), 76.

observed in any Sea-voyages." John Winthrop minimized the danger of one of his political blunders by reminding his critics of God's protection for the people of New England. He pointed out that "the Lord hath brought us hither through the swelling seas, through perills of Pyrats, tempests, leakes, fyres, Rocks, sands, diseases, [and] starvings." Should we now, asked Winthrop, abandon our confidence in God? [24]

The recurrence of nautical language in New England sermons reflects the importance of the Atlantic Ocean in Puritan society. To be sure, the idea of "raging seas" appeared in Puritan writing prior to the founding of New England.[25] But such metaphors appeared less frequently and lacked the experiential base which added to the poignancy of Puritan sermons in America. Shortly after the settlement of Hartford, Connecticut, Thomas Hooker employed the image of shipwreck to describe religious error. "Look we therefore at these desperate delusions," he preached, "not as Rocks and Sands where men may suffer Shipwrack and yet be recovered." Heretical thinking, he continued, directs one to a more final fate, "As a Ship that is foundred in the midst of the main Ocean

[24] "New Englands First Fruits" [1643], reprinted in Samuel Eliot Morison, *The Founding of Harvard College* (Cambridge [Mass], 1935), p. 440; John Winthrop to Richard Saltonstall and Others [c. July 21, 1643], *Winthrop Papers*, IV, 410. Winthrop had erred by supporting the claims of one Frenchman, La Tour, over those of his stronger rival, D'Aulany. For a discussion of this episode, see Morgan, *Puritan Dilemma*, Chapter XIII.

[25] See, for example, John Preston, *The New Covenant*, p. 64; John Winthrop to His Wife, February 14, 1629[/30], *Winthrop Papers*, II, 209; Perry Miller, *The New England Mind: The Seventeenth Century* (New York, 1939), pp. 11, 135. Babette May Levy, *Preaching in the First Half Century of New England History* (Hartford, 1945), pp. 104–106, suggests the importance of the sea in Puritan sermons. Michael Walzer in *Revolution of the Saints*, pp. 179–83, discusses the "ship of state" metaphor in Puritan political sermons.

without the sight of any succor, or hope of Relief." In another sermon, Hooker warned the Elect to shun the seductions of this world with similar language. Temptations, he intoned, are "as violent and boisterous winds, and raging waves, [which] force the Vessel out of the Channel" and lift "it upon the shore and shelves, where it is set on ground, if not split." [26] John Cotton preached of the Lord's control of human destiny. "The safety of mariners' and passengers' lives," he suggested, "lieth not on ropes or cables . . . , but in the name and hand of the lord." At the time of the Robert Child affair, Cotton urged the advocates of religious toleration to scuttle their plans to carry their petition to England and warned them "that the terrors of the Almighty shall beset the vessel wherein you are." To avoid a tragic ending, he counseled, "desist . . . and cast [your] petitions into the sea." [27] Peter Bulkeley, minister of the church at Concord, distinguished between the Covenant of Grace and the Covenant of Works with oceanic metaphors. "He that rests on works," wrote Bulkeley, "is like a wave of the Sea, tossed and tumbled up and down, and finds no rest." But "he that rests on grace is like one built upon a rock, and therefore cannot be shaken." John Norton similarly described the religious vicissitudes of New England in the 1650s. "People," he wrote, "will accept of a quiet harbor . . . rather then be afflicted with continual tossings in stormy seas." [28]

Although the Puritans reached "a quiet harbor," and thereby escaped the tossings of the seas, the ocean ex-

[26] Thomas Hooker, *The Application of Redemption* (London, 1657), p. 160; Thomas Hooker, *A Comment upon Christ's Last Prayer In the Seventeenth of John* . . . (London, 1656), p. 140.

[27] Cotton, "A Brief Exposition Upon Ecclesiastes," 103; John Cotton Sermon on *Canticles* 2:15, quoted in Mather, *Magnalia*, I, 283.

[28] Peter Bulkeley, *The Gospel Covenant; Or the Covenant of Grace Opened* . . . (London, 1646), p. 90; Norton, *Abel being Dead*, p. 48.

periences remained prominent in their minds. The career of Thomas Shepard typifies the significance of the ocean in this thought.[29] Silenced by the Laudian church and harried in England, Shepard resolved to sail for New England. Only the fervent desire to enjoy the ordinances of Christ enabled him to "overlooke all the dangers and difficulties of the vast Seas, the thought whereof," he later confessed, "was a terrour to many." On October 16, 1634, Shepard bade farewell to England and embarked for Massachusetts Bay. Off the coast of Yarmouth, however, less than two days at sea, a violent storm arose and nearly destroyed the vessel. Only "the infinite wisdom and power of god" preserved the Shepard family and permitted them to survive "such terrible stormes." But the mishap delayed Shepard's departure, and the following year, despite his increased apprehensions, Shepard boarded the *Defense* bound for America. This voyage, too, was not without its troubles. In mid-ocean the ship sprang a leak, endangering the lives of the terrified passengers. Fortunately the Lord delivered them from this crisis, but only to lead them into a serious storm. In subsequent sermons, Shepard alluded to his reaction to such dangers. A man at sea, wrote Shepard, is haunted by the thought, "What if I should fall in! and hence keeps close in the ship, whatever storms come, whatever calms come, for he sees death before him." "Men that sail upon the sea," he continued, "If they see nothing but waves, and vast raging of waters about them," confine themselves "though their cabins be but little." [30]

---

[29] There is no adequate biography of Shepard. John A. Albro, *The Life of Thomas Shepard* (Boston, 1847) merely strings together a variety of Shepard quotations. For the best modern sketch of Shepard, see Samuel Eliot Morison, *Builders of the Bay Colony* (Boston, 1930), Chapter IV.

[30] Thomas Shepard [and John Allin], "The Preface to the Reader," *A Defence of the Answer made unto Nine Questions or Positions sent from New-England,* third ed. entitled *A Treatise of Liturgies . . .* (London,

The memory of the "sad stormes and wearisom dayes" which characterized that voyage continued to influence Shepard's thoughts, and oceanic metaphors appeared frequently in his discourses. In the Massachusetts Bay election sermon of 1638, Shepard compared sins to the "raging Sea, which would overwhelm all if they have not bankes." In a later piece, he warned against succumbing to worldliness. "Your temptations are greater here," he exhorted, because "others are in storms, we in calms." In similar language Shepard denied that spiritual restlessness was equal in all persons. "No," he commented, "but just like some ships, some are carried with more rough winds," while others are guided to the harbor "with more gentle and still winds." [31] Shepard was also conscious of the role of the ocean in creating a sense of self-identity in New England. People have "passed through the waves . . . , and stood many a week within six inches of death," he reminded the settlers, "to see Christ here." "What shall we say of the singular Providences of God," he asked in another context, in "bringing so many Ship-loads of his people, through so many dangers, as upon Eagles wings, with so much safety from yeare to yeare"? He answered such questions by emphasizing the uniqueness of the New England Puritans. "We that dwell in America," insisted Shepard, have "motives [which] are proper to ourselves" to honor the Lord. We should "love and fear God," he asserted, because "of our redemption and de-

1653), p. 7; Shepard, "Autobiography," 352, 354–55, 384; Thomas Shepard, *The Parable of the Ten Virgins* . . . , reprinted in *The Works of Thomas Shepard*, ed. by John A. Albro, 3 vols. (Boston, 1853), II, 327–28, 592.

[31] Thomas Shepard, "Thomas Shepard's Election Sermon, in 1638," printed in *N.E.H.G.R.*, XXIV (1870), 363; Shepard, *Parable*, 258–59; Thomas Shepard, "A Brief Explication of John . . . ," printed in *A Short Catechism Familiarly Teaching the Knowledge of God and of our Selves* (Cambridge [Mass.], 1654), p. 38.

liverances from . . . the vast sea-storms," and "the tu-
mults of Europe." [32]

The Atlantic crossing, to which Shepard and his contemporaries ascribed so much meaning, continued to influence the Puritan mind later in the century. This interest in the ocean was sustained partly because of the
continuation of transatlantic voyages. Anne Bradstreet
expressed a mother's concern when her son embarked
for England: "Preserve, O Lord, from stormes and wrack/
Protect him there, and bring him back." Within four years
the Lord responded to her prayers and delivered her child
"From Dangers great." John Winthrop, Jr. reacted in
similar fashion when his son, Fitz-John, journeyed to England. The elder Winthrop reminded the youth to praise
God "for those many deliverances in that ship wherein
you went." To be sure, Fitz-John was already "very sensible" of these divine providences. A few years later, John
Winthrop, Jr. himself returned to England. "I heare what
a dangerous passage you had," wrote a correspondent
from New England; "it may put us in minde of the ex-
treame difficulties and hassards [which] doe attende our
pilgrimage" to our native land. For people traveling to
the New World for the first time, the ocean retained its
original significance. Edward Taylor, destined to become
the most important American poet of his age, filled a
travel diary with descriptions of oceanic novelties and
fierce storms. His notations differed only slightly from
the journals of earlier colonists.[33]

[32] Shepard, *Parable*, 180; Shepard [and Allin], "Preface," *A Defence*,
pp. 7–8; Thomas Shepard, *Theses Sabbaticae Or, The Doctrine of the
Sabbath* (London, 1649), Part I, 116.

[33] Anne Bradstreet, "Upon my Son Samuel his goeing for England, November 6, 1657," Anne Bradstreet, "On my Sons Return out of England,
July 17, 1661," both printed in *The Works of Anne Bradstreet in Prose
and Verse*, ed. by John Harvard Ellis (New York, 1932), pp. 25, 28–29
(first published in 1867); John Winthrop, Jr. to Fitz-John Winthrop, Sep-

Second- and third-generation New Englanders, who already had begun to deify the founding fathers, applauded the courage of their ancestors in surmounting the perils of the Atlantic Ocean. Puritan ministers extolled the munificence of God in carrying the first settlers "by a mighty hand, and an out-stretched arm, over a greater then the Red Sea." Increase Mather eulogized his father for transporting his family "over the rude Waves of the vast Ocean," while Michael Wigglesworth gratefully thanked his parents for taking him, at the age of seven, into New England despite the "many difficulties and hazzards" of the voyage. Cotton Mather's panegyric similarly exalted the first planters for undertaking the Atlantic migration.[34]

These later Puritan writers were also conscious of the social significance of the ocean voyage. Thus John Oxenbridge, preaching in Massachusetts Bay in 1670, reminded his hearers that "Gods hand hath been lifted up on one or other of you in a Storm at Sea" in order to bring repentance. The impact of the ocean was still so important at this time that Samuel Danforth admonished his listeners to remember that New England was unique *not* because of "our transportation over the Atlantick Ocean," but only as a result of "the fruition of . . . holy Ordinances" there. And Increase Mather significantly devoted

tember 9, 1658, Winthrop Mss., V, 20, Samuel Symonds to John Winthrop, Jr. [n.d. received by Winthrop March 26, 1662], Winthrop Mss., III, 35, Massachusetts Historical Society; Edward Taylor, "Diary," *Proc. M.H.S.*, XVIII (1880–81), 6–10.

[34] "Copy of a Petition to the Parliament in 1651," reprinted in Hutchinson, *History of Massachusetts-Bay*, I, 428; The General Court of Massachusetts Bay to Parliament, December 19, 1660, printed in *Recs. of Mass. Bay*, IV, Part I, 453; "A brief account . . . of the rights and settlements of the people of . . . Connecticut . . . ," July 22, 1675, printed in *Pub. Recs. Conn.*, II, 339; Increase Mather, *The Day of Trouble is Near . . .* (Cambridge [Mass.], 1674), p. 27; Increase Mather, *Life and Death*, p. 11; Michael Wigglesworth, "Autobiography," *N.E.H.G.R.*, XVII (1863), 137; Mather, *Magnalia*, I, 74, 145.

the first chapter of his compendium of divine providences to "Remarkable Sea Deliverances."[35]

The persistence of such ideas about the sea reveals the great impact wrought by the Atlantic upon New England society. Besides introducing the settlers to the wonders of the earth and conditioning them for the novelties of the wilderness, "the vast Ocean" created a lasting social bond. The terror associated with the crossings knit the passengers together and prepared them for their communal endeavors in the wilderness. America thereby became a refuge not only from the "fleshpotts" of England, but also from the turmoil and tossings of the sea.

[35] John Oxenbridge, *A Quickening Word for the Hastening a Sluggish Soul to a Seasonable Answer to the Divine Call* . . . (Cambridge [Mass.], 1670), p. 14; Samuel Danforth, *A Brief Recognition of New-Englands Errand into the Wilderness* (Cambridge [Mass.], 1671), p. 18; Increase Mather, *Essay for the Recording of Illustrious Providences* (Boston, 1684).

CHAPTER III

"A New World"

ON June 19, 1629, after endless weeks of long waiting upon the rolling decks of the *Talbot*, Francis Higginson reported, no doubt with a sigh of relief, that "some went up to the top of the mast, and affirmed . . . they saw land." But five days lapsed before he noted that his fellow passengers had "a clear and comfortable sight of America." As the three-hundred-ton *Talbot* sailed slowly along the New England coast, the weary travelers gazed anxiously at the land which would become their home. "We saw every hill and dale," related Higginson, "and every island full of gay woods and high trees." The "fine woods and green trees by land" and the yellow flowers which painted the sea, he continued, "made us all desirous to see our new paradise of New England, whence we saw such forerunning signals of fertility afar off." As the vessel slipped into the harbor at Cape Ann, four men disembarked for a nearby island and returned with "ripe strawberries, gooseberries, and sweet single roses." "Thus," proclaimed Higginson, "God was merciful to us in giving us a taste and smell of the sweet fruit . . . to welcome us at our first arrival." "And as we passed along," he added, "it was wonderful to behold so many islands, replenished with thick wood and high trees, and many fair, green pastures." [1]

[1] Higginson, "A True Relation," pp. 230–34.

One year later, John Winthrop stood at the rail of the *Arbella* and lavished similar praise upon the virgin continent before him. "It is very high land, lying in many hills very unequal," he wrote, "and there came a smell off the shore like the smell of a garden." Upon landing in Massachusetts, the passengers also partook of the luscious strawberries which awaited them.[2]

Unlike Higginson and Winthrop, however, other colonists, perhaps even a majority, were disappointed at the sight of the New England coast. The response of poetess Anne Bradstreet was a representative view. Upon arriving in America, she recalled, "I found a new world and new manners, at which my heart rose [i.e., rebelled]." Several contemporaries noted this dissatisfaction among other settlers. Writing of the expedition of 1630, John Smith declared that conditions in America contradicted their expectations, and many returned to their native land to spread ill rumors about New England. Only the fear of another ocean crossing, insisted Edward Johnson, prevented many more from deserting the colony in its infancy. William Wood later criticized those settlers who confused a fertile land with a settled country and therefore anticipated "walled townes, fortifications and corne fields." Such people, he added, "missing of their expectations, returned home and railed against the Country."[3]

The contradictory reactions to the New World reflect the ambiguity with which the Puritans originally viewed New England. The differences between a Winthrop and a Bradstreet betray the variations of Old World thought

[2] Winthrop, *Journal*, I, 47, 48, 50. The initial response of the Roanoke colonists to the American continent was strikingly similar. See, "Arthur Barlowe's Discourse of the First Voyage" [1584–85], printed in *The Roanoke Voyages: 1584–1590*, ed. by David Beers Quinn, 2 vols. (London, 1955), I, 93–94.

[3] Bradstreet, "Religious Experiences," *Works*, p. 5; Smith, "Advertisements For . . . New England," 40; Johnson, *Wonder-working Providence*, p. 57; Wood, *New Englands Prospect*, pp. 52–53.

about America. For the uninitiated who rely upon a map, remarked Peter Bulkeley of Concord, the wonders of nature "are seen darkly." Such outlines, he suggested, "are nothing to that when they are seen in their own beautie and greenesse." [4] Thus it appears that the initial impressions of the Puritans toward New England derived from their expectations and preconceptions rather than from the wilderness itself. The sight of America from the decks of Puritan ships merely confirmed or assaulted previous ideas.

The Puritan response to the American wilderness typified the reaction of most seventeenth-century colonials to the New World. Reflecting the contemporaneous interest in natural history and geography, the Puritan colonists devoted themselves to depicting the wonders of the American forest for their curious friends at home. The settlers, to be sure, frequently embellished their descriptions of the wilderness in order to satisfy their promotional inclinations. But more often they endeavored to portray with accuracy the natural life of America. At first, a lack of information about the varieties of nature in New England led the colonists to generalize disproportionately about the wilderness. But within a decade, New Englanders were sufficiently acquainted with the land to describe the country with more moderate metaphors.

In his history of New England, William Hubbard declared that the people who arrived in Massachusetts Bay in 1630 "were not much unlike the family of Noah at their first issuing out of the ark, and had, as it were, a new world to people." [5] The early responses of the Puritans to New England reveal this lack of familiarity with the American wilderness. Puritan commentators like Francis

---

[4] Bulkeley, *Gospel Covenant*, p. 121.
[5] Hubbard, "A General History," V, 134.

Higginson were forced to generalize from their limited experience. His description of New England, like his journal of the sea voyage, cataloged the varieties of natural life which he confronted for the first time. "This country aboundeth naturally with store of roots of great variety and good to eat," he wrote, and the "turnips, parsnips and carrots are here both bigger and sweeter than is ordinarily to be found in England." Higginson especially praised the excellence of the fruits that "grow in plenty here." Of the wildlife, he suggested the presence of bears and lions and extolled the abundance of "fowls of the air," many of which, he observed, were unknown in England. There is "abundance of sea-fish . . . almost beyond believing," he exclaimed, "and sure I should scarce have believed it except I had seen it with mine own eyes." Higginson also praised "the temper of the air," and concluded, "Experience doth manifest that there is hardly a more healthful place to be found in the world that agreeth better with our English bodies." [6]

Higginson's remarks, however, were based upon observations made during the summertime freshness of New England. It was therefore not difficult to praise the "fat black earth" of Massachusetts and the myriad signs of natural abundance.[7] But the seasonable wealth of America led Higginson to overlook what he called "the discommodities" of New England. He dismissed such nuisances as mosquitoes, snakes, and cold winters, and declared that the greatest problem was the lack of good Christians to subdue the fertile land. "Great pity it is," he maintained, "to see so much good ground . . . lie altogether unoccupied," while England remains desperately

[6] Francis Higginson, "New-Englands Plantation. Or a Short and True Description of the Commodities and Discommodities of that Countrey" [1630], reprinted in Young, *Chronicles*, pp. 246–47, 248–49, 251, 252–53.
[7] Higginson, "New-Englands Plantation," pp. 243, 245–46, 251.

overpopulated. In a subsequent letter to his friends in Leicester, Higginson was more realistic and confessed that the settlement of Massachusetts "shall be difficult at the first." This missive warned future colonists to be prepared for adversity. Yet even here Higginson betrayed the optimism of his limited perspective by concluding with news of an extremely successful fishing trip. Thomas Graves, an "Engynere" who accompanied the Higginson group to Salem, also wrote of the abundance of New England in extravagant terms. "I never came in a more goodly countrey in all my life," he stated flatly. After praising the vegetation of the area, Graves, like Higginson, acclaimed "the healthfulness of the country." [8]

The writings of Higginson and Graves belong properly with those of a long list of contemporary promotionalists. Though it is difficult to ascribe conscious motives to these early New England commentators, it is nevertheless apparent that they hoped to hasten the development of their colony by persuading potential settlers, including perhaps the Winthrop group, of the beneficence of the region about Massachusetts. Such ulterior purposes, however, did not diminish the contributions of these writers as chroniclers of the natural life of the New World. In this sense, their compilations whetted the intellectual appetites of their less adventurous compatriots in England.[9]

In describing the fauna and flora of Massachusetts,

[8] Higginson, "New-Englands Plantation," pp. 254–56; Higginson, "Some Brief Collections," pp. 261, 264; Thomas Graves, "A Letter sent from New-England . . ." [1629], reprinted in Young, *Chronicles*, pp. 264–66.

[9] Cawley, *The Voyagers*, pp. 290–91; Parry, *Age of Reconnaissance*, pp. 306–307. Similar promotional tracts, of varying value, emerged in nearly all the colonies. See, for example, Thomas Hariot, "A Briefe and True Report . . . of Virginia," printed in Quinn, *Roanoke Voyages*, I, 325–68, 382–87; Robert Horne [?], "A Brief Description of the Province of Carolina . . . 1666," printed in *Narratives of Early Carolina: 1650–1708*, ed. by Alexander S. Salley, Jr. (New York, 1911), pp. 66–73; Le Page Du Pratz, *The History of Louisiana* . . . (London, 1774), Book III.

Thomas Morton, an early non-Puritan settler of New England, devoted his promotional energies to depicting the region as a New Canaan. "Let the people have their desire," he urged, "who write to their friends to come out of Sodom to the land of Canaan, a land that flowes with Milke and Hony." Overlooking the contradiction that the milk was provided by the first inhabitants who transported their cattle to America, Morton lauded the lusciousness of the soil and the varieties of wildlife. The natural beauty and abundance of the wilderness, he remarked, "made the Land to mee seeme paradice: for in mine eie t'was Natures Masterpeece." Morton applied such superlative language to all of New England, but reserved his strongest accolades for the "Lake of Erocoise" which he placed three hundred miles west of Massachusetts Bay.[10] Despite his catalog of natural phenomena, Morton distorted and exaggerated the situation in New England. By ignoring the difficulties and hazards of settlement, he told but half the story. Other New Englanders were, at times, equally errant in their private correspondence and contended that the colony faced few significant problems.[11]

Not everyone, of course, responded as favorably to the necessities of the early years in Massachusetts as the promotionalists. Edward Johnson related that some of the settlers, afraid of poverty and hunger, supposed that "the present scarcity would never be turned into plenty [and] removed themselves away." Others who remained attested to the hardships of settling the unbeaten wilderness. Thomas Dudley, first Deputy Governor of the col-

[10] Thomas Morton, *New English Canaan*, ed. by Charles F. Adams, Jr. (Boston, 1883), pp. 110, 114, 230, 179–80, 234–35.

[11] See, for example, John Wiswall to George Rigby, September 27, 1638, printed in Historical Manuscripts Commission, *Fourteenth Report* (London, 1894), Appendix, part IV, 56.

ony in Massachusetts and father of Anne Bradstreet, bit-
ingly criticized the optimistic reports sent to England by
advance-guard colonists like Higginson and Graves. Such
letters, "by their too large commendations of the country and the commodities thereof," convinced aspiring
settlers to sail for New England despite the hardships
involved in simply remaining alive. Dudley stressed the
need for honesty "lest other men should fall short of their
expectations when they come hither, as we to our great
prejudice did." Although New England was well furnished
with natural blessings, Dudley advised that "if any come
hither to plant for worldly ends . . . , he commits an
error." There are sufficient "materials to build, fuel to
burn, ground to plant, seas and rivers to fish in," he continued, and a man "may find here what may well content
him." But clearly, the people of New England were not
a people of plenty. "In a word," he concluded, "we yet
enjoy little to be envied, but endure much to be pitied
in the sickness and mortality of our people." [12]

Another colonist was equally pessimistic about New
England. In a letter to his family in England, he discussed the difficulties of living in the wilderness and
maintained that "the cuntrey is not so [good] as we did
expect it." So great were the problems of settlement, that
he doubted whether the plantation would long endure.[13]
Significantly, both pessimistic appraisals were made during the first winter in Massachusetts Bay, a time when the
normal wilderness difficulties were compounded by in-
adequate food and housing and a serious epidemic. Like

[12] Johnson, *Wonder-working Providence*, p. 77; Dudley, "Letter to the
Countess," pp. 310, 324. For a contemporary satire of the promotional
missives directed to England, see, P. A. Kennedy, ed., "Verses on the Puritan Settlement of America, 1631," Thoroton Society, *Record Series*, XXI
(Nottingham, 1962), 37–39.
[13] —— Pond to William Pond, March 15, 1630[/31], *Winthrop Papers*,
III, 17–18.

Higginson and Graves, these commentators generalized on the basis of limited experience in America.

John Smith had warned New Englanders to avoid such statements about the land. A man who goes "at Christmas to gather cherries in Kent," he wrote, "may be deceived, though there be plenty in summer." This situation is equally valid in America, he maintained, where the vegetation is seasonable. As William Hubbard later explained, however, the men who first arrived in Massachusetts "chanced to be here in the first part of the summer, when the earth was only adorned with its best attire of herbs and flowers." Weather-beaten and forlorn, the travelers refreshed themselves with the wild fruits of the wilderness and "promised themselves and their successors a very flourishing country." [14]

The response of John Winthrop to the New England wilderness, though optimistic, was nevertheless tempered by greater realism. Despite the "many and great troubles" of settlement, Winthrop was confident that the Lord would "uphold us, and . . . give us hope of a happye issue." Although the New England soil is "very fertile," he informed his wife, "yet there must be tyme and meanes" to cultivate it. To his son, Winthrop reported that "the Country is exceeding[ly] good," and compared favorably to the climate of England. "Here is sweet aire[,] faire rivers and plenty of springs," he announced, and there "can be noe want of any thinge to those who bring meane[s] to raise [them] out [of] the earth and sea." The recognition that plenty would come only from hard work distinguished Winthrop from such extreme optimists as Higginson and Graves. "People must come well provided," insisted the Governor, "and not too many at

[14] Smith, "A Description of New-England," 121; Hubbard, "A General History," V, 23.

once." And although he could write to his wife that "we are heer in a Paradice," Winthrop acknowledged that plenty would emerge only from subduing the earth. As "soone as Mr. Winthrop was landed" in Massachusetts, stated an anonymous contemporary, "he presently fell to worke with his owne hands, and thereby soe encouradged the rest that there was not an Idle person to be found in the whole Plantation." [15]

Winthrop's realism, however, did not entirely diminish the enthusiasm of other optimists. The work of settlement "will require my best dilligence," wrote John Masters to England, but "the Country is very good, and fitt to receive Lords and Ladies." We have come to "as goodly a land as every mine eyes beheld," declared one minister to his flock in England. "I see," he assured his friends, "with industry and selfe denyall men may Subsist as well here as in any place." John Eliot cited the increase of cattle and the possibility of a good harvest and concluded, "I know nothing but is comfortable to a contented mind." Yeoman William Hammond described the variety and quantity of fish and fowl. "Thanckes be to god," he exclaimed, "it is like to be a floreisheing plantatyon." [16]

[15] John Winthrop to His Wife, July 16, 1630, John Winthrop to His Wife, July 23, 1630, John Winthrop to John Winthrop, Jr., July 23, 1630, John Winthrop to His Wife, November 29, 1630, *Winthrop Papers*, II, 302, 304, 306–307, 320; [Anonymous], "Narrative [addressed to Secretary Cooke?] concerning the settlement of New England—1630," *Proc. M.H.S.*, V (1862), 131. The optimism of Winthrop's correspondence to England convinced his wife "that it is the place whearin god will have us to settle in"; see, Margaret Winthrop to John Winthrop, Jr. [c. first week of May 1631], *Winthrop Papers*, III, 33.

[16] John Masters, "Letter to Lady Barrington and Others, March 14, 1630/1," *N.E.H.G.R.*, XCI (1937), 69; Master Welles to his people at Tarling in Essex [1633], Sloane Mss., 922, fol. 91; John Eliot to Sir Simonds D'Ewes, September 18 [1633], William Hammond to Sir Simonds D'Ewes, September 26, 1633, both printed in Franklin M. Wright, ed., "A College First Proposed, 1633: Unpublished Letters of Apostles Eliot and William Hammond to Sir Simonds D'Ewes," *Harvard Library Bulletin*, VIII (1954), 273, 262–65.

Aside from the works of self-conscious promotionalists, the exaggerated accounts which usually resulted from the initial contacts with the wilderness persisted as long as New Englanders were uncertain about their environment. The Puritans manifested their unfamiliarity with the wilderness by their interest in the novelties of "this strange lande." Despite the difficulties of wintering in New England, wrote Edward Johnson of the Endecott group of 1628, some of the settlers delighted "their Eye with the rarity of things present," and fed "their fancies with new discoveries." English correspondents were greatly interested in the novelties of the wilderness and requested their New England friends to transmit descriptions and specimens of the rarities of the New World. New Englanders answered these requests and studded their letters with details about the natural wonders of America and the contours of the land. Thomas Dudley, for example, depicted the migration of immense flocks of birds which darkened the skies.[17]

Besides representing the natural curiosity of the age, the Puritans' interest in such minutiae paralleled their response to oceanic novelty and revealed the difficulty of adjustment to life in the wilderness. Increased exploration and continued contact with the forest, of course, eventually diminished the shock of the wilderness. Soon after their arrival in New England, the Puritans commenced hesitant exploration of the lands about them. In October 1630 a pinnace which was sent to trade with the Indians located a region filled with wild grapes already rotted on the vines. The traders also observed a large island alleged by the Indians to be "a fruitfull

[17] Johnson, *Wonder-working Providence*, p. 45; John Winthrop to John Winthrop, Jr., March 28, 1631, Henry Jacie to John Winthrop, Jr., January 9, 1631[/32], Edward Howes to John Winthrop, Jr., March 25, 1633, *Winthrop Papers*, III, 21, 58, 115; Dudley, "Letter to the Countess," pp. 335–36.

place." But since the men lacked permission "for dis-
covery," they returned without visiting the island. John
Winthrop later related other exploratory trips into the
New England wilderness and described an extended voy-
age of discovery to the Isle of Shoals. And in 1639, the
Bay colony reimbursed one, Nathaniel Woodward, "for
his journey to discover the running up" of the Merrimack
River.[18]

This increased familiarity with the American continent
produced a gradual decline in generalizations about the
wilderness.[19] William Wood's promotional essay, *New
Englands Prospect,* which was published in 1634, described the bounty of America in superlative language.
Calling New England the "best ground and sweetest Climate" in the New World, Wood proceeded to discuss its
natural abundance in great detail. He praised the wealth
and variety of the nearby timber and assured future colonists that New England possessed sufficient fuel to
combat the chills of winter. Whatever "growes well in
England," maintained Wood, will prosper in New England's soil, "many things being better and larger." Besides
the fertility of the lands, he added, there are "thousands
of Acres that yet was never medled with." Wood denied
that such "discommodities" as wolves, rattlesnakes, and
"musketoes" presented important problems. Even the Indians, whom he described in elaborate detail, were portrayed as honest, courteous individuals.[20]

Superficially, it would appear, Wood resorted to gross
generalizations in attempting to lure colonists to New

[18] Dudley, "Letter to the Countess," p. 323; Winthrop, *Journal,* I,
73–74, 138, 153–54; *Recs. of Mass. Bay,* I, 261.

[19] A similar pattern emerged in Elizabethan literature about the New
World. Robert Cawley, in *The Voyagers,* p. 309, writes: ". . . the early
allusions [to America] tend to be general, vague, the later far more specific and accurate."

[20] Wood, *New Englands Prospect,* pp. 3, 4, 12, 15, 16–17, 49, 63–110.

England. Such, however, was not so. Although Wood denied that the ground was barren, he nevertheless believed that improvements would be necessary before American soil would be as productive as English lands. He also lamented the folly of people who expected to find a veritable Eden awaiting them in the wilderness. "Surely they were much deceived, or else ill informed," he argued, "that ventured" to New England "in hope to live in plenty and idleness, both at a time." He urged only the able-bodied to migrate to Massachusetts Bay because "all New England[ers] must be workers in some kinde." Denying rumors that even young boys could obtain sustenance easily, he wrote of the colonists that "howsoever they are accounted poore, they are well contented, and looke not so much at abundance, as a competencie." [21] John Winthrop, echoing this realistic appraisal in a letter to an acquaintance in England, discussed the natural resources and husbandry of New England in unsentimental terms. "Our ploughes goe on with good successe," he declared, but only hard labor would transform the wilderness into settled lands. [22]

The waning of generalizations about the land became a typical trend in Massachusetts Bay. The case of John Pratt of Newtown illustrates the change in New England attitudes and suggests that the transplanted Englishmen were slowly adjusting to their wilderness environment. On November 3, 1635, John Pratt was hailed before the Court of Assistants of Massachusetts Bay and interrogated about a letter he had transmitted to England. In this missive, according to John Winthrop, Pratt "affirmed divers things, which were untrue and of ill report, for the

[21] Wood, *New Englands Prospect*, pp. 13–14, 52–53, 54.
[22] John Winthrop to Sir Nathaniel Rich, May 22, 1634, *Winthrop Papers*, III, 166–67.

state of the country." He had reported, alleged Winthrop, "that there was nothing but rocks, and sands, and salt marshes, etc." [23]

The following day, with the permission of the Court, Pratt defended himself against these charges. His apologia, which won the endorsement of Thomas Hooker, then minister of the Newtown church, relied upon four basic arguments. Although Pratt did not deny the validity of the accusation, he insisted that his original statement describing the difficulties of sustaining life in New England was not intended "in respect of the whole country . . . , but onely of that compasse of ground" near the Bay. Despite the overcrowdedness of the area, argued Pratt, "I found that men did thinke it unreasonable that they should remove . . . into other parts of the Countrie," and therefore "I thought I could not subsist myselfe, nor the plantation, nor posteritie." The purpose of the questionable letter, maintained Pratt, was to unmask earlier accounts which "hadd made larger reports into England of the country then I found to be true." Finally, Pratt confessed that his criticism of the quality of the soil was based upon limited knowledge of America. Since the writing of the derogatory letter, he admitted, "there have been sundry places newly found out . . . which will afford good meanes of subsistence for men and beasts." Furthermore, he averred, his experiences taught him that the soil of New England, if properly husbanded, could produce plentiful harvests.[24] Despite the elements of coercion which probably influenced this retraction, Pratt's sober second thoughts reveal a deeper understanding of the land which surrounded him, a recognition that

[23] Winthrop, *Journal*, I, 165.
[24] "John Pratt's Answer to the Court" [November 5, 1635], *Recs. of Mass. Bay*, I, 358–59. See also, Sir William Martin to John Winthrop, March 29, 1636, *Winthrop Papers*, III, 240. For a discussion of the Pratt affair in the context of New England expansion, see Chapter VII.

the diversity of New England did not lend itself to mono-lithic denunciations.

Although the Pratt affair did not constitute an intel-lectual watershed, it nevertheless underscored the process of Puritan adaptation to the wilderness. Bold generaliza-tions based upon scant knowledge gradually gave way to tempered statements about the nature of the land. "The soyle I judge to be lusty and fat in many places, light and hot, in some places sandy botomed and in some loomy," observed one New Englander in 1638. In an otherwise optimistic report about the country, this com-mentator significantly distinguished the various types of soil without exaggerating their virtues or their vices. In 1642 the General Court of Massachusetts Bay dispatched two men to assess the suitability of the Shawshin area for the erection of a village. The surveyors reported that the site was inappropriate for such a settlement since there was "very little medow" and the uplands were "very barren." [25]

Such tendencies away from generalization about the land were made even clearer by the General Court the following year. Because of the frequency of disputes in the towns about the cultivation of the common lands, several men proposed that the General Court issue a broad statement regarding the husbandry of the soil. In rejecting this idea, the Court argued that "no generall order can provide for the best improvement of every . . . common feild," because "some consists onely of plowing ground, some [have] a great part fit onely for planting, [and] some [are only] meadowe and feeding ground." A general policy statement, the Court maintained, "may bee very wholesome and good" for one field, but "exceed-ing[ly] prejudiciall and inconvenient for another." The

[25] "Report of Edmund Browne," 77; *Recs. of Mass. Bay*, II, 10–11.

Court therefore urged that disputes about planting and sowing be settled by the individual towns.[26]

The decision of the General Court signified a subtle though ongoing shift in New England attitudes. Increased familiarity with the wilderness and the decline in the role of novelty had reduced the propensity to generalize. Thereafter descriptions of New England were more particularistic and subdued. This modification of ideas indicated a gradual reconciliation among the settlers to the wilderness lands around them. Though but an inchoate movement, this change represented an early stage in the process of provincialization. "Men doe now build, as looking on a setled Commonwealth," wrote John Winthrop's financial advisor in 1637, "and therefore, wee looke at posteryty and what may be usefull or profitable for them." [27] Despite the Puritans' unfamiliarity with the wilderness, New England was becoming their home.

[26] *Recs. of Mass. Bay,* II, 49.
[27] James Luxford to John Winthrop [c. December 1637], *Winthrop Papers,* III, 516.

PART II

THE SYMBOLIC WILDERNESS

WHILE the Puritans obviously lacked direct knowledge of the New World prior to colonization, they possessed nevertheless elaborate resources to interpret the meaning of their endeavors. Biblical references to the wilderness are manifold, and the Puritans well understood the significance of the wilderness in historical Christianity. Such metaphors provided the founders of New England with adequate standards to assess their wilderness adventure in America.

The wilderness of the Old Testament is often depicted as a desert or wasteland. In Exodus, the Lord led the Israelites through these arid areas in order to test their faith. The difficulties and hardships of this journey afforded the Puritans a useful precedent for explaining their problems in America. By viewing themselves as the children of Israel, the Puritans saw the hazards of settlement as part of a divine plan to purge the colonists of their iniquities before they could enter the Promised Land. The Puritans' need to surmount these temptations, moreover, constituted an important part of the moral battle against Satanic forces. Only by defeating the forces of evil concealed in the wilderness could the settlers of New England hope for salvation among the Elect.

Although a time of trial and temptation, the forty-year sojourn in the wilderness also signified an escape from the persecutions of Egypt. The concept of the wilderness as a sanctuary from worldly corruption persisted in Christian thought and influenced, in fundamental ways, the Puritans' understanding of their self-exile from Stuart England. While the political life of England deteriorated into civil war, the Puritans sang praises to the Lord for providing them with a secure haven protected by a Hedge of grace. And as this divine shield preserved the colonies from demonic threats in America, New Englanders were convinced that God would remain with His children as long as they retained their faith in Him.

Because of its isolation, therefore, the wilderness denoted a place of sanctuary as well as an area of trial. Both ideas implied that such regions lacked the amenities and impediments of human society. Since wilderness areas possessed none of the trappings of Christian civilization and, indeed, contained specific temptations for the Christian man, historical Christianity interpreted the wilderness as a state or symbol of sin. These metaphors remained vivid for seventeenth-century New Englanders, and the colonists of Massachusetts Bay applied such concepts to the wilderness lands around them. And as the Bible juxtaposed the wilderness with the Promised Land, the Puritans were persuaded that they could transform the sinful areas into gardens of the Lord. The spiritual metamorphosis of the wilderness thereby became a prime justification for converting the Indians and expanding the areas of settlement in New England.

Despite its inherent evil, however, the Biblical wilderness remained the site of religious insight. The trials and temptations of the wilderness were designed to purify and strengthen the faith of the Israelites. Moreover, it was in the wilderness that Moses received the Tabernacles from the Lord. In the New Testament, John the Baptist entered the wilderness to reinvigorate the faith. The Puritans of New England viewed these examples as literal precedents of their own experience. Like their ancestors, they too ventured into the wilderness to revitalize their religion. And, with the successful transplantation of churches in the New World, the Puritans were assured that their ecclesiastical institutions embodied the true pattern of God's will.

The persistence of Christian metaphors in Puritan thought enabled the colonists to examine their situation from traditional perspectives. Thus the applicability of Biblical rhetoric facilitated the Puritans' adjustment to the American wilderness and reduced, to a degree, the impact of the new environment.

The symbolic wilderness, to be sure, involved evident paradoxes. Yet by accepting these contradictions, the Puritans retained their identification with Christianity and viewed themselves as the heralds of the Protestant Reformation.

CHAPTER IV

"A Sorrowful Estate"

GREETED by a virgin forest and dense underbrush, the Puritan colonists were awed by the tasks awaiting them in America. Their background provided scant preparation for the difficulties of settling the untamed continent, and only a painful process of trial and error enabled the Puritans to adjust to life in the wilderness. William Hubbard expressed sympathy for the settlers who first confronted the rigors of American life and who, "for want of experience and judgment," exposed themselves to the hazards of an unknown wilderness. "These poor people," he stated, "met with much hardship . . . in their first settlement, before they were well acquainted with the state of new Plantations, and nature of the climate." The Puritans explained their unexpected difficulties with reference to the Biblical wilderness wherein the Lord tempted His people to test their faith. Although Thomas Shepard praised the peacefulness of New England, he acknowledged that the land remained "a place of tryall." For, as his eldest son, Thomas Shepard, Jr., declared, "In a wilderness there is not only want of many comforts, but there is a danger as to many positive evils." Shortly after the arrival of the Winthrop fleet in the summer of 1630, Francis Higginson preached his final sermon from Matthew 11:7: "What went ye out into the wilderness to see"? With his waning strength, he reminded the people that New England was founded primarily for religious purposes and admonished the colonists to be prepared for "the streights, wants, and various trials which in a wilderness they must look to meet withal." [1]

The difficulties of subduing the American forest profoundly influenced Puritan thought about the wilderness. Viewing themselves as the chosen nation, the Puritans interpreted their hardships in New England as part of a divine scheme to complete the Protestant Reformation in the New World. For the Saints, the troubles of colonization signified the process of humiliation necessary for everlasting salvation. Beset by immense dangers, they conceived of the wilderness experience as Armageddon, the final moral battle against the forces of the antichrist. But as a result of projecting their hostility for the external forces *of* the forest onto the wilderness itself, the Puritans regarded their condition in New England with obvious antipathy. To be sure, New Englanders frequently exploited their wilderness troubles for propaganda purposes in England. But the idea of the wilderness as the antithesis of civilization became increasingly influential as the Puritans attempted to explain their self-exile in America.

The Puritans regarded their wilderness adversity from their self-image as the chosen people and were therefore confident that the hardships of settlement would be transitory. On the eve of migration, John Winthrop assured his wife that God tries His children "with troubles or difficulties" in order to reveal his omnipotence.[2] As the Lord

---

[1] Hubbard, "A General History," V, 139; Shepard, "Autobiography," 391; Thomas Shepard, Jr., *Eye-Salve; Or, A Watch-Word From our Lord Jesus Christ unto his Churches* (Cambridge [Mass.], 1673), pp. 3–4; Mather, *Magnalia*, I, 363–64.

[2] John Winthrop to His Wife, March 10, 1629[/30], *Winthrop Papers*, II, 219.

had protected the Israelites in their exodus from Egypt, so, believed the Puritans, He would carry New Englanders safely through the perils of the New World. Such ideas sustained the Puritans during the early years of colonization, a time when they were plagued by hunger, disease, and general insecurity. Roger Clap, who arrived in Massachusetts Bay in 1630, recalled the hardships of the first months in New England when "mean Victuals . . . would have been sweet unto me." In defense of the migration to Massachusetts, Emmanuel Downing argued that the settlers "have ventured farr in respect of theire estates and hasard of theire lives, and there yet submit to manie dangers, both of their lives and goods." The "many troubles and adversityes," however did not dampen the optimism of John Winthrop. God "is pleased still to humble us," he wrote upon the untimely deaths of Lady Arbella Johnson, Francis Higginson, and others whose bodies proved too weak for the work at hand. Yet, added Winthrop, "he mixes so many mercyes with his corrections, as we are perswaded he will not cast us off." Such difficulties would persist, Winthrop conceded, but only until the Lord "hath purged our corruptions and healed the hardnesse and error of our heartes . . . that he may have us relye wholy upon himselfe." The burning of several dwellings during the first winter in Massachusetts merely assured Winthrop that God "will doe us the more good at the last." [3]

The problems which plagued the Bay colony in its formative stages were repeated as New Englanders pressed further inland and erected new plantations on

[3] [Roger Clap], *Memoirs of Capt. Roger Clap* (Boston, 1731), p. 4; Emmanuel Downing to Sir John Coke, October 12, 1633, *Proc. M.H.S.*, second ser., VIII (1894), 383; John Winthrop to His Wife, September 9, 1630, John Winthrop to John Winthrop, Jr., March 28, 1631, James Hopkins to John Winthrop, February 25, 1632[/33], *Winthrop Papers*, II, 312, III, 21, 105.

the expanding frontier. The establishment of the colony at Connecticut was, in many ways, more difficult than the founding of Massachusetts, for besides the problems of starvation and illness, the outbreak of the Pequot War swiftly challenged the safety of that inland settlement. "The tymes are dangerous, our beginnings raw, our encumbrances great [,] necessities many, our helps few, and these few weake," wrote the forlorn colonists at Hartford. Stressing the hardness of the first winter and the failure of the crops, Thomas Hooker reminded the men of Connecticut that only "the marcy of the Lord . . . preserved us against the malis of devils." In a sermon preached shortly after the settlement of Hartford, Hooker compared the New England Puritans with the Children of Israel. God's people "must come into, and go through a vast and roaring Wilderness, where they must be bruised with many pressures, humbled under many overbearing difficulties," he exhorted, "before they could possess that good land which abounded with all prosperity, [and] flowed with Milk and Honey." [4] These "overbearing difficulties" reappeared as other inland settlements blossomed in the wilderness. It was therefore fitting that John Davenport, in the first Sabbath celebrated at New Haven, devoted his morning sermon to the text, "Then was Jesus led up of the spirit into the wilderness to be tempted of the devil." [5]

But the Puritans did not limit the idea of wilderness temptations to the hardships of early settlement. As the

[4] The Church at Hartford to John Winthrop, July [1637], *Winthrop Papers*, III, 520; Thomas Hooker, "Thanksgiving Sermon," October 4, 1638, printed in Andrew Thomas Denholm, "Thomas Hooker: Puritan Teacher, 1586–1647" (unpublished doctoral dissertation, Hartford Theological Seminary Foundation, 1961), p. 431; Hooker, *Application of Redemption*, IX, 5.

[5] Matthew 4:1. See, Isabel M. Calder, *The New Haven Colony* (New Haven, 1934), p. 83.

Great Migration to New England tapered off in the early
1640s, a serious economic depression threatened the Puritan colonies. "God hath dealt with us as his people Israel,"
intoned Peter Bulkeley, for "we are brought out of a fat
land into a wilderness, and here we meet with necessities." In recent months "our props which we leaned upon,
are broken, our mony spent, our [e]states wasted, and
our necessities begin to increase upon us," he suggested,
"and now we begin to be full of cares and feares, what
we shall doe." But despite these problems, Bulkeley urged
his congregation to retain their faith in the Lord. "The
hardships which Israel suffered for awhile in the wilderness," he reminded them, were "recompenced with a
Land flowing with milke and honey." The Lord has not
brought us into the wilderness to destroy us, averred
Bulkeley, but He has designed the hardships of life in
the wilderness in order to purge the settlers of their iniquities. "Your hearts now sink," preached Thomas Shepard at this time. But God "brings his people into [a] very
low condition, to humble them and to show them more
of his grace." Shepard confided similar thoughts to his
diary. "I was tempted to think that I had been out of my
Way in occasioning any to come to this Wilderness among
so many snares," he wrote, but "I saw it was my Duty
[to] make the best of what is, because bad at best." [6]

Later Puritans extolled their ancestors for surmounting
the trials and temptations of the wilderness. The records
of Charlestown, rewritten in the mid-1660s, described
the arrival of the Endecott group in Salem "where . . .
they met with the dangers, difficulties, and [wants] at-
tending new plantations in a solitary wilderness, and so
far remote from their native country." And the narrator

[6] Bulkeley, *Gospel Covenant*, pp. 143, 144, 264, 268, 276; Shepard,
Parable, 105; Thomas Shepard, "Meditations and Experiences," printed
in *Three Valuable Pieces* (Boston, 1747), part III, 30-31.

depicted the area surrounding Charlestown as "an uncouth wilderness." [7]

The younger John Winthrop similarly recalled the problems of early settlement. "Plantations in their beginnings have worke ynough," he observed, and require "buildings, fencings, cleeringe and breakinge up of ground, lands to be attended, orchards to be planted, highways and bridges and fortifications to be made." In short, he concluded, the planters have "all thinges to doe, as in the beginninge of the world." Michael Wigglesworth later applauded his parents for departing "their native land, a new built house, a flourishing Trade, to expose themselves . . . to the Distressing difficulties of a howling wilderness." Edward Johnson similarly lauded the process of overcoming wilderness hardships. In great detail he described the painful exodus of Simon Willard and his fellow settlers through the dense wilderness to establish the town of Concord. After pushing through immense thickets and underbrush, they arrived at their destination, but only to commence the arduous task of building a town. As Johnson pointed out his readers, "the toile of a new Plantation [is] like the labours of Hercules"; it is "never at an end." "Thus," continued Johnson, "this poore people populate this howling Desert, marching manfully on . . . through the greatest difficulties, and forest labours that ever any with such weak means have done." [8]

The trials which beset this wilderness people, however, were not unrewarding, for the Puritans were assured that God would bring them to the promised land. Writing of the various crises of 1637—the Pequot War, bad harvests, and the Antinomian controversy—Johnson argued that

[7] "The Early Records of Charlestown," printed in Young, *Chronicles*, pp. 373, 374–75.

[8] John Winthrop, Jr. to Henry Oldenburg, November 12, 1668, Photostat, Winthrop Mss.; Wigglesworth, "Autobiography," 137; Johnson, *Wonder-working Providence*, pp. 112, 114, 115.

"the Lord surrounded his chosen Israel with dangers
deepe to make his miraculous deliverance famous
throughout . . . the World." God inspired "a small hand-
full of his people" to come into "a forlorne Wilderness,"
where they were stripped of "all humane helps" and
plunged into "a gulph of miseries [so] that they may swim
for their lives through the Ocean of his Mercies, and land
themselves safe in the armes of his compassion." Other
Puritans echoed this interpretation of wilderness hardships. Although the people of God in New England encountered manifold "wilderness trials, and straits and sorrows," the Lord refreshed and rewarded them with "the
beauties of holiness, where they have seen and met with
Him whom their souls love." [9] With such blessings, the
Almighty would recompense His children for the tenacity
of their faith in the wilderness.

Subsequent generations of New England Puritans ap-
preciated the difficulties of their forefathers because they
too seemed to be beset by similar wilderness temptations.
As religious zeal seemed to decline among the children
of the Elect during the later decades of the century, Puritan preachers argued against succumbing to the trials of
the wilderness. In 1660 the Massachusetts General Court
ordered a day of public humiliation in hope that the
Lord "would be pleased yett to continew the angell of
his presence with us in these our wilderness travailes."
"Let me tell you," declared John Norton in a posthu-
mously published lecture, "it is a greater matter to be
subject to" the ordinances of Christ "then to come over
the Seas, or to endure the troubles of a Wilderness." John
Allin, minister of the church at Dedham, compared the

---

[9] Johnson, *Wonder-working Providence,* p. 151; William Greenhill and
Samuel Mather, "To The Reader," in Thomas Shepard, *Subjection to
Christ in all his Ordinances, and Appointments, The best means to pre-
serve our Liberty* . . . , reprinted in *Works,* III, 275.

Puritans to the Biblical Israelites whom God led through "a terrible Wilderness" to test their faith. "Let us not be secure," he warned, for "the Lord may justly carry us through a wilderness of sore tryals, to purge his Churches of the Chaffe, and to take us off from the world." Only faith in the Lord, he insisted, would enable the Puritans to surmount their wilderness hardships. Although New England has been free from the domestic turmoils which have plagued old England, wrote Simon Bradstreet, "wee have not beene, nor yet are, free from our tryalls and troubles, for soe our god sees it good for us." At the end of the seventeenth century, John Higginson, one of the last surviving original settlers of Massachusetts, observed "that our wilderness-condition hath been full of humbling, trying [and] distressing providences." But God's purpose has been to determine "whether, according to our profession and his expectation, we would keep his commandments, or not." [10]

"It may be when you came into this Wilderness," intoned Jonathan Mitchel, minister to the souls of the Cambridge congregation, "you thought that this would be a place of your own, and that none would ever trouble themselves to come into this Corner to trouble you." "But alas," he added, "New-England is but earth and not heaven" and therefore not exempt from the machinations

[10] *Recs. of Mass. Bay*, IV, Part I, 418; John Norton, "The Evangelical Worshipper," in *Three choice and profitable sermons* (Cambridge [Mass.], 1664), p. 36; John Allin, *The Spouse of Christ Coming out of affliction, leaning upon Her Beloved* (Cambridge [Mass.], 1672), pp. 2, 6, 10; Simon Bradstreet to Richard Baxter, February 5, 1671[/72], printed in Raymond Phineas Stearns, ed., "Correspondence of John Woodbridge, Jr., and Richard Baxter," *New England Quarterly*, X (1937), 583; John Higginson, "An Attestation to this Church-History of New-England," in Mather, *Magnalia*, I, 16. For a brilliant interpretation of the decline of religious zeal in New England, see Perry Miller, *The New England Mind: From Colony to Province* (Cambridge [Mass.], 1953), particularly Part I.

of the devil. Several decades later, Cotton Mather agreed that the people of New England "have had, in almost every new lustre of years, a new assault of extraordinary temptation upon them; a more than common 'hour and power of darkness.' " The Puritans, to be sure, anticipated Satanic opposition to the settlement of Massachusetts, for the erection of true religion in America would challenge the kingdom of the devil. While still in England, Thomas Shepard warned that "The Divell will sometimes undermine and seek to blow up the strongest walls and bulwarkes." And one correspondent urged the younger John Winthrop to be careful "that ye become not a prey to the spoyler, and your children turne heathen." [11]

The Puritan colonists translated all adversity as signs of this diabolic opposition and conceived of the wilderness as the site of moral battle against Satan and his minions. To prevent the success of the Puritans' settlements, the devil could muster a variety of forces since all the reprobate of the world were at his disposal. Although other seventeenth-century people, including the colonists of Virginia, also believed in the potency of Satanic power, the Puritan sense of mission and the prevalence of wilderness difficulties led the settlers of New England to view themselves as special targets of the devil.[12] "Sathan bends his forces against us, and stirres up his instruments to all kindes of mischeife," wrote Governor Winthrop in one of

[11] Jonathan Mitchel, *A Discourse of the Glory To Which God hath called Believers By Jesus Christ*, second ed. (Boston, 1721), p. 14; Mather, *Magnalia*, II, 490; Thomas Shepard, *The Sincere Convert, Discovering the Paucity of True Beleevers* . . . (London, 1642), p. 3; Edward Howes to John Winthrop, Jr., November 9, 1631, *Winthrop Papers*, II, 55.

[12] For the widespread belief in the resourcefulness of the devil, see, Basil Willey, *The Seventeenth Century Background: Studies in the Thought of the Age in Relation to Poetry and Religion* (New York, 1955), pp. 60–61, first published in 1934; Miller, "Religion and Society in . . . Virginia," pp. 113–14.

his earliest letters from New England, "so that I thinke heere are some persons who never shewed so much wickedness in England as they have doone heer." Many of these dissatisfied colonists returned to England and continued to disparage the Massachusetts settlement. This criticism confirmed Winthrop's belief that such people were instruments of Satan and convinced other Puritans that the devil, threatened "soe mightily" by the transplantation of the true church, was attacking the infant colony "with all [h]is might and maine." In the summer of 1632 this moral battle was vividly symbolized by a prolonged struggle between a mouse and a snake at Watertown, in which "after a long fight, the mouse prevailed and killed the snake." The startled witnesses of this event informed John Wilson, "a very sincere, holy man," who was then pastor of the church at Boston, of the details of this remarkable conflict. Wilson, recorded Winthrop, "gave this interpretation: That the snake was the devil; the mouse was a poor contemptible people, which God had brought hither, which should overcome Satan here, and dispossess him of his kingdom." [13]

Despite the Puritans' conviction that they would ultimately defeat the forces of antichrist, they were nevertheless wary of succumbing to the diabolic temptations concealed in the wilderness. "Beware of Sathans wylye baites," advised Thomas Tillam, for "he lurkes amongs[t] you." New England "is a place . . . of tryalls," wrote Ezekiel Rogers, minister of the church at Rowley; "The devill is very buisy and I suppose and hope that you have angred him" by threatening to usurp his throne. After the initial hardships of settlement were overcome, wrote John Winthrop, "Lest we should, now, grow secure, our

[13] John Winthrop to His Wife, July 23, 1630; Edward Howes to John Winthrop, Jr., November 28, 1632, *Winthrop Papers*, II, 303, III, 101; Winthrop, *Journal*, I, 83–84.

wise God (who seldome suffers his owne . . . to be long without trouble)" permitted the devil to launch a new and more vicious attack upon His children, "which proved [to be] the sorest tryall that ever befell" the colony. This renewed attempt at "interrupting the passage" of the gospel into America which Winthrop referred to was the rise of Anne Hutchinson and her Antinomian coterie. Winthrop viewed this woman as "an instrument of Satan . . . fitted and trained for her service" to poison "the Churches here planted." Thomas Shepard, who incidentally was one of Mrs. Hutchinson's most vehement prosecutors, was less specific about the Satanic forces which challenged the establishment of true religion in the New World. "We are in fear (in this country) of enemies," he preached, who "are plotting to take us unawares." But, he added courageously, "it may be the Lord will help then." [14]

The idea of a moral battle in the wilderness was especially relevant to particular problems which confronted the New England Puritans. In the early stages of the English civil wars, for example, William Hooke suggested that New England could assist the Puritan party in the mother country through prayer to God. "I cannot but look upon the Churches in this Land," he maintained, "as upon so many severall Regiments . . . lying in ambush here under the fearne and brushet of the Wilderness." Although "our weapons [are] as invisible to the eye of flesh, as our persons are to all the world," he concluded, "we can fight this day with the greater safety to our selves, and danger to our enemies." Other Puritan ministers interpreted un-

[14] Tillam, "Uppon the first sight of New England," 331; Ezekiel Rogers to John Winthrop, November 3, 1639, *Winthrop Papers*, IV, 150; [John Winthrop], *A Short Story of the Rise, Reign, and Ruine of the Antinomians* [1644], reprinted in *Antinomianism in the Colony of Massachusetts Bay, 1636-1638*, ed. by Charles F. Adams (Boston, 1894), pp. 71, 228; Shepard, *Parable*, 422.

necessary removals beyond the hearing of the Lord's ordinances as submission to wilderness temptations. Criticizing the existence of "a wandering disposition" among
some of the colonists, Thomas Shepard and John Allin
argued that "the Lord hath exercised his people with various temptations, by liberties, by offers of large outward
accomodations, by wants and straits, by various opinions
vented by Satan and his instruments" to expand beyond
the confines of the religious society. Such people, they
felt, had retreated in the face of moral conflict.[15] In 1649
the Court of Deputies of the Bay colony urged their
friends at Plymouth to extirpate the cause of anabaptism
there. "Wee hope," concluded the missive; that "neither
Sathan nor any of his instruments shall, by theis, or any
other errors, disunite" our fellowship. Increase Mather,
later in the century, equated drunkenness with spiritual
conflict against the devil. "It is sad," he observed, "that
ever this Serpent should creep over into this Wilderness,
where threescore years ago he never had any footing."[16]

For most New Englanders, however, Satan's use of the
Indians as instruments of his malice was more pertinent
than the battlefields of England or the problem of inebria-
tion on the streets of Boston. The Puritans believed that
the Indians, like all unregenerate men, were in the clutches
of Satan. Furthermore, there was a consensus among New
Englanders that the natives actively sought comradeship
with the devil and worshipped him in their "pawawes."
The frequency of war scares in the New England colonies

[15] William Hooke, *New-Englands Sence, of Old-England and Irelands
Sorrowes* [1645], reprinted in Samuel Hopkins Emery, *The Ministry of
Taunton*, 2 vols. (Boston, 1853), I, 116; Shepard [and Allin], *A Defence
of the Answer*, pp. 182–83. For a fuller discussion of the problem of
frontier expansion, see Chapter VII.

[16] *Recs. of Mass. Bay*, III, 174; Increase Mather, *Wo to Drunkards* . . . (Cambridge [Mass.], 1673), p. 20.

convinced the Puritans that the Indians were in league with Satan to drive the English from the land and thereby disrupt the transmission of the gospel into America.[17]

The Lord would occasionally permit these forces of evil to surface, as when He allowed "Satan to stir up the Pequot Indians to kill divers English men" in the mid-1630s. On the eve of that conflict, Roger Williams reported that the Pequots did not fear the Puritan armies because the natives expected assistance from Satan. John Underhill, a captain of the New England troops in that war, referred to the Pequots as "these devil's instruments," and was certain that "the old serpent, according to his first malice, stirred them up against the church of Christ." "So insolent were these wicked imps grown," he continued, "that like the devil, their commander, they run up and down as roaring lions, compassing all corners of the country for a prey." Edward Johnson viewed the war as a "quarrell . . . as antient as Adams time, propagated from that old enmity between the Seede of the Woman, and the Seed of the Serpent, who was the grand signor of this war." [18]

Other Puritan commentators also regarded the war as part of the moral battle against antichrist. John Higginson, then surrounded by menacing Indians at the Saybrook plantation in Connecticut, urged the Bay colony to commence hostilities "to defend (not so much their lives and liberties . . .) as the glorious gospell of Jesus Christ." Thomas Shepard suggested that the Lord permitted the

[17] Wood, *New Englands Prospect*, pp. 92–94; Emmanuel Downing to John Winthrop [c. August 1645], *Winthrop Papers*, V, 38–39. For a more complete discussion of the Indian crises in New England, see Chapters VII and VIII.

[18] [Clap], *Memoirs*, p. 20; Roger Williams to John Winthrop [c. September 1636], *Winthrop Papers*, III, 298; John Underhill, "News from America" [1638], reprinted in *Colls. M.H.S.*, third ser., VI (1837), 9, 15; Johnson, *Wonder-working Providence*, p. 148. For the best treatment of the Pequot War, see Vaughan, *New England Frontier*, Chapter V.

devil to muster his Pequot forces to prevent the Puritans from relaxing their never-ending struggle against sin and temptation. "I believe," he preached, "we should not have had those Pequot furies upon us, but God saw we began to sleep." "The Lord . . . tried the faith and courage of his people," agreed John Hull, by "permitting some villanies and outrage against the English." But Hull was certain that the Almighty fought at the side of His children and enabled them to vanquish the diabolical heathen. In the aftermath of the Pequot War, the Puritans continued to conceive of the Indian as a tool of the devil. Thomas Hooker called them Satan's "emissaryes," and John Winthrop reported that "Hobbamock (as they call the devil)" appeared before the friendly Indians "in divers shapes" and attempted to persuade them "to forsake the English." [19]

The Puritans frequently articulated their subsequent distrust of the natives in terms of the moral battle in the wilderness. A promotional tract designed for English consumption assured readers that "we are wont to keep [the Indians] at such a distance, (knowing they serve the Devill and are led by him) as not to imbolden them too much, or trust them too farre." In 1645 a war with the Narragansett tribe was narrowly averted. "So Sathan may stir up and combyne many of his Instruments against the Churches of Christ," stated the delegates to the New England Confederation in defense of war preparations, "but . . . the Lord of Hostes, the mighty one in battaile," will preserve His people.[20]

[19] John Higginson to John Winthrop [c. May 1637], Thomas Hooker to John Winthrop [c. December 1638], *Winthrop Papers*, III, 405, IV, 78; Shepard, *Parable*, 376, 378; John Hull, "Diary of Public Occurrences," *Transactions and Collections of the American Antiquarian Society*, III (1857), 171–72; Winthrop, *Journal*, I, 260.

[20] "New Englands First Fruits," p. 428; "A Declaration of former passages . . . betwixt the English and the Narrohiggansets . . . ," in *Acts of the Commissioners of the United Colonies*, ed. by David Pulsifer,

John Eliot, the celebrated apostle to the Indians, was equally cautious about the natives because many of the tribal chiefs opposed the conversion of their subjects. He urged the English "not to be secure . . . for if the Adversary should discerne us naked and weak . . . who knoweth what their rage and Sathans malice may stirre them up unto to work us a mischief"? The Puritans, however, expected divine assistance in their quarrels with the heathen. In 1654, for example, the General Court of Connecticut ordered a day of public humiliation to seek the Lord's blessing for an expedition against the Narragansetts. New Englanders also viewed King Philip's War, which erupted in 1675 with fiery onslaughts upon the inland English settlements, as an attack of the devil. William Hubbard accused Satan of instigating the war, and Increase Mather referred to the "barbarous Indians (who like their Father the Devil are delighted in Crueltyes)." [21] Such metaphors undoubtedly reinforced the Puritans' basic distrust of the natives.

The hardships of the wilderness condition and the ongoing conflicts against Satan and his Indian associates were frequently exploited by New England apologists to rationalize Puritan behavior and policies. Thomas Shepard and John Allin repudiated charges made by English Puritans that New Englanders, by migrating to the New

2 vols. (Boston, 1859), I, 55–56. (Hereafter cited as *Acts of the Commissioners.*)

[21] John Eliot to Edward Winslow, October 21, 1650, printed in Henry Whitfield, "The Light appearing more and more towards the perfect Day. Or, A Farther Discovery of the present state of the Indians in New-England . . . ," reprinted in *Colls. M.H.S.*, third ser., IV, 142–43; *Pub. Recs. Conn.*, I, 263; William Hubbard, *A Narrative of the Troubles with the Indians in New-England*, ed. by Samuel G. Drake under the title, *The History of the Indian Wars in New England*, 2 vols. (Roxbury, Mass., 1865), I, 52–53; Increase Mather, *A Relation Of the Troubles which have hapned in New-England, By reason of the Indians there* (Boston, 1677), p. 57.

World, were running away from trouble. Declaring that the colonists did not embrace heretical separatism, or the complete rejection of the Church of England, they defended the settlers of New England who left "our accomodations and comforts . . . to go to a wildernesse, where wee could forecast nothing but care and temptations" solely for the pleasure of enjoying the holy ordinances. They denied that they were "deserters of our Brethren, and the Cause of Christ" because it would have been "far more easie unto many of us to have suffered" in England "then to have adventured hither upon the wildernesse sorrows wee expected to have met withall." [22]

John Eliot later defended the migration to New England along similar lines. "Assuredly, if any do come hither to greaten their wealth," he suggested, "I believe by such time as he had conflicted with our wildernesse wants, difficulties, uncertainties, temptations, and raw beginnings," he would have recognized "the great folly of coming out of an old settled and cultur'd land into a wildernesse." Most of the people who migrated to New England, he pointed out, did so "with a suffering minde," because "by coming hither" they "changed a comfortable being for the outward man into a condition full of labour, toile, sorrow, wants, and temptations of a wildernesse." Only men of intense devotion would "go into a wilderness," he maintained, "where nothing appeareth but hard labour, wants, and wilderness-temptations (stumble not countrymen, at the repitition of that word, wildernesse-temptations)." [23]

New Englanders capitalized on the propaganda value

[22] Shepard [and Allin], "The Preface to the Reader," *A Defence of the Answer*, pp. 7, 9. I am indebted to Professor Leon Howard of the University of California at Los Angeles for first suggesting this idea to me; see also his study, *Literature and the American Tradition* (New York, 1960), pp. 24–25.
[23] John Eliot, "The Learned Conjectures touching the Americas," in Thomas Thorowgood, *Jews in America, or, Probabilities That the Americans are of that Race* (London, 1660), pp. 21–22.

of such rhetoric in their petitions to England. In 1651 the Massachusetts General Court remonstrated for a new patent and reminded the members of Parliament that the settlement of New England "hazarded not only all our estates but alsoe the lives of ourselves and our posterity." After the Restoration of King Charles II, the Bay colony again requested permission to retain its traditional religious institutions for which the colonists had transported themselves "into the vast and wast wilderness, choosing rather the pure Scripture worship . . . in this poore, remote wildernes, amongst the heathens, then the pleasures of England." In a similar petition, the General Court of Connecticut reminded the king that the founders of that colony "undertooke a troublesome, hazardous and chargeable discovery of the more inland parts of the Country." [24]

In 1664, when a committee of the crown arrived to investigate the state of New England, the Massachusetts General Court protested the presence of the delegation and argued that their fathers had settled the colony "with great labour, hazards, costs, and difficulties" and, "for a long time" had wrestled "with the wants of a wilderness, and the burdens of a new plantation." The Court also rejected the idea of appointing a proprietor for the New England colonies. They argued that "the length and coldnes of the winters, the difficulty of subduing a wildernesse, [the] defect of a staple commodity, [and] the want of money" created much "poverty and meanesse" among the people of New England. Only "with hard labour," they maintained, could "men gett a subsistence for theire families." A decade later, New Englanders still believed in the efficacy of these arguments to persuade English politicians. The Council of Connecticut assured King Charles that the charter of 1662 strengthened "our hearts

---

[24] "Copy of a Petition to the Parliament in 1651," 428; *Recs. of Mass. Bay*, IV, Part I, 450, 453; *Pub. Recs. Conn.*, I, 582.

and hands" and enabled the people "to graple further with the difficulties of this severe wildernesse." Massachusetts Bay similarly defended its original charter and asserted that an exact survey of their lands "in so hideous a wilderness possessed by an enemy, would be the worke of a few yeares." [25]

Aside from such self-conscious political statements, the Puritans expressed little satisfaction with their wilderness condition. Thomas Shepard viewed the wilderness as "a sorrowful estate," and most of the Puritan settlers would have agreed that the New England forest was the antithesis of civilization as they understood it. Only the joys of his English ministry, rhymed John Cotton shortly after his arrival in Massachusetts Bay, enabled him to overlook "the grief to be cast out into a wilderness." William Wood juxtaposed "the vacant Wildernesse" with the more luxurious life of Europe, and Peter Bulkeley regarded the wilderness as "a low condition." A later colonist remarked with surprise that "our Condition . . . is much more Comfortable then I could expect . . . in a wildernesse." [26]

Seventeenth-century colonists throughout the New World repeatedly lamented the absence of European cultural institutions in America.[27] And like their contempo-

[25] *Recs. of Mass. Bay,* IV, Part II, 129–30, 132, 238, V, 110; *Pub. Recs. Conn.,* II, 341.

[26] Shepard, *Parable,* 281; [John Cotton], "Another Poem made by Mr. Cotton . . . upon his removal from *Boston* to this Wilderness," printed in Norton, *Abel being Dead,* pp. 29–30; Wood, *New Englands Prospect,* p. 30; Bulkeley, *Gospel Covenant,* p. 134; Edward Browne to Nehemiah Wallington, December 10, 1644, Sloane Mss., 922, fol. 144b. For a discussion of this theme, see Roderick Nash, *Wilderness and the American Mind* (New Haven, 1967), Chapter II.

[27] See, Cawley, *Unpathed Waters,* pp. 139–41; Hariot, "A Briefe and True Report," I, 323; Lescarbot, *History of New France,* I, 15; John Smith, "A Map of Virginia. With a Description of the Countrey . . ."

raries elsewhere, the Puritans often contrasted the poverty of life in New England to the "full-fed Land" they had left behind. John Hull suggested that the example of many respectable people forsaking "all to embrace such a wilderness condition" helped provoke the demand for reformation in old England. Edward Johnson depicted Francis Higginson's removal to Massachusetts Bay as a step "From fertill Soyle to Wildernesse of Rocks." In advising his son not to volunteer for any military ventures while in England, the younger John Winthrop urged the youth to be content "with a meane condition heere in this wildernesse." [28]

Puritan writers frequently viewed the wilderness state as incompatible with the amenities of civilization. Charles Chauncy, second president of Harvard College, regarded a "wast howling wilderness" as a place "without any ministry, or schooles, and means of education for . . . posterity." New Englanders often appealed to such definitions to apologize for their crudities. "That the discourse comes forth in such a homely dresse and course habit," inscribed Thomas Hooker in the preface of his masterful treatise on congregationalism, "the Reader must be desired to consider, *It comes out of the wildernesse,* where curiosity is not studied." Colonists, he added, "if they can provide cloth to go warm, they leave the cutts and lace to those that study to go fine." Jonathan Mitchel similarly pointed out the difficulty of obtaining scribes "in this wilderness." And the young Samuel Sewall requested a correspondent

[1612], printed in *Travels and Works of Captain John Smith* . . . , ed. by Edward Arber, 2 vols. (Edinburgh, 1910), I, 83.

[28] Johnson, *Wonder-working Providence,* pp. 62, 47; Hull, "Diary of Public Occurrences," 167–68; John Winthrop, Jr. to Fitz-John Winthrop, September 25, 1660, Winthrop Mss., V, 25; see also, Nicholas Street, "Considerations Upon The Seven Propositions Concluded by the Synod . . . ," in John Davenport, *Another Essay for the Investigation of the Truth in Answer to Two Questions* . . . (Cambridge [Mass.], 1663), p. 71.

to excuse his errata, because of "the writer's Wilderness-Condition." [29]

Such disclaimers also provided a useful shield for the General Court of the Bay colony. In the midst of the English civil wars, the Court appealed to Parliament for the right to legislate for itself. The petitioners, however, tactfully admitted that "the wisdom and experience of that great council" makes it "far more able to prescribe rules of government, and to judge of causes, than such poor rustics as a wilderness can breed up." Shortly after the death of John Norton in 1663, the General Court attempted to attract Dr. John Owen to replace him. In their letter to Owen, the Court confessed that "the condition of this wildernes doeth present little that is attractive as to outward things" and acknowledged the many trials of life in New England. Such candor apparently dissuaded Owen, for he rejected the position. At the time of the arrival of the royal commissioners, John Winthrop, Jr. assured Lord Clarendon that his majesty's representatives would be received respectfully "according to the capacity of this our wildernesse condition." [30]

The Puritan authorities also appealed to this low state to oppose unnecessary lavishness. The Massachusetts legislature enacted two laws which stated that excessive apparel was "unbecoming a wilderness condition." And William Leete, Governor of the colony at New Haven,

[29] Charles Chauncy, *Gods Mercy, shewed to his people in giving them a faithful Ministry and schooles of Learning for the continual supplyes thereof* (Cambridge [Mass.], 1655), pp. 15–16; Thomas Hooker, *A Survey of the Summe of Church-Discipline* (London, 1648), Preface; Jonathan Mitchel, "Preface" [1659], in Shepard, *Parable*, 8; Samuel Sewall to [Daniel Gookin?], March 16, 1671[/72], "Letter Book of Samuel Sewall," in *Colls. M.H.S.*, sixth ser., I–II (1886–88), I, 20.

[30] "Petition of the General Court of Massachusetts to the Earl of Warwick," quoted in Winthrop, *Journal*, II, 312; The General Court of Massachusetts to Dr. John Owen, in *Recs. of Mass. Bay*, IV, Part II, 98; John Winthrop, Jr. to Lord Clarendon, September 25, 1664, Photostat, Winthrop Mss.

remarked that "it might better have suited a wilderness state, in its infancy especially," if people were less ostentatious. This attempt to restrain extravagance reveals an interesting adaptation of wilderness rhetoric to more general social problems, for Englishmen at this time also resented common people who attired themselves in the garments of the socially superior. Thus in New England the symbolic wilderness reinforced the desire of Puritan leaders to maintain at least the forms of the traditional social structure.[31]

Several more sensitive New Englanders recognized the inability of a wilderness to sustain higher cultural achievements and lamented their isolation from England. John Winthrop, Jr., upon returning to New England in 1663 after a two-year sojourn in his native land, referred to "the English of this wildernesse" in a way which suggests his awareness of the low cultural state of New England. The following year, Winthrop articulated these sentiments more clearly in a letter to Sir Robert Moray, first president of the Royal Society in London. He confessed to have "sad and serious thoughts about the unhappinesse of the condition of a wilderness life so remote from the fountains of learning and noble sciences" and expressed gratitude that he could retain at least some contacts with recent intellectual currents through his correspondence. In a subsequent letter, Winthrop bemoaned his isolation from England and regretted that he could not be of more service in acquiring "such mean things as could be had in such a wilde place as this." In the younger Thomas Shepard, however, Winthrop found a kindred spirit. "It is no small part of our great unhappinesse who dwell in

---

[31] *Recs. of Mass. Bay,* IV, Part I, 60, Part II, 41; William Leete to Samuel Disbrowe, Esq., October 10, 1654, printed in *N.E.H.G.R.,* XLI (1887), 357; Peter Laslett, *The World We Have Lost* (New York, 1965), p. 35; Bridenbaugh, *Vexed,* p. 292.

these out-skirts of the earth," wrote Shepard upon receiving some missives of the Royal Society from Winthrop, "that we are so little acquainted with those Excellent things that are done, and found out in the world and discoursed of by those learned and worthy personages." John Woodbridge, Jr., of Killingworth, Connecticut, similarly bewailed the three thousand miles which separated him from the citadels of learning in England. "I have so long conversed with Oakes and Indians," he wrote to Richard Baxter, "that I find my selfe very much disenabled to manage any due and humble Intercourse with those that are so much exalted." [32]

Such murmurings suggest that the Puritans, like their Biblical predecessors, found the wilderness situation to be extremely uncomfortable. The continuing difficulties of settlement and the seemingly endless Satanic assaults combined with the sense of isolation to convince the Puritans that New England was a wilderness of sorrows. Although their faith in the Lord enabled them to persevere and surmount the variety of obstacles which they confronted daily, the Puritans nevertheless expressed their antipathy to the wilderness with disarming frequency. The New England colonists loved, not the wilderness itself, but the advantages which derived from being in that state.

[32] John Winthrop, Jr. to Peter Stuyvesant, June 17, 1663, Photostat, Winthrop Mss.; John Winthrop, Jr. to Sir Robert Moray, September 20, 1664, printed in *Colls. M.H.S.*, fifth ser., VIII (1882), 90; John Winthrop, Jr. to Henry Oldenburg, November 12, 1668, Photostat, Winthrop Mss.; Thomas Shepard, Jr. to John Winthrop, Jr., March 8, 1668/9, Winthrop Mss., XVIII, 59; John Woodbridge, Jr. to Richard Baxter, October 14, 1669, "Correspondence of Woodbridge and Baxter," 565.

CHAPTER V

"A Place of Safetie"

ALTHOUGH the Puritans believed that the Lord, in anger, would destroy the protective Hedge which surrounded England, they were confident that He would not forget His exiled children in the wilderness. With the transplantation of the true church to New England, they felt, the Lord would provide for the resurrection of a Hedge of grace in America and would construct new walls of safety around the Wilderness Zion. "Gods worke shall not be hindered," suggested John Cotton, because the Lord will protect His people though their enemies "are most strongly combined" to destroy them.[1] Throughout the seventeenth century, New Englanders continued to view their colony as a refuge from the havoc and chaos of Europe. The seeming decline of morality at home and the outbreak of the civil wars in England strengthened the Puritans' belief in the sanctuary blessings of the New World. Moreover, as the Lord delivered the colonists from Indian plots and wilderness difficulties, the idea of the refuge bulwarked the Puritans' sense of divine mission and reinforced the notion of uniqueness in New England.

The Puritans viewed the protective shield, upon which they placed so much hope, as an expression of political godliness. Wise and judicious laws, stated Thomas Shep-

[1] John Cotton, *Gods Mercie Mixed with his Justice,* ed. by Everett H. Emerson (Gainesville, Florida, 1958), p. 60.

ard, are "hedges and fences to safeguard both moral and ceremoniall precepts." "God would have all Nations preserve these fences for ever," he declared, because they eliminated the "danger of the treading down of those laws by the wilde beasts of the world and bruitish men." The General Court of Massachusetts Bay recognized the importance of such godly legislation, and in the introduction to the General Laws of that colony, the Court described its statutes as hedges which protect men from injury and preserve domestic tranquillity.[2] Thus the sense of security, though ultimately inspired by God, rested firmly upon human achievement.

Appropriate legislation, however, could be enacted only by pious, well-informed men. For this reason, the Puritans placed great emphasis upon their civil Magistrates. "The Christian Magistrate," wrote John Cotton, "is as a Wall" of protection. Such a wall, he contended, is "High to keep out invasions of enemies and other evils"; it is "Close, to keep the people within bounds from breaking out into disorders"; third, the wall is "Firm, whereon to erect any good course, for the publicke good of present and future ages"; finally, the Magistrate serves as a "partition, to divide between right and wrong, to give every man his civil right." Upon the election of the younger John Winthrop to the Court of Assistants of the Bay colony, an old friend, Edward Howes, praised him as "a cheife piller to the new Syon" and urged him to "helpe with councell and seasonable advice to reare the walles." Cotton pointed out, nevertheless, that the populace must not impede the work of the Magistrates. Since the Lord relied upon certain individuals to effect His will on earth, the masses must support wholeheartedly the work of their

---

[2] Shepard, *Theses Sabbaticae*, Part I, 27–28; *The Book of the General Lawes and Libertyes* [revised 1660], ed. by William H. Whitmore in *The Colonial Laws of Massachusetts* (Boston, 1889), p. 120.

rulers. If you "stint them where God hath not stinted them, and if they were walls of brasse," argued Cotton, your enemies "would beate them downe." But, he added, "give them the liberty God allows, and if it be but a wall of sand it will keep" the state inviolate.[3]

Committed to an organic world-view which grounded all behavior within a cosmic scheme, the Puritans recognized that such men were merely instruments of the divine will. Like other seventeenth-century Englishmen, they regarded civil order as a manifestation of God's grace and believed that faith in the Lord alone would enable them to locate and elect godly magistrates. These civil authorities could assure the continued presence of the Lord by administering the state according to religious precepts, but the Almighty God never relinquished His ultimate power to preserve or destroy a nation.

The settlers of New England were certain nevertheless that the Lord would shine upon His wilderness people and guarantee the sanctity of their refuge. The colonists at Salem transported "great ordnance . . . to keep out a potent adversary," wrote Francis Higginson, but "that which is our greatest comfort and means of defence above all others," he averred, "is that we have here the true religion and holy ordinances of Almighty God taught amongst us." And "if God be with us," he asked rhetorically, "who can be against us"? John Winthrop defended the migration of 1630 with similar language. In response to the objection that New England lacked natural fortifications, he replied that when God seated His people, He

[3] John Cotton, *A Brief Exposition with Practical Observations upon the Whole Book of Canticles* (London, 1655), pp. 226–27; Edward Howes to John Winthrop, Jr., June 5, 1633, *Winthrop Papers,* III, 124; John Cotton, *An Exposition upon the Thirteenth Chapter of the Revelation* (London, 1655), p. 73. See also, John Cotton, *A Brief Exposition of the whole Book of Canticles, or, Song of Solomon . . .* (London, 1642), pp. 252–53, and Cotton, "A Brief Exposition Upon Ecclesiastes," 108.

chose an unprotected site "besett with potent and bitter enemyes . . . , yet so long as they served him, and trusted in his helpe they were safe." In his farewell address to the Winthrop fleet, John Cotton assured the colonists that the people of God "shall enjoy their owne place with safety and peace." But he exhorted them to "ever let the name of the Lord be your strong Tower; and the word of his Promise the Rocke of your refuge." [4]

During their first decade in America, New Englanders emphasized the seeming protectiveness of the Lord for His people in the wilderness. The only overt threat to Puritan safety emerged with the outbreak of the Pequot War in 1637. The Puritans, however, were certain that the Lord would preserve the colonies despite that menace and thus allow the Hedge to remain unbroken. In the early stages of that conflict, John Higginson attempted to persuade the Bay colony of the wisdom of engaging in open war against the natives. He stressed the precarious position of the Lord's "pretious servants" settled along the Connecticut River and hoped that God "will make salvation unto them for walls and bulworks round about." "I see not how they could have been preserv'd without a miracle," he maintained, "had not the Lord in abundant mercy . . . kept the many hundreds of our enimies . . . from attempting any thing there as yet." Only "the rock of Israel will defend you," declared Roger Ludlow of Windsor to the isolated colonists at Springfield.[5]

The subsequent destruction of the Pequots convinced the Puritans that the Lord had assisted them in this wilderness conflict. John Winthrop viewed the tracking of

---

[4] Higginson, "New-Englands Plantation," p. 259; "Objections Answered: First Draft," 136; Cotton, "Gods Promise," 11, 15.

[5] John Higginson to John Winthrop [c. May 1637], *Winthrop Papers*, III, 405; Roger Ludlow to William Pynchon [May ?] 17, 1637, "Pincheon Papers," *Colls. M.H.S.*, second ser., VIII (1826), 235–37.

the Indian hoards as "a Divine Providence," and pointed out that the "defeat of the Pequods at Mistick happened the day after our general fast." As long as the Puritans stood with God, the Lord would stand with them and fight at their sides. Massachusetts Bay celebrated the victory with "a day of publick thanksgiveing to God for his great mercies in subdewing" their enemies. Thomas Shepard preached that the conquest of the Pequots signified the presence of the Lord among His people in America. With God as their captain, he assured the colonists, they would be able to crush the Indians, because the Lord shall make "your Enemyes . . . as grasshoppers." "Take leave of base feare . . . for this will divide you in times of danger," exhorted Shepard in 1638, and remember that God has preserved you "from Pekoat times that he could have made to have vex you." Despite dire warnings, wrote John Winthrop of the Pequot War, "in due time, the Lords hand appeared . . . and we felt but little of those great dangers which were justly to be feared." [6]

The protectiveness of the Lord was manifested in other ways during the early years of settlement. Thomas Hooker recalled the difficulties of the first winter at Connecticut and warned his congregation that "if once the hearts of men foresacke the way of God in his ordinances[,] truly marcy and truth will foresacke them." If "men doe not seek God and humble thire souls before him," he advised, "conclud that desolation is neare." The Lord had protected the colony in its infancy, maintained Hooker, and it was the duty of the settlers to prevent the departure of God. Upon his safe arrival at New Haven, Stephen Winthrop, a son of the Governor of Massachusetts, extolled

---

[6] Winthrop, *Journal*, I, 227, 221; *Recs. of Mass. Bay*, I, 204; [Thomas Shepard?], Sermons, August 1637–September 1638, pp. 11, 270, Miscellaneous Sermon Mss., Massachusetts Historical Society; Shepard, "Election Sermon," 366; John Winthrop to Richard Saltonstall and Others [c. July 21, 1643], *Winthrop Papers*, IV, 409.

the watchfulness of the Lord "when we were runinge rigt into great (though unknowen) danger." [7] Thus the Puritans ascribed their safety in New England to the protective hand of the Almighty.

The destruction of the Pequot Indians did not diminish the sense of insecurity in New England, for the natives continued to threaten the infant colonies. Despite this harassment, the Puritans placed their faith in the Lord and His protective shield. When "a people are in Covenant with God, and cleave onely to him," preached William Hooke, "hee enters himselfe presently [as] the Generall of all their forces, leades their Armies, and fights their Battails." Though our enemies be powerful and our defenses vulnerable, maintained Peter Bulkeley, yet "we shall be kept safe unto salvation by a divine power which is above all and over all. "I fear there is, at this day, as deep mischief plotting against New England as ever the sun saw," suggested Thomas Shepard in the early 1640s, but, he added, "the Lord shall be with us, as of late has he not been in the midst of us for a refuge"? And John Cotton exhorted the people of New England to look to the Lord for preservation in battle. "Trust not upon the experience of your Captaines or Souldiers to fight by Land and Sea," for "they are but the Arm of flesh." Faith in the Lord, he asserted, is the only sure defense in time of war.[8]

The Puritans articulated this confidence in divine assistance in their subsequent relations with the natives. In 1642, shortly after a rumored Indian plot proved to be unfounded, the Bay colony voted to restore the guns

[7] Hooker, "Thanksgiving Sermon," pp. 426, 430–31; Stephen Winthrop to Margaret Winthrop, January 7 [1638/39], *Winthrop Papers*, IV, 93.

[8] Hooke, *New-Englands Sence*, p. 114; Bulkeley, *Gospel Covenant*, p. 253; Shepard, *Parable*, 259; Cotton, *An Exposition upon . . . Revelation*, pp. 110–11.

which they had confiscated from the nearby tribes. Although reluctant to rearm these Indians, they realized that they had no legal right to these weapons. Therefore, noted John Winthrop, "we thought it better to trust God with our safety than to save ourselves by unrighteousness." Three years later, the Puritan settlements prepared for a war against the Narragansetts and commissioned Edward Gibbons to lead their troops. Asserting that God "is both our sword and sheild," the combined colonies assured Gibbons that the Lord would assist and bless this expedition "for his owne glory and his peoples safety and prosperitie in this wilderness." War did not come, however, and none was more gratified than William Pynchon, founder of the town of Springfield, who feared the toll of battle. But if war is inevitable, he added optimistically, God "will fight for us as he did in the Pequot war." [9]

Later Puritan commentators praised the name of the Lord for His protection of the wilderness communities. In 1646 the delegates to the New England Confederation suggested that the colonies compile a historical record of "the many speciall providences of God towards" the Puritans, for "in all respectes [He] hath bene a sun and shield to us." A decade later they issued a similar request so that the wonderful works of God for His wilderness people would be remembered. Edward Johnson's chronicle of New England, though not an authorized history, praised the magnificence of the Lord "in gathering together stones to build up the walls of Jerusalem" so that "his Sion [would] be surrounded with Bulworkes and Towres." [10] The sense of divine protection enabled the Puritans to oppose Oliver Cromwell's scheme to trans-

---

[9] Winthrop, *Journal*, II, 80; *Acts of the Commissioners*, I, 40; William Pynchon to John Winthrop, October 27, 1646, *Winthrop Papers*, V, 115.

[10] *Acts of the Commissioners*, I, 82–83, II, 176–77; Johnson, *Wonderworking Providence*, pp. 141, 227.

plant the New England saints in Ireland. "We know not any countrey more peaceable and free from warre," argued the Massachusetts General Court in criticizing the proposed abandonment of New England. Charles Chauncy later applauded the "great things" that God had done for the people in the wilderness. The Lord "hath subdued . . . all our enemyes, Indians and others," he preached, "whose hight was like the hight of Cedars, and they were strong as Oaks." [11]

Moreover, New Englanders recognized the advantages of their wilderness settlements as a refuge when they compared their situation to that of their native country. It appeared to the colonists in America that England, by proceeding in its sinful ways, was provoking the Lord to punish that nation. Prior to his migration to the New World, John Davenport wrote that the "want of christs government in this miserable land" is the "great cause of the wrath of god." [12]

Throughout the 1630s, numerous Englishmen repeated such gloomy appraisals in their correspondence to friends in New England. One writer complained "of badd times, and great fear of worse" and believed that God would chastise England. "We have not feared" the Lord "when he hath smitten us, except fainedly," wrote a friend to the younger John Winthrop, "and then [we returned] to our sins againe." Surely "It were just" if God proceeded "to deal wonderfully in his judgements against us." Another correspondent predicted "a stroake, for longe hath this nacion beene treasureing upp wrath, which . . . eare longe will fall full heavie uppon us." Referring to

---

[11] "Copy of a Letter to Oliver Cromwell in 1651, from the General Court of the Massachusetts," printed in Hutchinson, *History of Massachusetts-Bay*, I, 431–32; Chauncy, *Gods Mercy*, pp. 18–19.

[12] [John Davenport?], Essay on What the Visible Church is and The government of it [c. 1633], Davenport Mss., American Antiquarian Society.

the evils of the age and the departure of godly ministers to New England, a friend of the Winthrop family lamented "the heavy condition of this land that doe parte with such as showld hav been pilars to uphold it." In 1636 a smallpox epidemic ravaged the city of London and many people interpreted this crisis as a portent of worse catastrophes. Serious troubles begin "to peepe upon us soe frightfully, that mens harts faile them for feare," wrote Edward Howes, noting that several thousands had fled the city. A London tailor, John Smith, viewed the plague as a condemnation from the Lord, and Lucy Downing warned of future epidemics which she regarded as "the arguments of the allmighties controversie with us." [13]

To such people, England's future appeared bleak. "Things with us are dayly much worser," wrote one distressed correspondent, and "what another yeare may bringe forth the Lord knoweth." From his refuge in Dorchester, Richard Mather urged Englishmen to eradicate their religious iniquities before the Lord unleashed his fury. If the church of England does not reform itself, he warned, "then you know it might be just with God to cast off such utterly . . . so as never to walke among them any more." John Cotton suggested that bad rulers could desolate a state and observed that England was rapidly approaching this dangerous condition.[14]

While old England was apparently bent upon self-

[13] John Bluett to John Winthrop, Jr., March 14, 1632[/33], Henry Jacie to John Winthrop, Jr., December 17, 1633, Edward Revell to John Winthrop, April 20, 1636, Muriel Sedley Gurdon to Margaret Winthrop, May 5 [1636], Edward Howes to John Winthrop, Jr., June 21, 1636, John Smith to John Winthrop, September 10, 1636, Lucy Downing to Margaret Winthrop [c. March 1636/37], *Winthrop Papers*, III, 108, 142–43, 252, 258, 272, 307, 353.

[14] Robert Stansby to John Winthrop, April 17, 1637, *Winthrop Papers*, III, 391; [Richard Mather], *Church-Government and Church-Covenant discussed in an answer . . . to two and thirty questions . . .* (London, 1643), pp. 26–27; Cotton, "A Briefe Exposition Upon Ecclesiastes," 111–12, 113.

destruction, New Englanders cherished their refuge in the wilderness. Thomas Shepard suggested that religious purity itself was a refuge into which God had led His people to escape the jaws of death which would prostrate England. One correspondent compared "the wicked land" of England to "that blest land" in America which God had provided for His people. New Englanders agreed with this assessment, and Edward Howes reported several letters from the Bay colony which "tearmeth England to be babell and Sodome, and that it should shortly fall." Governor Winthrop referred to "many private letters" from friends in England which stated that "the departure of so many of the best [people] had bred sad thoughts in those behind of the Lord's intentions in this worke, and an apprehension of some evil days to come upon England." Such fears, intimated Winthrop, were responsible for the Privy Council's attempts in the mid-1630s to block further migration to New England and to revoke the patent of the Massachusetts Bay company.[15]

The Puritans were assured nevertheless that God would preserve His Hedge about New England and protect the colonies from such demonic threats. One correspondent advised New Englanders that a General Governor would be sent to America. But since God is "your protector," he added, "why should you feare"? Nathaniel Ward of Ipswich observed that New England was a sanctuary from the vices of England, and John Winthrop stressed the safety of Massachusetts in opposing a proposed transplantation to the West Indies. Despite their self-confidence that the Lord would uphold the Puritan settlements, many New Englanders continued to hope that God might yet bring England to reform itself. The Bay colony

---

[15] [Shepard?], Sermons, August 1637–September 1638, p. 167; Sir John Clotworthy to John Winthrop, Jr. [c. April 1635], Edward Howes to John Winthrop, Jr., March 18, 1632[/33], *Winthrop Papers*, III, 196, 112, note 1; Winthrop, *Journal*, I, 127.

held a general day of fast, partly because of "the calamities upon our native country" and the "famine and sword" which threatened old England.[16]

The declension in England which the Puritans had criticized for two decades climaxed in 1640 with the summoning of the first Parliament in eleven years. English Puritans were apprehensive about this shift in the political winds. After more than a decade of personal rule by Charles I, they hoped that the convening of a Parliament would pave the way for religious reformation; yet the seating of that body also signified the possibility of a bloody war against Protestant Scotland.

Englishmen expressed their cautiousness and trepidation in their letters to friends in New England. One correspondent predicted "troublesome times approaching both within and without the Kingdome," and a former neighbor of John Winthrop expressed hope that the Lord would favor the impending Parliament and guide its labors. Writing from London, however, Nehemiah Bourne, a supporter of the New England colonies, doubted that the coming Parliament would be successful. "The times that are approaching," he commented, "threaten heavy and sad things." "We are full of feares," confessed another friend of New England, "and have little ground of Comfort or hope of Good, save onlie in the Lord." Although "we are not yett come to open and common sufferings," he added, "yet our burdens within and without are manie." A London observer described the "dangerous times" that "nowe are in England," and expressed hope that prayers to God might deliver the nation "out of those jud[g]ments we dayly expect."[17]

[16] Samuel Reade to John Winthrop, Jr., March 5, 1635[/36], Nathaniel Ward to John Winthrop, Jr., December 24 [1635], *Winthrop Papers*, III, 234, 216; Winthrop, *Journal*, I, 333–34, 208.
[17] John Tinker to John Winthrop, February 26, 1639[/40], Thomas Gostlin to John Winthrop, March 2, 1639[/40], Nehemiah Bourne to

The troubles which beset England underscored the importance of the wilderness as a refuge. "Wee are full of feares gennerally," wrote William Bisbey to a friend at Hartford shortly after the dissolution of the Short Parliament, "but ould age and other infirmities" proscribe the possibility of seeking sanctuary in Connecticut. Two years later, when the full impact of the English civil wars began to be felt, another correspondent explained that the havoc erupted because "the whole land was over runne with Idoletry and popery and all manner of abominations." England was "in a most woefull and miserable Condistion," he confessed, but "many of you" in America "did foresee" the impending chaos "which did make you fly to New England as to a City of refuge for to preserve your selves." If the wars persist and "the clouds shoulde still increase, and threaten a further storme in that Land," wrote Ezekiel Rogers of Rowley to a fellow minister in England in 1646, "I would earnestly commende it to your deepest thoughts" that you seek "a resting place for yourselfe . . . among God's Exiles here," rather than continue "to expose yourselfe, in your age, to more dangers where you are." [18]

Although New Englanders stressed the sanctuary benefits of the wilderness condition, they were extremely sympathetic to their suffering brethren beyond the seas.

John Winthrop, March 4, 1639[/40], John Venn to John Winthrop [April 1640], John Tinker to John Winthrop, April 13, 1640, *Winthrop Papers*, IV, 205, 212, 214, 221, 223, 225. See also, Sir Simonds D'Ewes to Lady D'Ewes, in *Autobiography and Correspondence of Sir Simonds D'Ewes*, ed. by James Orchard Halliwell, 2 vols. (London, 1845), II, 263, 268.

[18] William Bisbey to George Wyllys, May 14, 1640, "Wyllys Papers," *Collections of the Connecticut Historical Society*, XXI (Hartford, 1924), 12; Nehemiah Wallington to James Cole [1642], Sloane Mss., 922, fol. 105; Rev. Ezekiel Rogers to Rev. Elkanah Wales, October 4, 1646, "Letters written by Rev. Ezekiel Rogers . . . , Rev. Daniel Rogers . . . , and Samuel Shepard . . . , 1626–1647," *Essex Institute Historical Collections*, LIII (1917), 222.

William Hooke's moving sermon, *New Englands Teares,
for Old Englands Feares,* preached in July, 1640, reminded the colonists of their special blessings in the wilderness but urged them not to express satisfaction at the
turmoil in England. "Of all the Christian people this day
in the world, wee in this Land enjoy the greatest measure
of peace and tranquillity," declared Hooke as he emphasized the need to be compassionate. The situation in
England, he maintained, is extremely grave for the
"swords that have hung a long time over their heads by
a twine thread, judgements long since threatned as foreseene by many of Gods messengers" are about to fall upon
that nation. War is usually God's last stroke upon a people who have ignored earlier warnings; and civil war
especially is the most severe of such chastisements. A
"land that is the garden of Eden before an enemy, behind
them is like a desolate Wildernesse," he concluded, "and
it is very wofull when people and land shall be wasted
together." [19] John Haynes, one-time Governor of the Bay
colony and a leading Magistrate in Connecticut, expressed
similar sentiments. Upon receiving "verry sadd" com-
munications from his native land, Haynes proposed a
monthly day of humiliation "to seeke the lord in behaulfe
of his poore Churches ther and elsewher." Although
Massachusetts did not implement such frequent days of
repentance, the Bay colony observed several fast days
because of the troubles in England and prayed that the
Lord might reconstruct a new Hedge there. Thomas
Shepard was equally sympathetic, although he felt that
England had brought destruction upon herself by ignoring the Lord's counsel. He expressed "Lamentation, for
them, that nation[,] that people, those churches[,] those

[19] William Hooke, *New Englands Teares, for Old Englands Feares.
Preached in a Sermon on July 23, 1640* . . . (London, 1641), pp. 7,
9, 13, 21.

persons" that now must rely entirely upon the transitory and impotent powers of men.[20]

Puritan sympathy for the condition of England did not obviate the desire among New Englanders for the reformation of religion in their mother country. George Cleeve of Casco Bay implied the true sentiments among the mass of people by indicting a man for supporting the king instead of the Parliamentary faction. Nathaniel Ward was more direct in encouraging the forces of reformation. "We your Brethren . . . on the American Sea-coasts," he announced to godly Englishmen, "will send up Armies of Prayers . . . in the day of Battel." [21]

Despite this compassion for their embattled friends, many Puritans were convinced that the civil wars were a just reward for a hard-hearted nation. John Endecott of Salem rebuffed a proposal to send delegates to England to obtain assistance for the economically-distressed settlements. Among his reasons for opposing such a mission was that it was "somewhat preposterous to goe from a place of safetie provided by God, to a place of danger under the hand of God to seeke reliefe." [22] Poetess Anne

[20] John Haynes to John Winthrop, December 1, 1643, *Winthrop Papers,* IV, 418; *Recs. of Mass. Bay,* I, 339, II, 38; Winthrop, *Journal,* II, 67, 81; Thomas Shepard, Sermon preached March 29, 1643, Shepard Mss., Houghton Library (Harvard College Library).

[21] George Cleeve to John Winthrop, January 27, 1643[/44], *Winthrop Papers,* IV, 434; [Nathaniel Ward], *The Simple Cobler of Aggawam in America* [1647], reprinted in *Tracts and other Papers Relating Principally to the Origin, Settlement, and Progress of the Colonies in North America . . . ,* ed. by Peter Force, 4 vols. (Washington, 1838–46), III, 49.

[22] John Endecott to John Winthrop [c. February 1640/41], *Winthrop Papers,* IV, 315. See also, Winthrop, *Journal,* II, 25–26, for a fuller discussion of Endecott's motives. Unlike Endecott, many New Englanders returned to their native land and participated in the political and religious controversies there. For a discussion of these men and their motives, see William L. Sachse, "The Migration of New Englanders to England, 1640–1660," *American Historical Review,* LIII (1948), 251–78.

Bradstreet developed this theme in a dialogue between the two Englands. "Alas dear Mother," queried the youthful land, "What ails thee" and makes "thee hang thy head, and cross thine arms": To which the suffering parent replied by describing her neglect of earlier warnings and her persistence in her wicked ways. Overlooking "sad *Germanyes* dismantled walls," the "starved Christians" of Rochel, and "poor Ireland bleeding," she confessed that

> Mine heart obdurate stood not yet agast.
> Now sip I of that cup, and just't may be
> The bottome dreggs reserved are for me.[23]

John Davenport agreed with this assessment and suggested that "Gods controversy" with England was prolonged "because they shaped their Course too much by Politike and nationall prudence, and held not strictly to the Rules of Gods worde." The Lord "may very justly" carry "the sword, Famine, Pestilence, or other plagues, upon England[,] Ireland, or other nacions," concurred Richard Mather, because "the corruptions of men are so many and great." Thomas Shepard justified the departure of God from England because the people of that country, by neglecting the holy ordinances, had already rejected the ways of the Lord. "I confesse I have long feared a Sword to come upon that pleasant Land," preached Shepard, "to make this unthankfull and evill generation understand, what they would not by the voice of [the] Gospel while it rid circuit amongst them." He added, however, that the tendencies toward religious toleration which emerged in the aftermath of the civil wars "is a certain presage . . . of worse dayes then ever yet England saw; Such cracks and flawes in the new building of Reforma-

---

[23] Anne Bradstreet, "A Dialogue between Old *England* and New; concerning their present Troubles, *Anno*, 1642," in *Works*, pp. 330, 334–35, 336–37.

tion," he concluded, "portent a fall." [24] The contrast between the two Englands was obviously not accidental.

With the outbreak of the civil wars in their native land, many New Englanders renewed their praise for the security of the wilderness condition. "When I thinke of the trublesom times and manyfolde distractions that are in our native Countrye," wrote Governor Winthrop's wife Margaret, "I thinke we doe not pryse our happinesse heare" as we should, because we live "in peace when so many troubles are in most places of the world." Thomas Shepard hailed the Lord for carrying him "to a land of peace" while "all England and Europe are in a flame." The Lord brought His children to New England, asserted Samuel Symonds, "To affourd a hiding place for some of his people that stood for the truth while the nation was exercised unto bloud." The idea of the refuge also entered the religious debates in New England. The petitioners for religious toleration in Massachusetts, led by Robert Child, praised the Almighty for procuring "the much desired fruits of peace and plenty" for the people in the wilderness, "while our native land[,] yea the Christian world[,] is sharply afflicted by the devouring sword and the sad consequents of intestine warres." And John Cotton responded to their challenge with similar rhetoric. The Lord "brought this people hither . . . and made this wilderness an hiding-place for them, whilst he was chastising our nation," preached Cotton, and "there is no question but He will defend us from the underminings of

[24] "John Winthrop's Discourse on Arbitrary Government," July 1644, marginal note, in *Winthrop Papers*, IV, 472; Richard Mather, The Summe of Seventie Lectures upon the first chapter of the second epistle of Peter, p. 113 (May 4, 1647), Mather Mss., American Antiquarian Society; Shepard, *Subjection to Christ*, 294–95; Thomas Shepard, *New Englands Lamentation for Old Englands present errours, and divisions, and their feared future desolations if not timely prevented* (London, 1645), pp. 1–2.

false brethren."[25] Samuel Danforth also lauded the wilderness as a haven from the turmoil of England. "Peace," he rhymed, is "The choisest garland that this Country wears."

> It bloom'd in Europe once, but now is gone
> And's glad to finde a desart-mansion,
> Thousands to buy it with their blood have sought,
> But cannot finde it: we ha't for nought.[26]

In explaining the Lord's wrath against England, however, Puritan ministers chided their congregations not to become overly secure in their wilderness refuge lest, by growing hard-hearted, they force God to withdraw from New England. On a day of public humiliation "in reference to the sad estate of the Lords People in England," Thomas Shepard exhorted New Englanders to be thankful that "the Lord should bring us hither, and give us peace in Church and Common-wealth." We must "look upon it as a rare and singular mercy of the Lord," he insisted, that God "hath kept us here in peace, and saved us from being poisoned with the Delusions in the world." He urged the people to be grateful for divine blessings, for while "Germany lies in blood, and . . . when England's lights and lamps are going out, no people have such peace" as New Englanders. Shepard, however, bemoaned the fact that "New England's peace . . . breeds strange

---

[25] Margaret Winthrop to John Winthrop, Jr., October 10, 1642, Samuel Symonds to John Winthrop, January 6, 1646[/47], *Winthrop Papers,* IV, 357, V, 126; Shepard, "Autobiography," 391; Petition to the Massachusetts Bay General Court, May 19, 1646, Miscellaneous Bound Mss., I, Massachusetts Historical Society; John Cotton sermon on Canticles 2:15, quoted in Mather, *Magnalia,* I, 283. See also, Edward Winslow, "New-Englands Salamander . . ." [1647], reprinted in *Colls. M.H.S.,* third ser., II, 128.

[26] Samuel Danforth, *MDCXLVIII An Almanack for the Year of our Lord 1648* . . . (Cambridge [Mass.], 1648) [p. 8].

security; and hence prayer is neglected here." Although he recognized that the temptation to slight the Lord was greater in New England because "others are in storms, we in calms," he nevertheless admonished the people not to provoke God to chastise them with divine wrath. "So I say," he proposed, "go to the Palatinate, go to Germany, France, go to the places whence you came, and 'see what the Lord had done'" to disbelievers. John Cotton stressed the role of ministers and magistrates as watchmen of the inner and outer man. But these pillars "need to watch over themselves" he advised, "lest they betray their trust" and defile the Hedge. Such a situation occurred in England, he maintained, and forced the Lord to depart from that nation. He implored his audience not to permit a recurrence of that withdrawal.[27]

The continued political turmoil in England which culminated in the restoration of the Stuart monarchy convinced the Puritans of their refuge blessings and reinforced their self-image as the chosen people. While the Lord had tried the inhabitants of England with pestilence and wars, He had spared His wilderness children. John Winthrop, Jr. thankfully acknowledged "the admirable goodnesse of the Lord, who hath beene an hiding place to" New Englanders "when their precious brethren have been so long under the hurries, hazards, and sufferings by civill warres." With the outbreak of "those sad and unhappy times of troubles and wars . . . in England, which we could only bewaile with sighs and mournfull teares," remonstrated the General Court of Connecticut, we have

---

[27] Thomas Shepard, *Wine for Gospel Wantons: Or Cautions Against Spirituall Drunkenness* (Cambridge [Mass.], 1668), p. 13; Shepard, *Parable,* 92, 170, 258–59, 244; Cotton, *A Brief Exposition with Practical Observations upon the Whole Book of Canticles,* p. 139; see also, Thomas Shepard, Sermon of October 4, 1648, Seaborne Cotton Mss., New-York Historical Society.

"hid our selves behind the Mountains, in this desolate desert." We chose "rather to sit solitary and wait only upon Divine Providence for protection," they added, "than to apply ourselves to any of those many changes of powers" in England. Michael Wigglesworth extolled the Lord in verse for providing a "hiding place" for His children "When th' overflowing scourge did pass/ Through Europe like a flood." While Englishmen bathed "In brother's blood," God crowned the gates of New England with peace. After depicting the ongoing troubles of Europe, Abraham Pierson of New Haven expressed hope that God would "appoynt his Salvation [to] be walls and Bulwarkes to his Sion" in New England.[28]

This self-consciousness among Puritans of God's "wall of defence" around New England heightened their feeling of uniqueness and strengthened the sense of social identity for later generations. Although "A wilderness is not hedged in, nor fenced about," preached the younger Thomas Shepard, the Lord has "given you those walls, such Defenders, Leaders, Instruments of safety, whereby you have been hedged about, walled in, and secured." New England alone, he added, has "had the blessing of peace, while others have been wasted with War." The Lord is "an high place of refuge . . . in time of trouble," intoned Shepard, and "his Name is a strong tower . . . to which" His people "may flee and be safe." In 1665 a petition signed by ninety-one inhabitants of the town of Hadley agreed that the Lord "hath in a day of danger in the world, bid us enter . . . a place of refuge and

[28] John Winthrop, Jr. to ———, September 19, 1660, Abraham Pierson to John Winthrop, Jr., March 13, 1666[/67], Winthrop Mss., V, 184, XVI, 111; Connecticut General Court to King Charles II [c. 1661], *Pub. Recs. Conn.*, I, 582–83; Michael Wigglesworth, "Gods Controversy with New England" [1662], reprinted in *Proc. M.H.S.*, XII (1873), 85, 87; see also, Simon Bradstreet to Richard Baxter, February 5, 1671[/72], "Correspondence of Woodbridge and Baxter," 583.

covert from the storm." "His eyes have been upon us," they declared, "his salvation for walls and bulworks," and He has blessed our dwellings with "his cloud and smoke and flaming fire." [29]

Other New England ministers also reminded the people of the blessings of their protective Hedge. "That Jerusalem have a Wall for the safety and preservation of it," preached Jonathan Mitchel in the Massachusetts Bay election sermon of 1667, "is requisite to the welfare of Israel." And John Oxenbridge urged New Englanders to remember that "the Lord hath contended with other Nations," while "you in this Land have had a Truce." God has carried you "to a place of Rest, and Peace, and Safety, and Liberty," maintained Urian Oakes. New England, he continued, is a "place of Retirement and Hiding . . . when other parts of the World have been embroiled," and our native land "hath been involved in Blood and Distractions." Yet "God hath found us in this Desert Land, and compassed us about, *and kept us as the Apple of his Eye.*" [30]

The shadow of the Lord thereby assured New Englanders of their special mission. In the face of wilderness adversity and the debacles of Europe, God permitted New England to thrive in tranquillity. Blessed by a Hedge of grace, the Puritans viewed their wilderness as an impregnable haven. As long as they retained the purity of their religion and maintained their faith in the Lord, New

[29] Shepard, Jr., *Eye-Salve*, pp. 5, 11, 14; Thomas Shepard, Jr., Sermon preached October 13, 1661, Discourses, IV, Shepard Mss., American Antiquarian Society; Petition of Hadley to the Massachusetts General Court, April 25, 1665, quoted in Sylvester Judd, *History of Hadley . . .* , second ed. (Springfield, Mass., 1905), pp. 73–75.

[30] Jonathan Mitchel, *Nehemiah on the Wall in Troublesom Times* (Cambridge [Mass.], 1671), p. 4; Oxenbridge, *A Quickening Word*, p. 14; Urian Oakes, *New-England Pleaded with, And pressed to consider things which concern her Peace, at least in this her Day* (Cambridge [Mass.], 1673), pp. 17, 20.

England would flourish and provide sanctuary for the spiritual exiles of the world. A wilderness of hardships thereby became a place of salvation, a citadel for the true religion amidst the corruption of man.

CHAPTER VI

"The Pleasant Gardens of Christ"

IF the Puritans believed that a Hedge of grace surrounded New England, they were equally confident
that similar barriers secured their church societies. Such
partitions, they felt, distinguished the Lord's Saints from
the reprobate of the world and preserved the churches
from unorthodox incursions. The younger Thomas Shepard declared that the existence of doctrinal purity within
the New England churches constituted a wall which separated the Jew from the Gentile, the saint from the sinner.
By excluding the unregenerate, this shield defended the
godly churches from the onslaughts of disbelievers. The
Lord preserved His churches "from being Licked and
swallowed up among these wilde beasts of the field," maintained John Cotton, "so as they that kicked, kicked against
a thorny hedge, and pricked and galled themselves at
length." Religion as well as civil order, suggested the General Court of Massachusetts Bay, protects Christians
"against the Injuries of men," and those enemies that assault the Hedge "will find [that] the thornes will prick
them." [1]

[1] Thomas Shepard, Jr., Sermons on Canticles, July 27, 1669, Shepard
Mss., American Antiquarian Society; Cotton, *A Brief Exposition with
Practical Observations upon the Whole Book of Canticles*, p. 36; *The*

The belief in a separating wall about the church reinforced the Puritans' sense of uniqueness and assured them that they differed considerably from the people beyond the boundaries of the Hedge, the lost souls who traveled wildly through the chaotic wilderness of the world. Such ideas moved orthodox colonists to oppose religious toleration in New England. Yet the paradoxical conception that the wilderness was also a place of religious insight compelled the Puritans to reexamine the symbolic image of the wilderness as a state of reprobacy. The desire to reconcile this contradiction and the commitment among Puritans to complete the Reformation in the New World led New Englanders to attempt to regenerate the doctrinally barren wilderness in America, in essence, to fill the land of spiritual darkness with divine illumination.

The sanctity of the ecclesiastical Hedge was as important as the secular wall in assuring social security. God's "precious truths" are "pulled up by the rootes and cast over the hedge," wrote John Davenport of the religious declension in England prior to his migration to America, "and weeds[,] thornes[, and] nettles" violate the purity of the church. Thomas Shepard urged New Englanders to preserve their doctrinal barrier, because "The enemies of the church did never yet hurt the church" as much as "the church's sins." "What would this despised country do," asked Shepard, if God should uproot His Hedge of grace and cover "the place with darkness, which through his presence is made light"? [2]

Such warnings underscored the distinction between the garden of the church and the world which lay beyond

---

Book of the General Lawes and Libertyes [1660], p. 120. See also, Thomas Cobbet to Increase Mather, December 13, 1681, "Mather Papers," *Colls. M.H.S.*, fourth ser., VIII (1868), 292.

[2] Davenport, Essay on What the Visible Church is; Shepard, *Parable*, 20, 377.

the confines of the Hedge. "All the world out of the Church is as a wildernesse, or at best a wilde field," preached John Cotton, "where all manner of unclean, and wilde beasts live and feed." Because of its disorder and unrestraint, the state of wilderness symbolized the sinful world of unregenerate man. "The Wildernesse is a cleere resemblance of the world," asserted Roger Williams, "heer greedie and furious men persecute and devoure the harmlesse and innocent as the wilde beasts pursue and devoure the Hinds and Roes." ³ Despite such seeming analogies with the American forest, these metaphors reflect the Christian tradition of the wilderness rather than the Puritans' experience in the New World. The murmurings of the Israelites in the Sinai wilderness signified the rejection of true religion, and historical Christianity associated this disbelief with the wilderness state itself. "This World's a Wilderness / To God's afflicted Saints," rhymed Michael Wigglesworth, a "place of Woes and Wants" where "Life's a very Death,/ At least a dying life." Thus, the Puritans viewed their sojourn in the temporal world as a necessary step on the road to everlasting salvation. We must "pass through a Wilderness of Miseries," asserted Increase Mather, "e're we can arrive at the heavenly Canaan." And his son, Cotton Mather, equated "this present evil world" with the wilderness which led to the Promised Land.⁴

Since the wilderness represented the world of reprobacy and sinfulness, Puritan theologians stressed the

³ Cotton, *A Brief Exposition with Practical Observations,* pp. 104–105; Roger Williams, *A Key into the Language of America* [1643], reprinted in *The Complete Writings of Roger Williams* [ed. by Perry Miller], 7 vols. (New York, 1963), I, 190.

⁴ Michael Wigglesworth, *Meat out of the Eater* (Cambridge [Mass.], 1670), p. 181; Increase Mather, *The Day of Trouble,* p. 3; Cotton Mather, *The Wonders of the Invisible World* (Boston, 1693), p. 63. For a discussion of the wilderness in the context of traditional Christian ideas, see Williams, *Wilderness and Paradise,* pp. 4–6, 98–113.

value of the Hedge as a shield from these corruptions. Describing the first planters of New England as the Lord's garden, William Stoughton, in the Massachusetts Bay election sermon of 1668, remarked that "God sifted a whole Nation that he might send choice grain over into this Wilderness" so that the unregenerate would not defile His church. John Cotton observed that the Lord "hath planted us not in the wildernesse of the world, but in the garden of his Church." "In our inclosure and separation" from the sinful world, he noted, we are "A garden enclosed, a fountaine sealed." Because of these partitions, Cotton reminded New Englanders, "We are not to grow wild, or unsavoury, or unclean." Appropriately, the seven regenerate men necessary for the establishment of a congregation in New England were referred to as the seven pillars of the church upon which the ecclesiastical order would rest.[5] The congregational Hedges thereby separated the well-ordered Garden of the Saints from the untamed Wilderness of the unredeemed. John Cotton suggested that the "evill members of the Church" acted as "bryers and thornes" to hedge and fence in the Elect and keep them "in a marvellous innocent frame." By enclosing His garden with such walls, the Lord prevented the saints from wandering and straggling in the wilderness of the world, where they would be susceptible to vicious corruptions.[6]

Puritan ministers in America elaborated on the idea of the wilderness as an unregenerate state and compared the unrestraint of reprobate souls to the uncultivated

[5] William Stoughton, *New-Englands True Interest; Not to Lie* (Cambridge [Mass.], 1670), pp. 25, 19; Cotton, *A Brief Exposition of the whole Book of Canticles*, p. 139; Cotton, *A Brief Exposition with Practical Observations*, pp. 110, 104–105. For a discussion of the establishment of one church, that of Dedham, see Kenneth A. Lockridge, "The History of a Puritan Church: 1637–1736," *New England Quarterly*, XL (1967), 399–424.

[6] Cotton, *Gods Mercie*, pp. 55, 57.

lands around them. John Cotton maintained that sins are like "the weeds that are cast in over the pale into a man's garden"; they "are not the weeds of the garden, till the soil give rooting to them, that is, consent." His colleague in Connecticut, Thomas Hooker, distinguished between "a gracious and a sanctifying knowledge, garden knowledge" which motivated the saints of the church and "a wild and a common knowledge" which directed the behavior of hypocrites. Sinners, he suggested, "are like wildernesses overgrown with weeds." Hooker explained that God, by denying His ordinances to the unregenerate, left them without help "and therefore they grew wild as a tree in the Wildernesse growes wild." Other New Englanders also grounded these Biblical metaphors in the experience of the American wilderness. Thomas Shepard insisted that a man who neglects prayer should not live in human society and deserves to dwell "among bears, and wolves, and beasts in the wilderness." The Commissioners to the New England Confederation also grappled with the problem of religious declension and criticized the lack of zeal in New England. The fruits of insincere devotion, they warned, were "nothinge better then the wild vines or brambles in the wildernes." [7]

The Puritans' belief in the enclosed garden surrounded by the wilderness led them to oppose religious toleration in New England. In a draft of the Cambridge Platform which defined the religious tenets of the New England Way in 1648, Richard Mather denied that "the doores of the church . . . stand so wide open, that all sorts of peo-

---

[7] Cotton, "A Brief Exposition Upon Ecclesiastes," 72; Thomas Hooker, "Culpable Ignorance, Or The Danger of Ignorance under Meanes," in *The Saints Dignitie and Dutie. Together with the Danger of Ignorance and Hardnesse . . .* (London, 1651), p. 206; Hooker, *Application of Redemption*, p. 380; Thomas Hooker, *The Covenant of Grace opened . . .* (London, 1649), p. 50; Shepard, *Parable*, 584; *Acts of the Commissioners*, I, 82.

ple whether good or bad may freely enter therein at their pleasure." On the contrary, he observed, "the church is compared to a garden enclosed and a fountain sealed." [8] John Cotton, a staunch critic of religious toleration, warned that the garden of the church "is made a wildernesse if you pull down the pales, take down the narrow watch of Officers, and let in all men." And in response to Roger Williams's allegation that the reprobate of the wilderness would not threaten the saints within the garden, Cotton asked, but "what if the weeds grow so neere the inclosure (or hedge) round about the garden, that they easily creep into the Garden, and . . . choak the good herbes"? It was better, felt Cotton, to insist upon strict religious conformity than to challenge the church's protective shield. Thomas Cobbet, of the church at Ipswich, also criticized the abatement of religious requirements and warned that religious toleration "breaketh the very Hedge and walls of a State." Such a policy, he admonished, would undermine "Gods gracious protecting providence" and weaken the fabric of society. Magistrates, concurred Edward Johnson, "are Eyes of Restraint set up for Walles and Bulworks, to surround the Sion of God," and they must not "open the Gates for all sorts." [9] According to these conservatives, such precautions were necessary lest the purity of the garden be overrun by the thorny weeds of the wilderness.

Although the wilderness was a region of spiritual corruption, it was also paradoxically the place for religious

[8] Canticles 4. Richard Mather, Modell of church-government, p. 55, Mather Mss., American Antiquarian Society.

[9] Cotton, *An Exposition upon . . . Revelation*, p. 92; John Cotton, *The Bloudy Tenent washed, And made white in the bloud of the Lambe* (London, 1647), p. 151; Thomas Cobbet, *The Civil Magistrates Power In matters of Religion Modestly Debated* . . . (London, 1653), pp. 93–94; Johnson, *Wonder-working Providence*, p. 32.

fulfillment. The Puritans founded New England primarily for religious ends in order that they might communicate with God in their own way. "It is better . . . [to] go into the wildernesse" to enjoy the Lord's ordinances, reasoned Richard Mather, than to live without them or to suffer persecution for enjoying them at home. The colonists emphasized the religious basis of the New England settlements and considered the ecclesiastic institutions there the choice blessings that God bestowed upon His children. Confident that they carried the Protestant Reformation to new pinnacles, the Puritans stressed the successful transplantation of true religion in America. Francis Higginson, in his last sermon, reminded the people that New England was established for religious purposes, and Thomas Shepard, paraphrasing the same text, "What went ye out into the wilderness to see"? responded that the settlers came "into this wilderness to see . . . more of Jesus Christ." [10]

This religious motivation served as a unifying force among the New England colonies, and the opening paragraph of the Articles of Confederation, which in 1643 loosely united Massachusetts Bay, Connecticut, New Haven, and Plymouth, emphasized this point. "Wee all came into these partes of America with one and the same end and ayme," commenced that document, "namely to advance the Kingdome of . . . Christ and to enjoy the Liberties of the Gospell in puritie with peace." In 1645 the delegates to the Confederation reiterated that "the most considerable part" of the settlers, "professe they came into these parts of the world" to enjoy the fullness of the holy ordinances of Christ. New Englanders praised the Almighty for permitting His people to erect such religious institutions. "The Lord hath brought us to a Good

[10] [Mather], *Church-government and Church-Covenant,* pp. 34–35; Mather, *Magnalia,* I, 363–64; Shepard, *Parable,* 179.

Land," rejoiced John Winthrop, "a Land, where we enjoy . . . above all, the Blessings of the Gospel." Two young ministers agreed that "One of the sweetest refreshing mercies" which God granted "to his New England people" was "the beauties of holiness" with which they "had familiar and full converse with him, above what they could then enjoy in the land from whence they came." [11] The successful rooting of the Puritan churches thereby confirmed the view that religion could prosper in the wilderness condition.

Later in the century, as the initial religious zeal of the founders waned, New England ministers urged their congregations to cherish their spiritual blessings in the wilderness and reminded the people of the original motives for colonization. In an attack upon the Quaker missionaries who were slowly infiltrating the Puritan colonies, John Norton exhorted New Englanders "always to remember, that Originally they are a *Plantation Religious.*" "The profession of purity of doctrine, worship and discipline, is written upon her forehead," he continued, and worldly successes "cannot denominate New-England." "All these notwithstanding," he insisted, "if shee fall away from her profession, call her *Ichabod, the Glory is departed.*" [12] The apotheosis of the first generation enabled the New England clergy to reaffirm the importance of religious purity. "Let us show it," preached Norton in the Massachusetts Bay election sermon of 1661, "that we mistook not our selves, pretending to come into the Wilderness to live under the Order of the Gospel." "We are out-casts . . . and reproached," he confessed, "but let us be such Out-

<hr>

[11] *Acts of the Commissioners,* I, 3, 50; John Winthrop to John Winthrop, Jr. [c. 1643], *Winthrop Papers,* IV, 366; Greenhill and Mather, "To The Reader," in Shepard, *Subjection to Christ,* 275.

[12] I Samuel 4:21. John Norton, *The Heart of N-England rent at the Blasphemies of the Present Generation* (Cambridg[e, Mass.], 1659), p. 58.

casts, as are caring for the Truth." Two years later, John Higginson, an original settler of the Bay colony, reminded New Englanders that their ancestors came into the wilderness for spiritual reasons alone. Praising the temporal wealth in the New England colonies, Higginson declared that these "are but additionall mercies," and "it was another thing and a better thing that we followed the Lord into the wilderness for." Other Puritan ministers also recalled the primary mission of the founding fathers. "It is our errand into the Wilderness to study and practise true Scripture Reformation," preached Jonathan Mitchel of Cambridge, "and it will be our Crown . . . if we finde it, and hold it without Adulterating deviations." And Samuel Danforth, pastor of the church at Roxbury, urged New Englanders not to forget this errand. "You have solemnly professed before God, Angels and Men," he declared, that you departed your native land and entered "this waste and howling Wilderness" to enjoy the purity of God's ordinances without human corruptions.[13]

By emphasizing this unique mission, the Puritan ministers implicitly suggested that the New England Way was the clearest manifestation of God's ecclesiastical plan. While all the world had gone astray, they argued, New England represented the last citadel of doctrinal purity. The New England orthodoxy supported this idea by stressing the value of the wilderness as a place of religious insight. When the Lord wishes to "speak to our heart," maintained Peter Bulkeley, He "will allure us . . . into the Wildernesse" rather than converse "in the throng of a City." As the Lord gave Moses the pattern of the tabernacle in the wilderness, suggested John Norton, God often

[13] John Norton, "Sion the Out-cast healed of her Wounds," in *Three choice and profitable sermons*, p. 14; John Higginson, *The Cause of God and his people in New England* (Cambridg[e, Mass.], 1663), pp. 14, 10–11; Mitchel, *Nehemiah on the Wall*, p. 28; Danforth, *A Brief Recognition*, pp. 9–10.

"transplants many of his faithfull servants into this vast wilderness" because its remoteness makes it "so much the fitter for the fuller inquiry . . . of all his holy ordinances." Samuel Danforth pointed out that the apostle John "began his Ministry, not . . . in any famous City . . . , but in the Wilderness." By withdrawing into "a woody, retired and solitary place," he was able to escape "from the envy and preposterous zeal of such as were addicted to their Old Traditions" and could lead "the people aside from the noise and tumult of their secular occasions and businesses, which might have obstructed" their interest in his doctrines.[14]

Other New England ministers applied these ideas to the churches planted in the American wilderness. "God doth sometimes raise up a Church out of a wildernesse," maintained John Cotton, "To take us aside from disturbances, and temptations in populous Cities," and he urged New Englanders "To behould the like favour of God to us (in some measure) in this wildernesse." Increase Mather cited an observation of the English theologian Thomas Brightman that "some faithful ones in a Wilderness should have the most clear Discoveries of the Abominations of the Man of Sin" and suggested that these remarks "applied unto these worthy confessors in New England" who migrated into the wilderness "for the Testimony of Jesus." In a subsequent work, *The Mystery of Israel's Salvation . . . ,* published in 1669, Mather maintained that "such of us as are in an exiled condition in this wilderness" are better able to understand the arcane truths of God and shall bear witness against those hypocrites who permitted human inventions to corrupt the Lord's holy ordinances. "God hath led us into a wilderness," assured Mather, "not because the Lord hated us, but because he loved us." "Who knoweth,"

---

[14] Bulkeley, *Gospel Covenant,* p. 305; Norton, *Abel being Dead,* p. 19; Danforth, *A Brief Recognition,* p. 1.

he asked rhetorically, "but that he may send down his spirit upon us here, if we continue faithful before him"? [15]

The Puritans combined this idea of the wilderness as a place of intense religious perceptivity with its antithesis, the notion of the wilderness as a state of sin, to produce a significant intellectual synthesis: the desire among New England Puritans to spiritually transform the wilderness into a garden by expanding the range of the gospel. Several years before the founding of the Massachusetts Bay colony, the Anglican poet, George Herbert, developed the idea of the westward movement of religion in "The Church Militant." Commencing in the exotic Orient, Christianity had followed the sun into Europe and England and now "stands on tip-toe in our land,/Readie to passe to the *American* strand." New Englanders were very impressed with Herbert's interpretation of the transit of religion into the wilderness and frequently quoted these lines in moments of self-analysis.[16] Referring to the churches "here planted in these western parts of the world," Thomas Shepard suggested that many people "have taken their flight hither" in order to follow the sunshine of the gospel as it

[15] Cotton, *A Brief Exposition with Practical Observations*, p. 71; Increase Mather, "An Apologetical Preface to the Reader," in Davenport, *Another essay*; Increase Mather, *The Mystery of Israel's Salvation Explained and Applyed* . . . (Cambridge [Mass.], 1669), pp. 163, 164.
[16] George Herbert, "The Church Militant," in *The Works of George Herbert*, ed. by F. E. Hutchinson (Oxford, 1941), pp. 190–98, lines 235–36. For examples of this poetry in New England writing, see Ezekiel Rogers's eulogy to Thomas Hooker, in Hooker, *A Survey* [p. xiv] and Daniel Gookin, "Historical Collections of the Indians in New England," reprinted in *Colls. M.H.S.*, first ser., I (1792), 160. See also, Loren Baritz, "The Idea of the West," *American Historical Review*, LXVI (1961), 635–37. The idea of the passage of religion from east to west should not be confused with the so-called lure of the West as a factor in frontier expansion. While New Englanders found the former concept relevant to the transformation of the wilderness, it is doubtful that the latter idea was equally pertinent. For a fuller discussion of this problem, see Chapter VII.

set in the west. An anonymous promotional tract similarly compared the passage of the sun in the sky with the transit of religion westward into America.[17] The Puritans believed that the importation of Christianity into the spiritually barren New World would destroy the noxious weeds of the wilderness and cause the land to flower as a garden.

Prior to the migration to America, the Puritans articulated their desire to redeem the wilderness. If the Lord removes our vineyard, preached John Cotton while still in England, "wee shall carry our roote with us . . . and our fruite will bee more sweet and savoury." The pastor of the church at Boston, John Wilson, in a conversation with John Winthrop, remarked that on the eve of his departure from England "he dreamed he was here, and that he saw a church arise out of the earth, which grew up and became a marvellous goodly church." [18] The successful transplantation of the Protestant church in America convinced the Puritans of their mission to regenerate the barren soil. James Hopkins, a friend of Winthrop's, compared the Governor to Moses and Joshua not only for guiding "a people into a good land through many hard adventures," but also "for plantinge . . . gods worshipp in an heathenish place, whereby . . . it was made the fertilist land upon earth, though naturally montanus and rockie." The promotionalist Thomas Morton lauded the settlers of New England for furnishing the country "so commodiously in so short a time" with godly institutions and assured readers that "posterity will taste the sweetnes of it, and that very sodainly." [19]

The process of transforming the wilderness into a garden required both the importation of religious institutions and

[17] Shepard, *Parable*, 65, 243; "New Englands First Fruits," pp. 430–31.

[18] Cotton, *Gods Mercie*, p. 65; Winthrop, *Journal*, I, 83–84.

[19] James Hopkins to John Winthrop, February 25, 1632[/33], *Winthrop Papers*, III, 106; Morton, *New English Canaan*, p. 181.

the extension of the area of the gospel by erecting churches in new plantations. Frontier expansion and church settlement went hand in hand in New England as each inland town provided for the spiritual solace of the saints in the wilderness. Moreover, religious discord in settled towns occasionally motivated dissatisfied saints to depart to the frontier in hope of preserving what they considered ecclesiastical purity; for this reason, for example, Elder William Goodwin led a portion of the Hartford congregation from Connecticut to Hadley, Massachusetts.[20] These frontier churches also served as instruments of social control, and John Cotton, in a series of proposed statutes, suggested that "noe man shall set his dwelling house" more than a "half a myle, or a myle at the farthest, from the meeting house of the congregation." Cotton urged the people who established new plantations to "sit downe no where without good Ministers, if it be possible, and sure possible it is, else Christians may resolve to tarry where they are." [21]

Such admonitions, however, were ordinarily unnecessary, for the frontier settlers usually selected ministers before they pulled up stakes at home. In the first Sabbath celebrated at New Haven in 1638, Peter Prudden, who shared the pulpit with John Davenport, appropriately preached on the text, "The voice of one crying in the wilderness, Prepare ye the way of the Lord, make his paths straight." [22] The other New England colonies also provided

[20] For a discussion of the role of religious dissension as a factor in frontier expansion, see Robert A. East, "Puritanism and New Settlement," *New England Quarterly*, XVII (1944), 255–64.

[21] John Cotton, "An Abstract of the Laws of New England," in [Hutchinson], *A Collection of Original Papers*, p. 168; John Cotton, *The Powring Out of the Seven Vials: Or, An Exposition of the Sixteenth Chapter of the Revelation* . . . (London, 1645), p. 52. For a discussion of the relation between social institutions and inland settlement, see William Haller, Jr., *The Puritan Frontier: Town Planting in New England colonial development, 1630–1660* (New York, 1951). For an analysis of frontier expansion, see Chapter VII.

[22] Matthew 3:3. Calder, *New Haven Colony*, p. 83.

for adequate religious institutions in the frontier settlements. Shortly after the establishment of New London, the younger John Winthrop went to great pains to attract a suitable minister to care for the spiritual needs of that plantation. Massachusetts Bay was equally vigilant in safeguarding the souls of its frontiersmen. In 1650 the Court of Deputies ordered the abandonment of the plantation at Nashaway (Lancaster) because the settlers were unable to support a ministry there.[23]

Because the Puritans placed great emphasis upon the need to extend the influence of the gospel as a means of fulfilling their divine mission, New Englanders often employed such arguments to convince their conservative governments of the value of inland settlements. In recommending the New Haven region as a suitable site for a plantation, Israel Stoughton, a commander of the Massachusetts army during the Pequot War, admitted his reluctance to support unnecessary expansion. Yet, he added, "so far as it may tend to public utility, and the enlargment of Christ's kingdom, I hope I should not hinder so good a work." In 1653 several colonists in Connecticut, with the support of some of the inhabitants of Springfield, petitioned the General Court of Massachusetts Bay for permission to erect a town at Northampton. They cited the advantages of "further inlarging . . . the territories of the Gospell" and maintained that the site would afford "a Comfortable Subsistence whereby people may Live And Attend upon god in his holy ordinances without distraction." At this time, an ambitious group of New Haven men

[23] Amos Richardson to John Winthrop, Jr., October 6, 1649, Marmaduke Matthews to John Winthrop, Jr., October 7, 1649, *Winthrop Papers*, V, 378–79; *Recs. of Mass. Bay*, III, 203. One reason for the absence of a ministry at Nashaway was that, unlike other inland plantations, it was settled primarily for economic purposes. See, Samuel Eliot Morison, "The Plantation of Nashaway—An Industrial Experiment," *Publications of the Colonial Society of Massachusetts*, XXVII (1932), 204–22.

sought support for a settlement on the Delaware Bay. In rationalizing their proposed departure from New England, they stressed the advantages of enlarging the kingdom of Jesus Christ, spreading the gospel, "and the good of posteritie therein." [24]

The Puritans also recognized that they could achieve the spiritual transformation of the wilderness by converting the inhabitants of that land of darkness, the Indians.[25] Numerous New England commentators believed that the natives worshipped the devil and advocated instructing them in the doctrines of Christianity to liberate them from the shackles of Satan. Though it was often suggested, the Puritans responded slowly to this missionary task prior to John Eliot's dramatic breakthrough in the mid-1640s when he preached several sermons in the Indian language and claimed to have converted several of the natives. John Wilson explained this retarded interest in the Indians' souls by comparing the natives to the "woody and rocky soile" of New England. When the colonists first arrived in Massachusetts Bay, he noted, "there was scarce any man that could beleeve that English grains would grow, or that the Plow could doe any good . . . till experience taught them otherwise." "So wee have thought of our Indian people," observed Wilson, "and therefore have beene discouraged to put plow to such dry and rocky ground." He hoped nevertheless that Eliot's early successes would prove that "they are better soile for

[24] Israel Stoughton to the Governor and Council of Massachusetts [August 14, 1637], *Winthrop Papers*, III, 483; Petition to the General Court of Massachusetts Bay [c. May 1653], quoted in James Russell Trumbull, *History of Northampton Massachusetts . . .* , 2 vols. (Northampton, 1898), I, 5–6; *Records of the Colony or Jurisdiction of New Haven, from May 1653, to the Union*, ed. by Charles J. Hoadly (Hartford, 1858), pp. 128–29. (Hereafter cited as *N.H. Recs.*, II.)
[25] For elaborate discussions of the Puritans' missionary activities, see Vaughan, *New England Frontier*, chapters IX–XI and William Kellaway, *The New England Company: 1649–1776* (London, 1961).

the Gospel then wee can thinke." Thomas Mayhew of Martha's Vineyard served as another early apostle to the Indians of New England. In 1651 the Commissioners of the New England Confederation praised his labors among "the poore Indians" and hoped that "good corn may abundantly Spring up and this barran Wildernes become a fruitful feild[, yea,] the garden of God." [26]

Second-generation New Englanders lauded the various steps which had illuminated the wilderness with the lights of the gospel. Michael Wigglesworth acclaimed the establishment of true religion in America whereby "The dark and dismal western woods . . . /Beheld such glorious gospel-shine." The inhabitants of Northampton employed similar metaphors in urging the Bay colony to defend its traditional liberties when the royal commissioners of 1665 threatened the charter of that colony. The Lord has transformed New England from "a wilderness [to] a fruitful field," they argued, "wherein wee have enjoyed much of the presence of God . . . for so long a time." [27] Puritan ministers extolled the metamorphosis of New England in reminding their congregations of the need to uphold the faith. The younger Thomas Shepard surmised that the Lord had transplanted their fathers in New England "that so this land might not be a land of darkness and wilderness." And Urian Oakes assured his congregation that New England was indeed a Canaan "though a Wilderness." "Yea, the Lord hath given us his good Spirit to instruct us, and hath not withheld Manna from us," concluded Increase

[26] [John Wilson?], "The Day-Breaking, if not the Sun-Rising of the Gospell with the Indians in New-England" [1647], reprinted in *Colls. M.H.S.*, third ser., IV (1834), 15; The Commissioners of the United Colonies to Thomas Mayhew, September 12, 1651, in *Acts of the Commissioners*, I, 205.

[27] Wigglesworth, "Gods Controversy," 84; Inhabitants of Northampton to the General Court of Massachusetts Bay, April 19, 1665, quoted in Trumbull, *History of Northampton*, I, 156–57.

Mather, "but hath turned this Wilderness into a Canaan, and here hath he given us Rest." [28]

Within twenty years of the founding of New England, it was apparent that the enclosed gardens of the church would flourish in the wilderness. Praising the work of the Lord "in raising up these Churches," John Cotton extolled the multiplication of "one garden into many, one Church into above a score." Since congregational theology provided for the independence of its churches, Cotton significantly viewed the new settlements as separate enclosed gardens which thrived in the wilderness. The younger John Woodbridge later explained that the contours of the land proscribed the possibility of establishing a presbyterian system in New England. In a letter to Richard Baxter in 1671, he observed that "the plantations . . . are too remote for Convenient Assembling," and "the good Land lying in Independent spots seemes to be cut out for Independent churches." And the elders of the Massachusetts Bay colony warned that the decline in religiosity in New England betrayed "a dangerous tendencie to utter devastation of these churches, turning the pleasant gardens of Christ into a wilderness." [29]

More often, however, New Englanders overlooked the distinctions of congregationalism and lauded the transformation of the wilderness as a whole. In criticizing the loosening of morality in New England, Increase Mather subtly transposed the Biblical metaphors of original sin. "It is sad," he remarked, "that ever this Serpent should

[28] Shepard, Jr., *Eye-Salve*, p. 11; Oakes, *New-England Pleaded with,* p. 20; Increase Mather, "To The Reader," in Samuel Torrey, *An Exhortation unto Reformation* . . . (Cambridge [Mass.], 1674).

[29] Cotton, *A Brief Exposition with Practical Observations*, pp. 222, 166; John Woodbridge, Jr. to Richard Baxter, March 31, 1671, "Correspondence of Woodbridge and Baxter," 577; Letter of the Elders to the General Court of Massachusetts Bay, May 31, 1671, in *Recs. of Mass. Bay*, IV, Part II, 490.

creep over into this Wilderness, where threescore years ago he never had had any footing." No longer a barren wilderness, New England now blossomed with the flowers of Christianity, and Cotton Mather regarded it as the Lord's "Almost only Garden . . . in the vast continent of America." [30]

[30] Mather, *Wo to Drunkards*, p. 20; Cotton Mather, *The Present State of New-England* . . . (Boston, 1690), p. 37.

PART III

A WILDERNESS SOCIETY

WHILE the Puritans employed the symbolic wilderness to interpret their experiences in New England, they were less successful in adapting their social theories to the wilderness condition. Metaphorical extension can be explained by an intellectual lag, an unwillingness or inability to discard traditional language. But social theory, to remain vital, must solve explicit problems in the world of action. The failure of Puritan social theory to function in the wilderness reflects not so much a lack of will, for this we shall see was quite evident, but rather the irrelevance of these ideas in the new environment.

Like most Puritan concepts, the social ideals transported to America reflected centuries of Old World experience. In brief, the founders of New England endeavored to erect a medieval city in the wilderness, a society in which all men could live together with a natural harmony of interests. The Puritans replaced the stone walls which surrounded the medieval town with the idea of God's Hedge, but for all practical purposes, the wilderness society was to be a static community.

This ideal commonwealth suited the interests of the colonists as long as they distrusted the wild forest about them. Thus the hazards of life in the wilderness reinforced the early commitment to a collective society. But at the same time, certain divisive forces began to appear. Besides the problem of vertical mobility, which is beyond the realm of this study, the possibility of geographic dispersal slowly undermined the social aspirations of the Puritan leaders. Within a few years of settlement, the influx of new inhabitants and the discovery of favorable inland locations created continued pressure for frontier expansion. Resolved to perpetuate a cohesive society, the Puritan authorities attempted to inhibit these disintegrating tendencies. But for the most part, these forces, once put into play, could not be restrained.

The external factors behind frontier expansion—overpopulation and the desire to settle in more fertile areas—were strengthened, moreover, by an internal paradox within Puritan thought. From the beginning of colonization, the Puritans emphasized the importance of transforming the wilderness into cultivated acreage. This mission served as a rationale for inland expansion and accelerated the breakdown of the organic community envisioned by the first settlers of Massachusetts Bay. Although the Puritans recognized the contradiction in ideals by the end of the century, they were unable to resolve the conflict. Thus the generation of Cotton Mather groped, in vain, for a solution to a dilemma which first appeared during the lifetime of John Winthrop.

This inability to select alternatives is, perhaps, the most suggestive aspect of Puritan thinking in America. The socially disintegrating pressures, by about 1640, had demonstrated the bankruptcy of the ideal of a collective society in the wilderness. In 1643 the Puritan leaders attempted to restructure their model society by establishing the New England Confederation. Even this compromise proved unsatisfactory in the wilderness environment. Yet at the end of the seventeenth century, Puritan leaders still believed that an organic society would best fulfill their needs in America. Despite the experience of three generations, these people attempted to persuade the colonists of the viability of social cohesion.

Although the wilderness eroded the social theories of the founding fathers, it offered no substitutes for their original vision. And despite the obvious need, no new synthesis emerged to liberate Puritan thinkers from the bonds of their Old World values. While grappling for solutions to ongoing social problems, therefore, New Englanders were compelled to fall back upon anachronistic patterns of thought. These models, however, provided the Puritans with unsatisfactory answers to basic social questions and left them, to the end of the seventeenth century, on the horns of an insoluble dilemma.

CHAPTER VII

"The Welfare of
This Commonwealth"

THE seventeenth-century migration to New England
embodied both a physical relocation and an intellectual transplantation. Along with their worldly goods, the
colonists transported sophisticated ideas about the nature
of society into the wilderness. In the early years of settlement, the Puritans endeavored to incorporate these views
into their Wilderness Zion and, for a time, these ideas
guided New England policymaking. The Pequot War of
1637, however, unleashed a series of events which undermined this intellectual edifice. Thereafter the wilderness
experience threatened more and more the social ideals of
the founding fathers and compelled them to adapt their
thinking to the realities of America.

Drawing upon the medieval tradition of the organic
state, Puritan social and political theory stressed the value
of cohesion and collectivity. This view of society emphasized the interdependence among the members of a commonwealth and expected all men to accept their social
responsibilities along with their privileges. To preserve
the health of the body politic it was imperative that the
members of society worked for the common good, or, as

John Winthrop stated it, "the care of the publique must oversway all private respects." As in a living organism, all the parts of society existed for the benefit of the body and each appendage performed some necessary function. Balanced and well-ordered, such a society would promote the welfare of all. These ideas, to be sure, were shared by most Englishmen. In a sermon preached before King James on his birthday in 1621, William Laud, destined to become the strongest opponent of English Puritanism, declared that any person who is "so addicted to his private [interest], that he neglect[s] the common good . . . is void of the sense of piety and wisheth peace and happiness to himself in vain. For whoever he be," concluded Laud, "he must live in the body of the Commonwealth and in the body of the Church." [1]

The Puritans, moreover, bolstered their commitment to social cohesion by affirming the compact theory of society. Ten years after the settlement of Massachusetts Bay, John Winthrop argued that "it is the nature and essence of every society to be knitt together by some Covenant, either expressed or implyed." Such an agreement not only brought a society into being, but also served to strengthen the social bond. Since "no man [is] constrained to enter into such a condition, unlesse he will," reasoned Thomas Hooker, the social covenant acts as "that *sement* which soders [*sic*] them all" together. In the aftermath of the Antinomian controversy in Massachusetts, Winthrop underscored the importance of "the consent of a certaine companie of people" in the formation of a body politic and Hooker noted that any person who chooses to enter a society "must . . . willingly binde and ingage himself

---

[1] Winthrop, "A Modell," 45; [William] Laud, "A Sermon Preached Before His Majesty" [1621], reprinted in *The Works of . . . William Laud*, 7 vols. (Oxford, 1848–60), I, 28–29. For a study of the organic world view, see E. M. Tillyard, *The Elizabethan World Picture* (London, 1943).

to each member of that society to promote the good of the whole, or else a member actually he is not." [2]

The sense of mission which pervaded the migration to New England strengthened the cohesiveness that was implicit in Puritan social theory. "Goe forth, every man that goeth, with a publick spirit," exhorted John Cotton to the departing colonists in 1630, and look "not on your owne things onely, but also on the things of others." As the *Arbella* bobbed perilously upon the Atlantic waves, John Winthrop reiterated the need for Christian love in the New World. "Wee are a company professing ourselves fellow members of Christ," asserted Winthrop to his fellow passengers, and "wee ought to account ourselves knitt together by this bond of love, and, live in the exercise of it." Recalling the uniqueness of the Puritan venture, he reminded the people of their obligations to the Lord. "We are entered into Covenant with Him for this worke," intoned Winthrop, and, "For this end, wee must be knitt together . . . as one man." [3]

Superficially, the emphasis upon social cohesion in Puritan thought suited the needs of a wilderness society in which the dangers of life, both real and imagined, confirmed the advantages of collective behavior. As long as these social values retained their pragmatic significance, they went unchallenged and were put into practice. But

[2] John Winthrop to Henry Paynter [c. 1640], [John Winthrop], "A Declaration in Defense of an Order of Court Made in May, 1637," *Winthrop Papers*, IV, 170; III, 422–23; Hooker, *A Survey*, part I, 50. For fuller analyses of the social covenant, see Perry Miller, *Orthodoxy in Massachusetts, 1630–1650* (Cambridge [Mass.], 1933); Miller, *The New England Mind: The Seventeenth Century*, Book IV; Larzer Ziff, "The Social Bond of the Church Covenant," *American Quarterly*, X (1958), 454–62.

[3] Cotton, "Gods Promise," 14; Winthrop, "A Modell," 44, 46. For a perceptive analysis of Winthrop's mid-ocean address, see Darrett B. Rutman, *Winthrop's Boston: Portrait of a Puritan Town, 1630–1649* (Chapel Hill, 1965), Chapter I.

almost immediately, other socially disruptive forces were also set into motion. The boundless expanse of the American wilderness constantly beckoned to the Puritan settlers, luring them beyond the secure confines of the Hedge. And the desire of the Puritan leaders to strengthen the community by inviting newcomers and by establishing defensive outposts along the frontier often worked to serve cross-purposes. Peter Bulkeley of Concord, in recounting the promises that the Lord made to His children, perceptively articulated the essential paradox of Puritan society in America: "Whereas they might feare, that being but few, and a small number, they might be scattered and come to nothing, therefore the Lord tells them . . . that *Jerusalem shall be inhabited without walls;* meaning that it should not be able to containe the people in it, for the multitude. A second promise, is that he would be a protection unto them; *I will be a wall of fire about you. . . .* A wall of safe defence to you, and a fire to burne up your enemies, if any invade you." [4] Although the tendency toward expansion was almost inevitable, given the nature of the Puritans' enterprise and their view of the wilderness as a refuge from the chaos of Europe, a Jerusalem without walls nevertheless was incompatible with the social and political ideals of the Puritan leaders. The rival forces of cohesion and disintegration coexisted in a tenuous equilibrium during the early years of settlement as the Puritan authorities attempted to reconcile the principles of the organic society with the perennial demands for inland expansion.

Although the Puritan colonists believed that their ultimate safety would derive from the Hedge which surrounded New England, they were sufficiently realistic to take appropriate precautionary measures to protect their wilderness community. The advance-guard colonists who

[4] Zechariah 2:4, 5. Bulkeley, *Gospel Covenant*, p. 2.

departed from England in 1629 transported arms for one hundred men and planned to erect a fort in New England. Francis Higginson subsequently reported that the Salem plantation possessed "great ordance, wherewith we doubt not we shall fortify ourselves in a short time to keep out a potent adversary"; but there is no evidence that the settlers ever completed such designs.[5] The following year, John Cotton admonished the Winthrop group to "Neglect not walls, bulwarkes, and fortifications." While still in England, the leaders of the 1630 expedition drafted elaborate plans for the defense of their colony and commissioned the younger John Winthrop to study the fortifications and gunnery at Harwich and note its dimensions and structural design; they also arranged to convey heavy artillery to Massachusetts. The founders of the Bay colony expected to use Winthrop's diagrams as a model for a fortified town in the wilderness. Such a community, not unlike the medieval walled town, would satisfy the requirements of Puritan social thought by grouping the majority of the population within strong walls.[6] In addition, a garrisoned town would provide sanctuary from Indian assaults upon the infant colony. New Englanders well remembered the Indian uprising in Virginia of 1622 and regarded the local

[5] *Recs. of Mass. Bay*, I, 26, 29; Higginson, "New-Englands Plantation," p. 259.

[6] Cotton, "Gods Promise," 15; Isaac Johnson to John Winthrop, December 17, 1629, John Winthrop, Jr. to John Winthrop, January 18, 1629[/30], *Winthrop Papers*, II, 177–79, 193–94; Winthrop, *Journal*, I, 54; Dudley, "Letter to the Countess," p. 320. For a discussion of the the desire to settle in one town, see Rutman, *Winthrop's Boston*, appendix I. The interest among New Englanders in erecting a fortified town may reflect the influence of earlier colonial endeavors. Richard Hakluyt had recommended the immediate construction of fortifications, and the colonists at Plymouth had impaled their town to protect them from Indian assaults. See, Richard Hakluyt, "Discourse of Western Planting . . . , 1584," printed in *The Original Writings & Correspondence of the Two Richard Hakluyts*, ed. by E. G. R. Taylor, 2 vols. (London, 1935), II, 274–75, 277; E[dward] W[inslow], *Good Newes From New-England* . . . (London, 1624), pp. 4, 13.

tribes with circumspection. Mathew Cradock, Governor of the New England Company, urged John Endecott to keep "a watchfull eye for your owne saftye, . . . and not to bee too confident of the fidellitie of the salvages." In subsequent missives, the New England Company recommended that all the settlers be trained in the use of arms and prohibited the sale of guns to the natives. On the eve of Winthrop's departure, a correspondent similarly advised him of the dangers "when pryvate Soldiers . . . sell their swoordes[,] there powder and shott to trade with the Savages." [7]

Upon their arrival in New England, the colonists expressed considerable distrust of the wilderness environment. The presence of ravenous wolves constituted a serious menace to the Puritan settlements. Roving by day and by night, the wolves devastated New England livestock throughout the century. John Winthrop, Jr. imported several wolf dogs and experimented with traps, and nearly every town authorized bounties for these nuisances. But the wolves swarmed through the countryside, and New England commentators continued to lament the damage wrought by these beasts. The Court of Deputies of the Bay colony described them as "ravenous[,] cruell creatures, and daily vexations to all the inhabitants of this collony." Although the wolves attacked cattle and not men, these animals added to the general sense of insecurity which permeated the formative period of colonization. The elder Winthrop, for example, reported that he carried a gun during his evening strolls about Boston, "supposing he might see a wolf, (for they came daily

[7] Mathew Cradock to John Endecott[?], February 16, 1628[/29], "First General Letter of the Governor . . . of the New England Company . . . to [John Endecott], April 17, 1629, *Recs. of Mass. Bay,* I, 385, 392–93, 39; Robert Ryece to John Winthrop [c. 1629], *Winthrop Papers,* II, 131.

about the houses. . . .)" [8] The Puritans also betrayed their distrust of the wilderness by credulously affirming the existence of other dangerous animals in America. Several people "being lost in [the] woods," wrote William Wood, "have heard such terrible roarings, as have made them much agast; which," he supposed, "must eyther be Devills or Lyons." [9]

"Another thing that gave them no little exercise," wrote Cotton Mather of the massive problems which beset the founders of New England, "was *the fear of the Indians,* by whom they were sometimes alarmed." During the first year of settlement, Francis Higginson maintained, "we neither fear [the Indians] nor trust them." But in later years, the Puritans expressed solicitude about the natives more frequently. One colonist described the Indians as "a crafty . . . suttell peple," and an early chronicler of New England recalled that the settlers were "constrained by [the Indians'] conspiracies yearly to be in arms." [10] Fear, more than anything else, shaped the Puritans' relations with the natives, and rumors of Indian plots ran rampant through the colonies. During the first winter in Massachusetts, the colonists recompensed several Indians who claimed that the English had burned their wigwams lest they "depart discontentedly from us." And Thomas Dudley recorded an episode in which a man attempted to rescue his calf from the clutches of wolves by discharging his musket. These gunshots were heard three miles away by the inhabitants of Roxbury who "took an alarm, beat up their drum, armed themselves, and sent in post" to Boston

[8] *Recs. of Mass. Bay,* I, 81, 102, 156, III, 10; Edward Howes to John Winthrop, Jr., August 5, 1633, April 18, 1634, *Winthrop Papers,* III, 134, 164; Wood, *New Englands Prospect,* pp. 22, 27; Winthrop, *Journal,* I, 68.

[9] Wood, *New Englands Prospect,* p. 21.

[10] Mather, *Magnalia,* I, 78; Higginson, "New-Englands Plantation," pp. 257–58;—Pond to William Pond, March 15, 1630[/31], *Winthrop Papers,* III, 17; "Early Records of Charlestown," p. 378.

to alert the populace.[11] This almost-comic incident reveals the pervasive state of insecurity which dominated the early days in New England.

Similar panics occurred at varying intervals. In May 1631 another gunshot in the night aroused the Puritans from their beds shortly after they were notified of an imminent Mohawk uprising. While standing guard near the town of Linn, Lieutenant Walker, "a man indued with faith, and of a couragious spirit," narrowly escaped death when an Indian arrow pierced his coat. "Seeing this great preservation," the sentinels stood nervously at their posts "expecting the Indians to come upon them every moment," and in the morning fired their large guns to frighten the Indians away. The following year, John Winthrop reported that "There was much suspicion, that the Indians had some plot against the English." "We doubled our guard," he noted, "and kept watch every day and night." [12]

The colonists, of course, had anticipated some of these dangers prior to their departure from England, and a fortified town might have reduced their anxiety in the wilderness. But, as Thomas Dudley observed, rumors "of some French preparations against us" and the outbreak of disease forced the settlers "to change counsel, and . . . to plant dispersedly" around the Bay. The scattering of the towns during the first winter "troubled some of us," remarked Dudley, "but help it we could not, wanting ability to remove to any place fit to build a town upon." [13] Fear in the unknown continent thereby produced the Puritans' first compromise with wilderness conditions; instead of one godly commonwealth, there were now several.

The dispersal of the settlements undermined the Puri-

[11] Dudley, "Letter to the Countess," pp. 338, 339–40; Winthrop, *Journal*, I, 60.

[12] Johnson, *Wonder-working Providence*, p. 79; Winthrop, *Journal*, I, 63, 91–92.

[13] Dudley, "Letter to the Countess," pp. 312–14.

tans' primary plan for collective safety, and the colonists were compelled to rely upon other lines of defense to preserve their wilderness enterprise. They responded by placing the burden of security upon each individual. By the spring of 1631, the General Court of Massachusetts Bay established a system of watches, ordered that all men except ministers and magistrates be "furnished with good and sufficient armes," and instituted compulsory military training. Subsequently the Court enacted additional measures providing for the construction of fortifications and for the expansion and enforcement of existing legislation.[14]

The Puritans' distrust of the natives manifested itself in numerous provisions for the regulation of Indian affairs. The Massachusetts Court prohibited the trading of guns and ammunition to the natives, regulated the use of Indians as servants, and ordered the erection of trucking houses in each town "whither the Indians may resorte to trade, to avoide there comeing to severall howses." [15] The promotionalist William Wood believed that this "needlesse feare" of the Indians "is too deeply rooted in the conceits" of many Englishmen, but he nevertheless advised aspiring settlers to bring adequate arms, "because security hath beene the overthrow of many a new plantation, [and] it is their care . . . to secure themselves . . . as well as they can." Aside from military preparations, the Bay colony also required its inhabitants to affirm a loyalty oath in which the residents promised to "give speedy notice . . . of any sedition, violence, treacherie, or other hurte . . . intended against" the commonwealth.[16] The Puritans, in this manner, attempted to preserve their community from external assailants.

---

[14] *Recs. of Mass. Bay,* I, 85, 84, 87, 93, 102, 105, 113, 120, 123–25, 137.

[15] *Recs. of Mass. Bay,* I, 76, 83, 96, 99–100.

[16] Wood, *New Englands Prospect,* pp. 78; 58–59; *Recs. of Mass. Bay,* I, 115–16.

The most serious menace to Puritan society, however, was more subtle than the wolves which devoured New England livestock and more enduring than the Indian hoards which the settlers imagined beyond the horizon; it was the existence of the wilderness itself. Whether as a safety valve or as a place for personal advancement, the vacant area around the New England plantations continuously lured the colonists beyond the limits of the Hedge. The "thousands of Acres that yet was never meddled with" thereby challenged the cohesive tenets of Puritan social theory and threatened to destroy the godly commonwealth in the wilderness.[17]

The propensity for expansion in the seventeenth century should not be confused with a mystical lure of the West. Although the colonists recognized that New England was geographically to the west of Europe, they never ascribed special significance to westward extension in America. Edward Johnson revealed the true direction of New England's interest when he warned that the settlers would prefer "to dwell on the *backside* of this Desert (a place as yet unaccessible)" rather than accept religious toleration. As New Englanders faced the Atlantic and the nations beyond its waves, they turned their backs on the westward lands of the wilderness. The absence of a specific direction, of course, did not impede the socially disruptive qualities of "the vast wilderness in America."[18]

---

[17] Wood, *New Englands Prospect*, p. 12. For a recent discussion of early frontier expansion, see Douglas Edward Leach, *The Northern Colonial Frontier: 1607–1763* (New York, 1966), chapter 3.

[18] Johnson, *Wonder-working Providence*, p. 145 (itals. added); John Blackleach to John Winthrop [August 3, 1637], *Winthrop Papers*, III, 476. In 1638, substantially after the settlement of Connecticut, Hugh Peter of Salem wrote, "our plantations do reach a great way South and East . . . ," and Cotton Mather, at the end of the century, described the New Haven region as "the southern parts of the country." Such statements indicate that New Englanders viewed inland expansion without reference to a particular geographical direction; see, Hugh Peter to

In the first years of settlement, the Puritan leaders responded to the problem of expansion in various ways. Although they were unable to avoid the initial dispersal of the towns around the Bay, they resolutely opposed further needless expansion. In September 1630, barely two months after arriving in Massachusetts and prior to the abandonment of the plan for a single community, the authorities ordered several stragglers who had settled at the future site of Ipswich "to come away" and plant within the community.[19] In rejecting a proposal made by several English Puritans that the settlers withdraw from the region about the Bay, the leaders of the infant colony further revealed their commitment to social cohesion. Betraying a great deal of misinformation about American geography, these well-meaning friends had urged the leaders of the Bay colony to hasten "the discoverie of some fitter place more to the South, where you may enjoye greater Comfort in respect of milder winters and fruitfuller . . . harvests." They recommended as alternatives the Narragansett region, where "there is farr lesse Cold and snow than where you are," and the area about the Hudson River. And they advised that unless the settlers agreed to remove, certain influential parties might withdraw their support of the entire adventure. There is no record of the New England response to these missives. But apparently the English writers accepted the dispersal of the towns as sufficient sign of expansion, for in April 1631 one of these correspondents expressed pleasure that the colony had "begunn to remove and plant some what higher up the river into the land among the woods." [20]

Patrick Copeland, December 10, 1638, *Winthrop Papers,* IV, 85; Mather, *Magnalia,* I, 152.

[19] *Recs. of Mass. Bay,* I, 76.

[20] Emmanuel Downing to John Winthrop, December 8, 1630, John Humfrey to Isaac Johnson, December 9, 1630, John Humfrey to John Winthrop, December 12, 1630, Emmanuel Downing to John Winthrop, April 30, 1631, *Winthrop Papers,* II, 324–25, 329, 333, III, 30.

Other inducements for expansion were more realistic. In the spring of 1631, a sagamore from Connecticut visited the Bay colony and endeavored, by offers of land and beaver skins, to entice the colonists "to come plant in his country." Governor Winthrop, however, flatly rejected this offer and noted subsequently "that the said sagamore is a very treacherous man." Two years later, Winthrop similarly disposed of a proposal made by Plymouth Colony to enter jointly the fur trade in Connecticut. "The place was not fit for a plantation," maintained Winthrop, and "we thought not fit to meddle with it." But the people of Massachusetts Bay could not resist the lure of beaver wealth, and less than two months later, they dispatched a ship to trade at Connecticut.[21] Despite Winthrop's acquiescence to economic expansion, it is significant that as a representative of the existing system, he prevented the establishment of a settlement at Connecticut and thus repudiated unnecessary dispersal.

There was, however, one exception to this anti-expansionist attitude in Massachusetts. Though the Puritans opposed inland plantations because they weakened the social fabric, they were prepared to sanction new settlements for the protection of the colony. And early in 1633 rumors of an impending attack by the French resulted in a change of policy. In response to this crisis the Puritan leaders agreed to erect a fortified town at Natascott, "partly to be some block in an enemy's way, . . . and especially to prevent any enemy from taking that passage

[21] Winthrop, *Journal*, I, 61, 103, 107–108. Governor Bradford of Plymouth presented a slightly different version of the negotiations with the Bay colony. The Massachusetts delegates "cast many fears of danger and loss and the like, which was perceived to be the main obstacles, though they alleged they were not provided of trading goods"; see, William Bradford, *Of Plymouth Plantation: 1620–1647*, ed. by Samuel Eliot Morison (New York, 1967), p. 258.

from us." They also endorsed a plantation at Agawam "least an enemy, finding it void, should possess and take it from us." Although the Puritans were compelled to compromise their principles at this point, they exercised great care in maintaining control of this expansion and thereby hoped to restrain the forces of social disintegration. After inspecting the area near Natascott, they concluded that the erection of a fort there would be too costly "and of little use; whereupon the planting of that place was deferred." The proposal to settle at Agawam proved more feasible, and in March 1633 John Winthrop, Jr. led a contingent of twelve men to plant there. But within a month the Massachusetts legislature ordered that "noe person whatsoever shall goe to plant or inhabitt att Aggawam, without leave from the Court, except those that are already gone." [22] In this manner, the Massachusetts authorities surmounted, temporarily, the disrupting forces of the wilderness.

The Puritans' conception of the wilderness as a refuge, by stimulating the migration of new colonists from England, aggravated the problem of social cohesion. John Cotton had defended the 1630 migration because "the hive of the Common wealth is so full, that Tradesmen cannot live one by another," and John White argued by analogy that "trees flourish faire, and prosper well . . . in a large orchard, which would otherwise wither and decay, if they were penned up in a little nursery." In Massachusetts, John Winthrop urged that the land be divided equitably so that newcomers could obtain sufficient quantities, since "it would be very prejudicial to the commonwealth, if men should be forced to go far off for land." The constant influx of new settlers, however, betrayed the futility of such counsel and, as William Hubbard later recalled, the Bay

[22] Winthrop, *Journal*, I, 97–98, 99; *Recs. of Mass. Bay*, I, 103.

colony was "overpressed with multitudes of new families, that daily resorted thither, so as . . . there was a necessity that some should swarm out." [23]

The efforts of the Massachusetts authorities to regulate these expansionist impulses produced a serious crisis in 1634. In May of that year, the inhabitants of Newton (Cambridge), led by their minister Thomas Hooker, complained of a "straitness for want of land," and received permission from the General Court "to look out either for enlargement or removal." Unimpressed with the offerings at Agawam and Merimack, the people of Newtown commissioned six men to view possible sites for a plantation in Connecticut, and by September they resolved to remove there.[24] Though other historians have examined the nature and origins of the debate which then ensued, the response of the Bay authorities is of particular interest.[25] John Pratt of Newtown, who regretfully noted that "theis townes are so thicke sett togeather," discovered that "men did thinke it unreasonable that they should remove or disperse into other parts of the countrie." The Bay officials expressed this opposition formally at the autumn session of the Massachusetts General Court. Appealing to the sanctity of the political covenant, they argued that the Newtown group "ought not to depart from us, being knit to us in one body, and bound by oath to seek the welfare of this commonwealth." The opponents of expansion supported this point by emphasizing the exigencies of the wilderness. The departure of the Hooker congregation was inexpedient, they maintained, because

[23] Cotton, "Gods Promise," 8; White, "Planter's Plea," 373; Winthrop, *Journal*, I, 144; Hubbard, "A General History," VI, 305–306.

[24] Winthrop, *Journal*, I, 124, 126, 128, 132–33; *Recs. of Mass. Bay*, I, 119.

[25] For perceptive treatments of this crisis, see Perry Miller, "Thomas Hooker and the Democracy of Connecticut," *Errand Into the Wilderness*, Chapter II, and Charles M. Andrews, *The Colonial Period of American History*, 4 vols. (New Haven, 1934–40), II, chapter III.

the Bay colony was "now weak and in danger [of being] assailed." They also protested that the establishment of a Puritan settlement in Connecticut would not only deprive Massachusetts of needed manpower, "but also [would] divert other friends that would come to us." Such a colony, they entreated their neighbors, would be exposed to "evident peril" from the Dutch and Indians, as well as "our own state at home, who would not endure they should sit down without a patent." And they concluded by reminding the proponents of expansion that "the removing of a candlestick is a great judgment, which is to be avoided." [26]

The proposed migration to Connecticut thereby forced the Puritan establishment to redefine its conception of the collective society, and it is significant that at this time the conservative groups reinforced their appeal to covenant theory with a realistic appraisal of the wilderness dangers. The commitment to community in Puritan Massachusetts represented more than a theoretical exercise; it also satisfied the needs of a frontier society. Although the pragmatic appeal may have been secondary to the desire to preserve their organic society, the Puritan authorities nevertheless articulated these ideas in a language relevant to the wilderness situation. These strenuous supplications convinced the Newtown group, for a time at least, to remain in the vicinity of the Bay. After weeks of bitter invective, the congregation of Newtown "accepted of such enlargement as had formerly been offered them by Boston and Watertown," wrote Winthrop, "and so the fear of their removal to Connecticut was removed." But the agreement of September 1634 produced, at best, a temporary interlude. By the following summer, Winthrop conceded that "we are putt to rayse new Colonys about 100 miles to the west of us, upon a very fine river and a

[26] "John Pratt's Answer," 358; Winthrop, *Journal*, I, 132–33.

most fruitfull place." And by autumn, the settlers commenced, in earnest, the arduous trek to Connecticut.[27]

The continued migration of colonists to New England
augmented the problem of overcrowdedness and further
weakened the cohesiveness of Puritan society. Although
the magistrates opposed "removall and spredding further
into other partes," observed John Pratt with understand-
able satisfaction, "they afterwards [conceived] it neces-
sarie that some should remove into other places, here
and there, of more inlargement."[28] In 1634 a group of
newcomers settled directly at Agawam and the General
Court authorized several Scottish and Irish gentlemen
who intended to migrate to New England "to sitt downe
in any place upp Merimacke Ryver." The following year,
the inhabitants of Ipswich, Watertown, and Roxbury obtained permission to plant inland, because "all towns in
the bay began to be much straigtened by their own
nearness to one another." The Court subsequently approved other plantations to accomodate the tidal wave
of newcomers.[29]

But throughout this period of rapid growth, the Massachusetts authorities pursued a cautious policy regarding
inland removals. The General Court resolved that "the
major parte of the magistrates shall have power . . . to
dispose of the sitting downe of men in any newe plantation," and ordered "that none shall goe without leave
from them." Though the Bay colony officials consented to
these expansionist demands, they diligently discouraged
unnecessary departures. In 1636 the Court proclaimed a

[27] Winthrop, *Journal*, I, 133–34, 163, 180; *Recs. of Mass. Bay*, I,
129–30; John Winthrop to Sir Simonds D'Ewes, July 20, 1635, *Winthrop Papers*, III, 200.

[28] "John Pratt's Answer," 358. For a discussion of the Pratt affair, see
above Chapter III.

[29] Winthrop, *Journal*, I, 125–26, 151, 154, 158; *Recs. of Mass. Bay*,
I, 129, 147, 148, 149.

day of general fast, in part because of "the removal of other churches." Nathaniel Ward of Ipswich criticized the younger John Winthrop for migrating to Connecticut. "I am in a dreame[,] att least not awake," he wrote, "if it be the way of God for so many to desert this place . . . to seeke the good of their cattell more then of [the commonwealth]." [30]

Besides opposing organized expansion, the Puritans of Massachusetts also objected to unwarranted dispersal. This attitude reflected the belief that unsanctioned plantations were beyond the pale of God's protection. To avoid such exposures and to promote social control, the General Court ordered that the squatters who had settled at Winetsemet should combine themselves with either Boston or Charlestown "as members of that towne." And subsequently the Massachusetts legislature announced that no dwellings should be erected more than half a mile from the meeting house. The belief that the frontier was the wrong side of the Hedge also influenced the abortive decision to transport Roger Williams to England rather than consent to a plantation at Narragansett Bay. The Massachusetts orthodoxy had feared that such a settlement would promote religious dissent, and "the infection would easily spread into these churches." [31]

The flurry of town-planting in New England ironically stimulated new concern for collective security, as the frontier settlers, no longer within the protective shield of the Bay, sought to preserve their budding plantations. After his mid-winter journey to Rhode Island, Roger Williams requested Winthrop's counsel about the drafting of

[30] *Recs. of Mass. Bay*, I, 167; Winthrop, *Journal*, I, 175; Nathaniel Ward to John Winthrop, Jr., December 24 [1635], *Winthrop Papers*, III, 216–17. For an analysis of the regulated expansion in New England, see Haller, *Puritan Frontier*.

[31] *Recs. of Mass. Bay*, I, 119–20, 157, 181; Winthrop, *Journal*, I, 168.

a civil covenant for that colony. He reported that "some young men" who had been invited to settle there for security purposes now "seeke the Freedome of Vote allso." "Beside[s]," he continued, "our dangers (in the midst of these dens of Lyons) now especially, call upon us to be Compact in a Civill way." Williams thus employed the rhetoric of wilderness realities to make the abstract theory of collectivity meaningful. In the other New England colonies, frontiersmen also consented to similar "plantation covenant[s]" to preserve their "civill order." [32] "We consider our Towne as a sey or porte towne of the land[,] remote from neighbours," wrote Nathaniel Ward of Ipswich, and we "neede to be strong and of a homogeneous spirit and people, as free from dangerous persons as we may." And his fellow townsmen attempted to lure John Winthrop, Jr. back to Ipswich because their remoteness from the Bay "hath made us earnest for the company of able men and as loath to loose them." Massachusetts promoted the security of its inland plantations by requiring military training in each new settlement.[33] The exposed settlers at Connecticut also provided for the safety of their plantations by transporting artillery from Massachusetts, establishing compulsory military training in the towns, and prohibiting the traffic of arms with the natives.[34]

The rising of the Pequot Indians in 1637 confirmed

[32] Roger Williams to John Winthrop [c. September 1636], *Winthrop Papers*, III, 296–97; *The First Century of the History of Springfield: The Official Records from 1636 to 1736*, ed. by Henry M. Burt, 2 vols. (Springfield, Mass., 1898), I, 156–58; *Pub. Recs. Conn.*, I, 20–21; *Records of the Colony and Plantation of New Haven, from 1638–1649*, ed. by Charles J. Hoadly (Hartford, 1857), p. 12. (Hereafter cited as *N.H. Recs., I.*)

[33] Nathaniel Ward to John Winthrop, Jr., December 24 [1635], "Petition of the Inhabitants of Ipswich," June 21, 1637, *Winthrop Papers*, III, 216, 432; *Recs. of Mass. Bay*, I, 141, 157, 179–80.

[34] *Recs. of Mass. Bay*, I, 148, 160; *Pub. Recs. Conn.*, I, 1, 2, 4.

the wisdom of these precautions. Particularly vulnerable to Indian assaults, the newly-settled plantations in Connecticut endured staggering hardships during the war. "We watch every other night never puttinge of[f] our Clothes," reported Lion Gardiner from the besieged fort at Saybrook, "for the Indians show them selves in troupes aboute us every day." Other isolated settlements recorded similar problems.[35] As insecure outposts, they looked to the Bay for support and attempted to arouse that colony from its lethargy. Gardiner requested the younger John Winthrop "to stirr up our freinds in the bay out of their dead sleep of securytie" and warned of the perils of procrastination. Edward Winslow of Plymouth urged Massachusetts to challenge the Pequots lest the Indians enter "a stronger confederacy to the further prejudice of the whole English." From Saybrook John Higginson wrote of the dangers of "that deeply-rooted securitie, and confidence in our owne supposed strength" and cautioned that "the eyes of all the Indians in the countrey are upon the English . . . ; and all may be assured . . . that if some . . . speedie course be not taken to tame the pride . . . of these now-insulting Pequots . . . , we are like to have all the Indians in the countrey about our ears." [36] The Connecticut settlers, perhaps because of their sense of isolation, underestimated the preparedness of their brethren, for by early spring the Bay colony adopted elaborate protective measures. The dangers of the war alarmed not only the frontier communities, but also the

---

[35] Lion Gardiner to John Winthrop, Jr., March 23, 1636[/37], *Winthrop Papers,* III, 381–82. For some contemporary accounts of the war on the frontier, see John Higginson to John Winthrop [c. May 1637], *Winthrop Papers,* III, 404–405; Roger Ludlow to William Pynchon [May?] 17, 1637, "Pincheon Papers," 235–37.

[36] Lion Gardiner to John Winthrop, Jr., March 23, 1636[/37], Edward Winslow to John Winthrop, April 17, 1637, John Higginson to John Winthrop [c. May 1637], *Winthrop Papers,* III, 382, 391–92, 404–405.

coastal settlements. John Winthrop urged Plymouth Colony to enter the war against "a common enimie," and warned that a Pequot victory would lead "to the rooting out of the whole nation." [37]

As an immediate effect, the commencement of hostilities stimulated a reemphasis upon the need for collectivity among the Puritan settlements. At the height of the Pequot tension, John Higginson suggested that the Lord had aroused the Indians against His children in order "to make them cleave more closely togither, and prize each other . . . , and stop their now beginning breaches." [38] The general state of fear which pervaded the colonies at this time probably encouraged social cohesion, but the long-range impact of the conflict upon Puritan social attitudes was more significant. In three important areas—Indian-white relations, intercolonial cooperation, and frontier expansion—the war forced a reconsideration of Puritan social theory.

In the aftermath of the Pequot War, the Puritan colonists continued to express their distrust of the Indians. Roger Williams urged Winthrop to treat their Indian allies fairly, yet warned him to "deale with them wisely as with wolves endewed with mens braines." To prevent surprise attacks, the Massachusetts General Court established a system of watches during peacetime as well as in "times of sudden danger" and reiterated the prohibition of the gun trade with the Indians. The colonies of Connecticut and New Haven were equally vigilant in their relations with the natives.[39] The Puritans revealed

[37] *Recs. of Mass. Bay,* I, 187, 188, 190; John Winthrop to William Bradford, May 20, 1637, *Winthrop Papers,* III, 417.

[38] John Higginson to John Winthrop [c. May 1637], *Winthrop Papers,* III, 404.

[39] Roger Williams to John Winthrop [July 10, 1637], *Winthrop Papers,* III, 445; *Recs. of Mass. Bay,* I, 293, 308, 312, 322–23; *Pub. Recs. Conn.,* I, 46–47, 49; *N.H. Recs.,* I, 33–35, 40.

their distrust of the natives by an increased tendency to relate Indian troubles to the machinations of the devil.[40]

Moreover, rumors of Indian conspiracies coursed through New England with striking regularity. The frequency of these false alarms indicates the depth of Puritan suspicion of the Indians and suggests that New Englanders, despite the victory of 1637, remained insecure in the wilderness. In July 1637 Israel Stoughton, a leader of the expedition against the Pequots, reported that the Narragansetts, erstwhile Puritan allies, became increasingly obstreperous and were likely to fill the power vacuum left by the vanquished enemy. The following spring Roger Williams denounced the resettlement of the Pequot survivors and urged Massachusetts to commence a war to disperse them. Shortly thereafter he informed the Bay colony of an approaching Indian war at Connecticut.[41] The frontier settlements again broached the possibility of hostilities against the Indians the following year and dispatched soldiers to destroy the corn planted by the Pequot remnants. In the autumn of 1640, John Haynes of Connecticut and William Bradford of Plymouth advised the Bay colony of an Indian conspiracy against the English settlements. Though the Massachusetts authorities doubted the veracity of these allegations, they nevertheless strengthened the watches in all the towns and disarmed the local Indian tribes.[42] And, like the other rumored cabals, this threat proved to be imaginary.

This long series of unsubstantiated panics climaxed in

---

[40] For a discussion of this aspect of Puritan thought, see Chapter IV.

[41] Israel Stoughton to John Winthrop [c. July 6, 1637], Israel Stoughton to the Governor and Council of Massachusetts [August 14, 1637], Roger Williams to John Winthrop, April 16 [1638], September 10 [1638], *Winthrop Papers*, III, 441–44, 482, IV, 26, 58.

[42] *Pub. Recs. Conn.*, I, 31–32; William Bradford to John Winthrop, June 29, 1640, August 16, 1640, Roger Williams to John Winthrop, July 21 [1640], *Winthrop Papers*, IV, 258–59, 275, 269; Winthrop, *Journal*, II, 6–7.

the Indian scare of 1642. In late August the Connecticut General Court notified the Bay colony that it had unearthed an Indian combination designed to remove the English from New England. Other missives from the frontier confirmed these tidings.[43] In response to this menace, each of the New England colonies instituted stringent precautionary measures. Massachusetts, "to strike some terror into the Indians," disarmed the tribes within its jurisdiction and summoned an emergency session of the General Court.[44] Unlike their more militant brethren at Connecticut, the officials of the Bay colony tended to discredit the accusations, particularly when direct consultation with the natives revealed no evidence of a conspiracy. Winthrop surmised that the enmity between two rival Indian chiefs instigated these rumors because "like reports [have] been raised almost every year since we came" to New England, and such information usually was transmitted "by the opposite faction among the Indians." But despite such levelheadedness, a general sense of fear filtered through the colonies. One correspondent reported that "the court [is] aconsulting what to doe about the Ingines. wee are in fare of thim." This insecurity passed slowly, and the Bay colony did not suspend the watches until mid-October, nearly two months after Connecticut first reported the danger.[45]

The continued sense of distrust and the desire for increased certainty in the wilderness modified Puritan attitudes about social cohesion. Though the Massachusetts leaders never embraced expansionism, they were suffi-

[43] Winthrop, *Journal*, II, 64, 74; *Pub. Recs. Conn.*, I, 73. For the details of the alleged conspiracy, see "Relation of the Plott-Indian" [1642], printed in *Colls. M.H.S.*, third ser., III (1833), 161–64.

[44] *Recs. of Mass. Bay*, II, 24–27; *Pub. Recs. Conn.*, I, 73, 74, 75; *N.H. Recs.*, I, 78; Winthrop, *Journal*, II, 74–75.

[45] Winthrop, *Journal*, II, 75–81; Martha Symonds to John Winthrop, Jr., September 27, 1642, *Winthrop Papers*, IV, 355; *Recs. of Mass. Bay*, II, 32.

ciently pragmatic to realize that, for the most part, they could not reverse the process of dispersal. Thus they endorsed a new pattern of collectivity, based upon intercolonial cooperation, which culminated in the formation of the New England Confederation. The quest for security in the wilderness, more than anything else, stimulated collaboration among the New England colonies. Despite petty bickering over jurisdictional issues, the Puritan leaders recognized that they were brethren "in the same work of God, in the same Community of perill, under the same envious observation." [46] Accordingly they were usually willing to assist one another in time of danger. The Pequot War greatly accelerated this tendency. In that crisis, Massachusetts Bay, Connecticut, Plymouth, and Rhode Island shared men, munitions, and information to defeat the common enemy.

These colonies, with the exception of the heretical settlement at Rhode Island, attempted to formalize their cooperation in later years. A league of friendship, they felt, would mitigate the danger of Dutch settlements in Connecticut and, even more important, would provide increased security from the Indians. The Connecticut representatives who visited Massachusetts in 1638 urged "that before the Indians we should in all things appear as one." But, as the New Haven legislature later recalled, the conference "ended without fruit, and the four jurisdictions [Massachusetts, Connecticut, New Haven, and Plymouth], though knitt together in affections . . . [remained] free from any express covenant or combination." Impeded by minor disputes, negotiations for a formal confederation dragged on until 1642. The Indian crisis of that

---

[46] John Winthrop to Thomas Hooker [c. March 1638/39], Roger Ludlow, in Behalf of the General Assembly of Connecticut to the Governor and Assistants of Massachusetts, May 29, 1638, *Winthrop Papers,* IV, 100, 36.

year, however, forced a reappraisal of intercolonial cooperation. Faced with the specter of large-scale Indian
attacks, the New England colonies abandoned their internecine quarrels. The Massachusetts General Court instructed a delegation to inform the natives "that wee
account the English at Plimoth, Connectecot, Newhaven,
and other parts of the country . . . as all one with our
selves." The Bay colony also approved a Connecticut proposal to enter a confederation and recommended the in-
clusion of Plymouth and Sir Ferdinando Gorges's province
of Maine. Only the coming of winter delayed the con-
summation of the compact and postponed the final negotiations until the following spring.[47]

The Pequot War also enhanced the colonists' interest
in frontier expansion by opening up new areas for settlement. The military excursions into Connecticut fostered
the discovery of many choice locations. John Mason, a
leader of the Puritan army, admitted to "being altogether
ignorant of the Country" in Connecticut prior to the war,
and John Underhill's history of the conflict cataloged
twelve newly-found areas suitable for settlement. Nearly
every military leader extolled the fertility of the surrounding lands and proposed the establishment of plantations
there. Israel Stoughton lavished special praise upon the
New Haven area and stressed the advantages of expansion to that region. Though he claimed to "affect not scattering" and preferred to "part stakes at home," Stoughton
cited "the goodness of the land, . . . the fairness of the
title," and warned that "an ill neighbor may possess it,
if a good do not." [48] The nature of the acquisition of the

[47] "John Winthrop's Summary of his letter to Thomas Hooker," August
28, 1638, *Winthrop Papers*, IV, 53; *N.H. Recs.*, II, 5–6; Winthrop,
Journal, I, 231–32, 301, II, 82; *Pub. Recs. Conn.*, I, 10, 30, 31; *Recs.
of Mass. Bay*, II, 23–24, 31.

[48] John Mason, "A Brief History of the Pequot War," reprinted in
Colls. M.H.S., second ser., VIII (1819), 133; Underhill, "News from

Pequot lands near the future site of New London also promoted expansionist tendencies. The Connecticut General Court, in June 1637, ordered thirty men to the Pequot territory "to maynteine our right that God by Conquest hath given to us." The Bay colony accepted this logic and agreed to divide these lands with Connecticut.[49]

Despite the attractiveness of the Pequot country, the leaders of the Bay colony, concerned primarily with social cohesion, pursued a conservative policy toward inland plantations. To be sure, the continued migration of new colonists from England forced them to countenance some dispersal, and in 1640 the General Court repealed the law which prevented the erection of buildings more than half a mile from the meeting house.[50] But the Massachusetts leaders, chagrined perhaps by the departure of influential Puritans to Connecticut, were much less willing to condone expansion beyond the boundaries of the colony. Thomas Hooker accused the Bay authorities of deliberately discouraging migration to Connecticut and reproached the Puritans of Massachusetts for exaggerating the difficulties of frontier settlement and for directing newcomers to other sites. Although John Winthrop attempted to placate Hooker, he nevertheless insisted that John Pratt "opened the doore to all that . . . followed" and charged that Connecticut had aggravated the dispute by trying "to drawe Mr. Shepherd and his wholl Church from us." [51]

America," title page; Daniel Patrick to the Governor and Council of War in Massachusetts, June 19, 1637, Israel Stoughton to the Governor and Council of Massachusetts [August 14, 1637], *Winthrop Papers*, III, 431, 483.

[49] *Pub. Recs. Conn.*, I, 10; *Recs. of Mass. Bay*, I, 216.

[50] *Recs. of Mass. Bay*, I, 210, 291; John Woodbridge to John Winthrop, March 22, 1640[/41], *Winthrop Papers*, IV, 327–28. In 1638 John Winthrop recorded that "There came over this summer . . . at least three thousand persons, so as they were forced to look out new plantations." Winthrop, *Journal*, I, 274.

[51] Thomas Hooker to John Winthrop [c. December 1638], John Win-

Desirous of retaining celebrated ministers, Massachusetts officials similarly opposed the colonization of New Haven by John Davenport and Theophilus Eaton. To distract attention from Connecticut, the Bay leaders offered to accommodate the Davenport company at alternate sites within Massachusetts, which were "pressed with much importunity by some." After lengthy deliberation, however, Davenport and Eaton rejected these proposals and in March 1638 departed for New Haven. Although Winthrop attempted to rationalize the defeat of the leadership by acknowledging the defensive advantages of settling in that region, he continued to disapprove of the venture.[52] And when John Cotton contemplated removing to New Haven at this time, it is likely that his neighbor, John Winthrop, was one of the "chief Magistrates" who persuaded him to remain in Massachusetts. "I then layed down all thoughts of removall," declared Cotton subsequently, "and sat down satisfied in my aboad." [53] In similar fashion, the Bay colony convinced Ezekiel Rogers, "a man of special note in England," to settle in Massachusetts rather than at New Haven. Although several of Rogers's friends had already traveled to Connecticut, the Bay colony promised them extensive tracts of land at Rowley in order to win them back. In later years Rogers justified his boundary demands, claiming that without

throp to Thomas Hooker [c. March 1638/39], *Winthrop Papers,* IV, 76–77, 99. See also Hooker, Thanksgiving Sermon, p. 431.

[52] Winthrop, *Journal,* I, 231, 265; John Davenport and Theophilus Eaton to the Massachusetts General Court, March 12, 1638, *Winthrop Papers,* IV, 19–20. William Hubbard noted that the Davenport company originally intended to settle "within the proper precincts" of Massachusetts, but the group was unable to find a place "of meet capacity for them." "A General History," VI, 317–18.

[53] John Cotton, *The Way of the Congregational Churches Cleared,* printed in Hooker, *A Survey,* part I, 52–54. For a discussion of Cotton's influence at New Haven, see Isabel M. Calder, "John Cotton and the New Haven Colony," *New England Quarterly,* III (1930), 82–94.

such a grant "we woulde upon no termes accept of a Plantation here." [54]

Besides opposing expansion to Connecticut and New Haven, the Massachusetts authorities also denounced schemes for the colonization of the West Indies. In 1640 a group led by John Humfrey and supported by Lord Say and Sele contemplated withdrawing to the West Indies. The attempt to win a mass following, however, aroused the displeasure of the Massachusetts establishment. The elders, led by John Wilson, urged the would-be colonists to desist, and the General Court, relying upon pragmatic rhetoric, warned them of the dangers of resettlement and defended the concept of social cohesion.[55] Although the failure of this enterprise brought a temporary lull, other socially disruptive forces appeared to challenge the Puritan community.

The economic depression which engulfed Massachusetts Bay and her sister colonies in 1640 and the outbreak of the English civil wars (which, in part, accounted for the economic decline by reducing the amount of migration to America) continued to draw people away from New England.[56] Thomas Shepard of Cambridge nearly departed for Connecticut because of the severity of the depression in Massachusetts. "For why should a man stay until the house fall on his head"? queried Shepard's father-in-law Thomas Hooker in support of such a removal, "and why continue . . . there where in reason he shall destroy

[54] Winthrop, *Journal,* I, 298, II, 16; Ezekiel Rogers to John Winthrop, October 5, 1640, Emmanuel Downing to John Winthrop, March 2, 1638[/39], *Winthrop Papers,* IV, 290–91, 103; *Recs. of Mass. Bay,* I, 289.

[55] Winthrop, *Journal,* I, 333–35; Mather, *Magnalia,* I, 315; Lord Say and Sele to John Winthrop, July 9, 1640, *Winthrop Papers,* IV, 263, 266.

[56] For a discussion of the people who returned to England at this time, see Sachse, "The Migration of New Englanders."

his substance"? After much agonizing prayer and a grant of additional land to Cambridge, however, Shepard decided to remain at the Bay. The Cambridge congregation desired "to sit still and not to remoove farther," wrote Shepard several years later, "partly because of the fellowship of the churches[,] partly because they thought there lives were short and remoovalls to new plantations full of troubles." [57]

The difficulties of resettlement, however, did not diminish the propensity to expand along the frontier, and dispersal continued to challenge the idea of a collective society. John Cotton expressed scorn for the "men [who] think they are forced to la[u]nch out in building and planting" and advised the frontiersmen "to provide fresh water" for their souls as well as their bodies. He implored New Englanders to be content to live "under the shadow of the Almighty, and never look for more" and suggested that "there is some sinne that lyes in the breast still, for which the Lord pursues men with a restlesse frame." Cotton lamented the fact that "every occasion puts us to a new plantation, and when we are there we cannot rest." Such removals, he admonished, signified that "there is no Spirit of Reformation, at least, not of Resurrection." But John Winthrop presented the most sophisticated plea for social unity. In criticizing the weak-hearted who "crept out at a broken wall" to improve their outward estates, Winthrop combined the idea of a covenant society with the realistic needs of a frontier society. Those people who "come together into a wilderness," asserted Winthrop, "where [there] are nothing but wild beasts and beastlike

[57] Thomas Hooker to Thomas Shepard, November 2, 1640, Shepard memoranda in "The Confessions of diverse propounded . . . ," both quoted in Lucius R. Paige, *History of Cambridge, Massachusetts: 1630–1887* (Boston, 1877), pp. 46–52; Shepard, "Meditations and Experiences," 10; *Recs. of Mass. Bay*, I, 306, 330, II, 62; Shepard, "Autobiography," 384–85.

men, and there confederate in civil and church estate"
implicitly "bind themselves to support each other, and
all of them that society . . . whereof they are members."
The tendency toward expansion, he warned, would leave
both the church and commonwealth "destitute in a wilderness, exposed to misery and reproach." [58]

Winthrop's plea significantly coincided with the rumors
of the Indian conspiracy of September 1642. The dangers
he wished to avoid were not vague and imaginary; they
were products of the wilderness condition. As in 1634,
Winthrop defended the imperiled colony by grounding
the notion of the social covenant in the pragmatic realities of the forest. He thereby made a predetermined
scheme of social values relevant to a new series of experiences. In this manner, the wilderness modified the
original idea of an organic society.

[58] Cotton, *An Exposition upon . . . Revelation,* pp. 239–40; Cotton,
The Powring Out of the Seven Vials, pp. 51, 52–53; John Cotton, *The
Churches Resurrection, or the Opening . . . of the Revelation* (Lon-
don, 1642), pp. 21, 26; Winthrop, *Journal,* II, 83–84.

CHAPTER VIII

"The Unity of
the English Colonyes"

A S the forest blossomed in the spring of 1643, seven
men from the New England plantations at Plymouth,
New Haven, and Connecticut arrived at Massachusetts
Bay to consummate the confederation of their colonies.
Each settlement assigned to its most eminent inhabitants
the task of reaching a judicious agreement. In consultation, the representatives "encountered some difficulties,"
wrote John Winthrop, but since all were "desirous of
union and studious of peace," he added, "they readily
yielded each to [the] other in such things as tended to
common utility" and after "two or three meetings they
lovingly accorded" to the Articles of Confederation.[1] Despite the retention of autonomy by the separate colonies,
the treaty of 1643 enabled the Puritans to expand the
notion of the collective society to account for the changes
wrought by the wilderness experience. The New England Confederation thereby served as a viable social insti-

[1] Winthrop, *Journal*, II, 98. At the negotiations of May 1643, Edward
Winslow and William Collier represented Plymouth, John Haynes, Edward Hopkins, and George Fenwick acted for Connecticut, and Theophilus Eaton and Thomas Grigson served the interests of New Haven.
The Massachusetts Court appointed Winthrop, Thomas Dudley, Simon
Bradstreet, Edward Gibbons, William Tyng, and William Hathorn to
treat with these delegates.

tution, for it permitted the colonists to reconcile the counter forces of disintegration and cohesion. Furthermore, by assiduously regulating Indian-white relations, the Confederation provided an effective mechanism to cope with the serious problem of social insecurity in the wilderness.

"We came into these partes of America with one and the same end and ayme," commenced the Articles of Confederation, but "in our settleinge . . . we are further dispersed upon the Sea Coasts and Rivers then was at first intended, so that we cannot . . . with convenience communicate in one Goverment [sic]." "We live encompassed with people of severall Nations and strang languages," the compact continued, and therefore we believe it is "our bounden duty . . . to enter a present Consotiation . . . , for mutuall help and strength in all our future concernementes." The migrations to Connecticut and New Haven in the mid-1630s had sundered the idea of an organic society surrounded by a protective Hedge. We "were here scattered at a great distance," asserted the Massachusetts General Court two decades after the founding of the Confederation, and we "had no walled tounes or garrisons of souldiers for . . . defence." The colonies compensated for the dispersal of the settlements by subscribing to "a league of amity," which, in effect, recast the pattern of Puritan social theory. Although the member governments retained their independence of action, the New England Confederation, by merging the colonies in a larger body politic, enabled the Puritans to redefine the limits of the Hedge.[2]

Massachusetts Bay, by expanding the idea of the protective barrier beyond its jurisdictional boundaries, could

[2] "Articles of Confederation," printed in *Acts of the Commissioners,* I, 3; The General Court of Massachusetts Bay to the King's Commissioners, May 1665, *Recs. of Mass. Bay,* IV, Part II, 231.

sanction frontier extension for the first time, without jeopardizing the ideals of the organic society. Thomas Shepard and John Allin, who generally disapproved of needless dispersal, observed "that removals from one towne and Church to another and from full to new Plantations, are frequently practised amongst us, with [the] consent and approbation" of the appropriate authorities. John Eliot maintained that "every order" of society should "cohabit together . . . as neer as may be; because that doth tend to facilitate the watch, and work of the Lords Government." The commitment to community, however, no longer proscribed the possibility of expansion. If any person "shall remove his habitation to a more remote place," argued Eliot, "meet it is that he do change his Rulers." Thus, he continued, people should undertake such removals only with the "approbation of the Rulers whence he goeth, and with the acceptance of those to whom he removeth, lest by [some] unstable changes," warned Eliot, "they . . . slip out from under the Government of the Lord."[3] The New England Confederation provided an institutional framework which made such transplantations legitimate and kept the frontier settlements within the Hedge.

The defeat of the Pequots in 1637 released a large tract of land for colonization. Both Connecticut and Massachusetts Bay claimed this territory according to the right of conquest. In the autumn of 1645, the younger John Winthrop traveled through these lands "looking for a suitable spot for a colony" and eventually decided to erect a plantation at the mouth of the present Thames River. In June 1646 the Massachusetts General Court granted

---

[3] Shepard [and Allin], *A Defence of the Answer*, pp. 182–83; John Eliot, "The Christian Commonwealth: or, The Civil Policy of the Rising Kingdom of Jesus Christ" [1659], reprinted in *Colls. M.H.S.*, third ser., IX (1846), 149.

power to Winthrop and Thomas Peters to govern this settlement until Connecticut and the Bay colony resolved their boundary dispute. But, as the elder Winthrop remarked, "it mattered not to which jurisdiction it did belong, seeing the confederation made all as one." Samuel Symonds of Ipswich, a friend and neighbor of the Winthrop family, advised John, Jr. not to quarrel "in case it be agreed . . . that that place shall belonge to . . . Connecticut and not to the Bay" and urged him to "joyne with them in the worke of god . . . to reconcile the Indians amongst themselves." And although Emmanuel Downing admonished Winthrop "not to burye [his] talents in those obscure parts," he subsequently endorsed the migration of "usefull working men" to Winthrop's plantation.[4] The New England Confederation thereby enabled the Massachusetts conservatives to accept expansion beyond the borders of that colony. In 1659 the secession of several members of the Wethersfield church in Connecticut reversed this process. In response to a petition from these settlers, the Bay colony approved the erection of a plantation at Hadley and endeavored to remove some of the obstacles which impeded the growth of that town.[5]

By the mid-1640s the authorities of the Bay colony generally abandoned their traditional objections to inland extension. Thereafter the Massachusetts General Court,

[4] William R. Carlton, ed., "Overland to Connecticut in 1645: A Travel Diary of John Winthrop, Jr.," *New England Quarterly*, XIII (1940), 504–505; *Recs. of Mass. Bay*, II, 160; Winthrop, *Journal*, II, 275; Samuel Symonds to John Winthrop, Jr. [c. September 1646], Emmanuel Downing to John Winthrop, Jr., December 17, 1648, *Winthrop Papers*, V, 100, 289; Emmanuel Downing to John Winthrop, Jr., February 24, 1650[/51], Winthrop Mss., II, 39.

[5] *Recs. of Mass. Bay*, IV, Part I, 368, 380; Sherman W. Adams and Henry R. Stiles, *The History of Ancient Wethersfield, Connecticut*, 2 vols. (New York, 1904), I, part I, 162–65. See also, East, "Puritanism and New Settlement."

responding to the needs of an expanding population, approved the establishment of new plantations without major debates. Petitioners for inland towns usually cited the problem of overcrowdedness as a justification for removals. But the coming of age of new generations, internal disputes, and the quest for economic advancement also accounted for the founding of new settlements. Dissatisfied with conditions in the older towns, energetic men could remove to the frontier in hope of better opportunities.[6] The colony of Connecticut similarly supported inland extension, particularly in the years after 1670. Like its sister colony at the Bay, however, Connecticut pursued a cautious policy regarding removals and carefully regulated the composition of its new towns. In 1650, for example, the General Court approved the founding of Norwalk provided that the settlers "make preparations and provisions for theire owne defense and safety," so "that the country may not be exposed to unnecessary trouble and danger in these hazardous times."[7]

Spread along the northern coast of the Long Island Sound, New Haven colony consisted of several dispersed towns which in 1643 agreed to merge as one jurisdiction. Several of the inhabitants of New Haven later attempted to establish a trading colony upon the Delaware Bay. Although they won limited support from their own government, the resourceful New Haven men could not earn the endorsement of the New England Confederation. The commissioners of the United Colonies argued that the Puritan settlements lacked sufficient manpower "to carry

[6] *Recs. of Mass. Bay,* II, 212, 273, 283, III, 181, IV, Part I, 136–37, 402, 421, 423–24, 445, Part II, 91, 557, V, 35, 36–37; Petition of the Inhabitants of Sudbury to the Massachusetts General Court [1656], quoted in Alfred Sereno Hudson, *The History of Sudbury, Mass.* (Sudbury, 1889), p. 160. See also, Sumner Chilton Powell, *Puritan Village: The Formation of a New England Town* (Middletown, Conn., 1963), Chapter VIII.

[7] *Pub. Recs. Conn.,* I, 210, II, 145, 148, 210, 224–25.

on theire necessary ocations" and hence rejected the proposed settlement at Delaware. The delegates, in opposing this scheme, significantly stressed the need to maintain the social order in New England.[8] Thus the desire to preserve the ideal of an organic society still constituted a prime obstacle to the establishment of remote settlements.

In Massachusetts Bay, frontier expansion and social security usually went hand in hand. The General Court in 1645 encouraged twenty families of Braintree to settle near the border of Plymouth Colony, for, as John Winthrop observed, "it was of great Concernment to all the English in these parts, that a strong plantation should be there as a bulwork . . . against the Narragansetts." The following year the elder Winthrop supported, in almost identical language, his son's enterprise in the Pequot country, because it would "be a curb to the Indians." In 1669 a committee advised the Massachusetts General Court to erect a town twelve miles west of Marlborough in order "to unite and strengthen the inland plantations." Besides planting defensive outposts in the wilderness, the Court frequently expressed concern for the safety of the inhabitants on the frontier and devised numerous policies to protect the inland settlements. "In regard to the great danger that Concord, Sudberry, and Dedham wilbe exposed unto, being inland townes and but thinly peopled," ordered the General Court in preparation for a war with the Narragansetts, "no man now inhabiting" in these plantations "shall remove to any other towne" without the approval of a magistrate. At the height of another war scare in 1653, the Court transferred some artillery from Roxbury

---

[8] *N.H. Recs.*, I, 199–200, II, 130–32; *Acts of the Commissioners*, I, 140–41, 212; John Mason to John Winthrop, Jr., January 28, 1654[/55], February 5, 1654[/55], Winthrop Mss., III, 117. The New Haven men attempted to settle at Delaware Bay, but were expelled by the Dutch who claimed the territory. Many of these people later migrated to Newark, New Jersey. See Calder, *New Haven Colony*, pp. 253–56.

to Dedham because the frontier settlements "maybe in more danger than some others are." To strengthen the collectivity among its inland plantations, the Bay colony created a separate county for the remote towns of Springfield, Northampton, and Hadley. In 1667 the inhabitants of Hadley settled along the west bank of the Connecticut River petitioned the General Court for permission "to be a society of ourselves." The exposed townsmen remonstrated that they had to cross the river to attend the Lord's ordinances and "leave our relations and estates lying on the outside of the colony, joining to the wilderness, to be a prey to the heathen, when they see the opportunity." In response to this appeal, the Court subsequently established the town of Hatfield.[9] Such measures indicate the marked concern for security upon the frontier throughout the seventeenth century.

"When Gods Israel hath to doe with many potent, subtill, most wicked and desperate enemies," preached William Hooke in 1645, "they had need to enter into a covenant of mutuall helpe and assistance." A people "united by confederacie," he concluded, "is not easily vanquished" because all men share their interests and engagements.[10] The New England Confederation, by reconciling dispersal with unity, provided a communal response to the dangers of the wilderness. The distances between plantations and colonies had diluted the original ideal of an insulated, organic society. But the Confederation transcended these divisive forces and enabled the New England colonies to coalesce in times of trouble. "If any of

[9] Winthrop, *Journal*, II, 261, 275; *Recs. of Mass. Bay*, II, 122, IV, Part I, 138, Part II, 435, 52; John Browne to John Winthrop, June 26, 1644, *Winthrop Papers*, IV, 464–65; Petition from Hadley to the General Court, May 3, 1667, quoted in Judd, *History of Hadley*, pp. 79–80.

[10] Hooke, *New-Englands Sence*, p. 111.

our Confederats . . . [brings] a Just warre upon them-selvs," declared John Winthrop shortly after the signing of the Articles of Confederation, and "if they call to us for helpe, . . . we must not leave them to destruction." [11]

While the existence of the Confederation provided some forms of institutional protection, New Englanders betrayed the depth of their insecurity in the wilderness by enacting various measures to strengthen their planta-tions. At the first meeting of the United Colonies, the delegates recommended that all the settlers possess fully equipped arms "to be ready upon all occations," and each of the colonies subsequently passed appropriate legisla-tion. The settlements supplemented these orders by ex-empting certain isolated residents from militia drills in order to protect their houses, and assigned soldiers to appear fully armed on Sabbath and lecture days. The col-onies also provided elaborate procedures for military af-fairs.[12] In 1645 the Bay colony proposed that the youth of New England should be trained in "the art and prac-tice of armes" (including bows and arrows) and inaug-urated this education for boys between ten and sixteen years of age.[13]

The savages of America constituted the most serious external threat to the Puritan colonies in the wilderness. The commissioners of the United Colonies, reacting to the interest of most of the settlers, attempted to reduce the Indian menace by prohibiting the trade of guns and ammunition to the natives. Besides chastising the shop-keepers of the Bay colony for furnishing the Indian allies with weapons, the Confederation also urged the nearby French and Dutch to curtail the arms trade to the Indians.

[11] John Winthrop to Richard Saltonstall and Others [c. July 21, 1643], *Winthrop Papers*, IV, 408; see also, Winthrop, *Journal*, II, 133–34.

[12] *Acts of the Commissioners*, I, 12; *Recs. of Mass. Bay*, II, 38, 42–43, 67, 221–22; *Pub. Recs. Conn.*, I, 196, 222, 150; *N.H. Recs.*, I, 399–400.

[13] *Recs. of Mass. Bay*, II, 99.

If the Indians "finde us divided and att difference" on the issue of the gun trade, wrote Governor Theophilus Eaton of New Haven to Peter Stuyvesant in 1648, "they will grown insolent and full of provocations." Each of the New England colonies reaffirmed its disapproval of the arms traffic, and Massachusetts attempted to eliminate the vagaries of the fur trade which enabled the natives to acquire weapons.[14] The New England settlements also hoped to diminish the martial strength of the Indians by preventing the trade or sale of horses and boats to the natives.[15]

Although the Confederation enabled the colonies to establish a uniform Indian policy and thereby afforded some security for the settlers, New Englanders frequently articulated their distrust of the natives. While informing the younger John Winthrop of the convening of the United Colonies in 1647, Edward Hopkins of Hartford wondered "how safe itt may be for all the Indyans . . . to be acquainted with the direct tyme of our travelling through the cuntrey." Two years later, Roger Williams expressed delight at the internecine quarrels among the natives which contrasted with "the oneness and securitie of the English." And in 1656 a resident of Springfield suggested that mastiff dogs "might bee of good use against the Indians incase of any desturbance from them." The Puritans distrusted not only the heathenish Indians, but also those natives who claimed to have been converted by the teachings of Christ. "Growth of Grace is very slow," observed John Brock of the natives upon the Isle of Shoals, and

---

[14] *Acts of the Commissioners,* I, 21–22, 65, 105; *Recs. of Mass. Bay,* III, 208–209, IV, Part I, 291–92; Theophilus Eaton to Peter Stuyvesant, October 9, 1648, printed in *N.H. Recs.,* I, 529; *Pub. Recs. Conn.,* I, 138.

[15] *Recs. of Mass. Bay,* IV, Part I, 255–56, 277; *The Book of the General Lawes and Libertyes* [1660], p. 158; *Pub. Recs. Conn.,* I, 284; *N.H. Recs.,* II, 217.

"The professing Indians are not to be trusted." John Eliot, the famed Indian missionary, remarked that during a war scare in 1653 many of the colonists erroneously believed "that even these praying Indians were in a conspiracy with others . . . to doe mischief to the English." "Wee ever have . . . put a great difference betwixt Indians whoe professe Jesus Christ and others who declare against him," claimed the commissioners of the United Colonies, "but many Indian professors" proved to be "lose and falce." The delegates therefore thought that it was "not safe to furnish them promiscqusly [*sic*]" with weapons.[16]

Although the New England Confederation managed to prevent the outbreak of a serious Indian war in the four decades after the Pequot conflict, the colonists enjoyed little tranquillity. From the founding of the Confederation in 1643, Indian machinations combined with Puritan nervousness to produce war scares nearly every year. The cautiousness and high-mindedness of the commissioners of the United Colonies prevented the overt commencement of hostilities. But the long series of Indian "plots" and colonial panics betrays the hesitancy with which the Puritans adjusted to their wilderness environment.[17]

Since the Indian scare of 1642 had hastened the establishment of the New England Confederation, it was appropriate that at the first session of that body the delegates resolved to punish the perpetrators of that conspir-

[16] Edward Hopkins to John Winthrop, Jr., May 5, 1647, Roger Williams to John Winthrop, Jr., October 25, 1649, *Winthrop Papers*, V, 156, 375; *Acts of the Commissioners*, II, 168; Brock, "Autobiographical Memoranda," 102; John Eliot, "A Late and Further Manifestation of the Progress of the Gospel amongst the Indians in New-England" [1655], reprinted in *Colls. M.H.S.*, third ser., IV, 270; The Commissioners of the United Colonies to John Eliot, August 29, 1655, printed in *Acts of the Commissioners*, II, 140.

[17] For a complete discussion of Puritan-Indian relations under the New England Confederation, see Vaughan, *New England Frontier*, Chapter VI.

acy. During the summer of 1643, Unkas, chief of the Mohegan tribe, captured his rival, Miantonomo, leader of the Narragansetts, and conveyed him to Hartford. The commissioners thereupon accused Miantonomo of "treacherous plotts . . . to engage all the Indians . . . to cutt of[f] the whole body of the English in these parts" and, after lengthy deliberation, recommended that Unkas be permitted to execute his opponent. During the captivity of Miantonomo, however, the commissioners reported that the Narragansetts had summoned the Mohawks to attack the English and their Mohegan allies. These rumors spread through the colonies and alarmed all the Puritan settlements. Despite the "sharp weather," the Bay colony established a system of watches, and not until mid-February did the New England authorities acknowledge that these reports were without foundation. Although William Pynchon of Springfield dismissed the likelihood of a Mohawk invasion, he nevertheless advised the leaders at the Bay to beware of the Narragansetts, who were bent on revenge and determined to "make lamentable havock." [18]

The rumors of a Narragansett conspiracy persisted through the summer of 1644. "Alas! Alas! We look for a Skermish with the Indians," exclaimed John Brock, then a student at Harvard College. And in October John Winthrop noted, with justifiable relief, that the colonists no longer feared a war with the Narragansetts.[19] At this time, the Indians in the vicinity of New Haven committed

---

[18] Winthrop, *Journal*, II, 135; *Acts of the Commissioners*, I, 10–11; John Haynes to John Winthrop, December 1, 1643, February 17, 1643 [/44], John Mason to John Winthrop, December 1, 1643, Edward Winslow to John Winthrop, January 7, 1643[/44], Benedict Arnold to John Winthrop, January 19, 1643[/44], William Bradford to John Winthrop [c. February 1643/44], William Pynchon to John Winthrop, February 19, 1643[/44], *Winthrop Papers*, IV, 418, 507, 419, 427–28, 431–32, 437, 443–44.

[19] Brock, "Autobiographical Memoranda," 100; Winthrop, *Journal*, II, 204, 175; *Recs. of Mass. Bay*, II, 72.

"sondry Insolencies and outrages" against the settlers there, particularly at the exposed plantation of Stamford. A magistrate of that town warned that "the Indians being so bolde and insolent are misceivously bent to begin a warr against the English," and the General Court of New Haven responded by enacting various defensive policies.[20] Such dangers, whether real or imagined, reveal the general state of insecurity which pervaded the New England colonies under the Confederation. For the Puritans, therefore, the wilderness remained an inhospitable environment.

The enmity between the Mohegans and the Narragansetts continued to plague the Puritans' relations with the natives. In the summer of 1645, the Narragansetts attacked their tribal enemies, and the English were obliged to intervene to check this aggression. The commissioners of the United Colonies, who endorsed an expedition against the Narragansetts, drafted an elaborate justification of the war, "A Declaration of former passages . . . betwixt the English and the Narrohiggansets . . . ," in which they recounted the deplorable behavior of that tribe. In rejecting a peace mission from the Confederation, the Narragansetts had insisted that the English withdraw their troops from Unkas. They threatened to "lay the English cattell on heapes as heigh as their houses," and warned "that no English man should stir out of his doore to pisse, but he should be killed." As the Puritan colonies prepared for war, fear spread through New England. "A warr with the Narraganset is verie considerable to this plantation," declared Emmanuel Downing. The General Court of New Haven advised "all those that goe abroad in the woods or meddowes . . . to carry their armes with them, and to worke as neare together as may bee." Fortunately, however, the Narragansetts, when

[20] *Acts of the Commissioners*, I, 26; *N.H. Recs.*, I, 119, 134–36.

confronted with a show of power, preferred to negotiate rather than fight. Although the commissioners averted a war, the preparation for hostilities revealed the underlying insecurity which permeated the New England colonies.[21]

❚ The pact between the Puritans and the Narragansetts failed to solve the problem of security in New England. In 1646 neither the Narragansetts nor their allies, the Nianticks, fulfilled their treaty obligations. The delegates to the Confederation claimed to have "good evidence" that the Narragansetts sought to engage the Mohawks "in some designe against the English and Uncas." The following year, the commissioners convened two months early because they were "enformed credibly" that the Narragansetts were conspiring with the local tribes to attack the English. Exasperated by the refusal of the Narragansetts to comply with the treaty and fearful of a possible Indian cabal, the commissioners dispatched twenty soldiers to compel the natives to pay the wampum in arrears. Once again, the Indians chose the peaceful course and accepted the English demands.[22] ❚

Meanwhile, other Indian troubles continued to aggravate the instability of the New England colonies. Shortly after the founding of New London by John Winthrop, Jr., Unkas attacked the local Indians there and imperiled the settlers of that infant plantation. The following year, Unkas's brother hovered near this settlement "in a suspitious manner . . . to the affrightment not onely of the

[21] *Acts of the Commissioners,* I, 33, 41, 50–51, 53–55; Emmanuel Downing to John Winthrop [c. August 1645], Thomas Peters to John Winthrop [c. May 1645], William Pynchon to John Winthrop, September 15, 1645, *Winthrop Papers,* V, 38–39, 20, 45; *N.H. Recs.,* I, 168–69; *Recs. of Mass. Bay,* II, 121–23, III, 39–40.
[22] *Acts of the Commissioners,* I, 74, 85, 145, 168; Roger Williams to John Winthrop, Jr., October 9, 1650, October 17, 1650, "Letters of Roger Williams, 1632–1682," ed. by John R. Bartlett, in *Complete Writings,* VI, 200–202, 203–204.

[friendly] Indians . . . but of diverse of the English themselves." [23] At this time, the settlers at Hartford uncovered an Indian plot to murder several of the magistrates there, and Connecticut narrowly avoided a war over this issue. In 1649 the colonists of New Haven and Connecticut prepared to revenge the murder of John Whitmore of Stamford and enacted numerous defensive measures. [24] These bellicose reactions underscored the fundamental insecurity of the New England settlements.

In the spring of 1653, "intelligence of a plot between the Dutch and the Indians to cut off all the English" filtered into the Bay colony and instigated a serious panic in the Puritan colonies. Although the reports of a Dutch-Indian conspiracy eventually proved to be unfounded, the response of New Englanders to these rumors reveals that the settlers were extremely uneasy at this time. Upon learning of the alleged plot, the Massachusetts Council summoned an emergency session of the New England Confederation, and the Court of Deputies, declaring its belief in "the reallitie of the plott," acknowledged "the speciall favour of God in the discovery thereof." Each day fresh reports arrived describing further Indian machinations against the English. Disquieted by the propinquity of the Dutch, New Haven and Connecticut endeavored to convince the Bay colony to commence hostilities. Edward Norris of Salem also urged the commissioners to declare war because a hesitant policy would make the neighboring Indians more insolent and bold in "future time." And Major General Daniel Dennison of Massachusetts Bay, "to

[23] John Winthrop to Unkas, June 20, 1646, John Winthrop, Jr. to Thomas Peters, September 3, 1646, "Petition of the Inhabitants of New London to the Commissioners of the United Colonies" [c. September 15, 1646], "Protest of the Inhabitants of New London Against Unkas," [c. 1647], *Winthrop Papers*, V, 82–83, 100–101, 111, 124; Winthrop, *Journal*, II, 287; *Acts of the Commissioners*, I, 101, 102.

[24] *Acts of the Commissioners*, I, 66; Winthrop, *Journal*, II, 348–49; *N.H. Recs.*, I, 481–84, 496; *Pub. Recs. Conn.*, I, 197.

quiet the minds of the inhabitants," ordered a party of soldiers to investigate the allegations of an Indian plot. At the height of the tension, former Governor Richard Bellingham, in dissenting from Massachusetts' policy of watchful waiting, lamented the inability of New Englanders to achieve a semblance of social security in the wilderness. "Itt were a sad hand of God," he remarked with chagrin, that "the Country [is] to be worne out with feares [and] watchings." [25]

The continuation of wars among the Indian tribes of New England impaired the Puritans' quest for safety in subsequent years. In the course of their bloody quarrels, the Indians inevitably created a tense situation in the colonies. The inland settlements, near which much of the fighting took place, were particularly alarmed. "I fear the Indeans may have some deepe plott against the Inglishe," suggested Governor Thomas Welles of Connecticut after the murder of some friendly Indians. For years, the Indians committed a variety of outrages which threatened the safety of the inhabitants of Connecticut. In 1660 the General Court of that colony reminded New Englanders of the unbending Indian policy of the founding fathers and urged the New England Confederation to undertake a war against "these beastly minded and mannered Creatures." But Connecticut's cautious neighbors refused to be cajoled into war.[26] In 1665 the New England colonies

---

[25] Hull, "Diary of Public Occurrences," 174; *Acts of the Commissioners*, II, 3, 23; *Recs. of Mass. Bay*, III, 314–15, 321, IV, Part I, 165; *Pub. Recs. Conn.*, I, 238–40, 244; *N.H. Recs.*, II, 11, 16; John Haynes to John Winthrop, Jr., May 31, 1653, Winthrop Mss., III, 132; Edward Norris to the Commissioners of the United Colonies, May 3, 1653, printed in *Acts of the Commissioners*, II, 58; Massachusetts Bay Council Minutes, April 26, 1653, printed in *Acts of the Commissioners*, II, 428–29.

[26] Thomas Welles to John Winthrop, Jr., March 25, 1659, Winthrop Mss., II, 186; Connecticut General Court to the Commissioners of the United Colonies, June 9, 1660, printed in *Pub. Recs. Conn.*, I, 576–77.

again prepared for an attack from the Mohawks, but the warning later proved to be unsubstantiated.[27]

{ Although the New England Confederation could not solve the underlying problems of uncertainty in the wilderness, it nevertheless served as a symbol of collective achievement. Despite the precariousness of peace in New England, the Confederation averted a major catastrophe. Since the defeat of the Pequots, the Indians have "put us to a considerable charge and trouble," declared the General Court of Massachusetts in 1665, "yet no massacre hath been amonge us from that day to this, blessed be God for it." [28] Moreover, the New England Confederation had unified the Puritans' efforts to convert the Indians. Serving as a clearinghouse for assistance from England, it dispensed money and supplies among the missionaries and the Christianized Indians.[29]

By the mid-1660s, however, the New England Confederation began to wane in importance. Plagued by "sundry agitations and troublesome motions," particularly the dispute over the absorption of New Haven by Connecticut, the Confederation declined in effectiveness. In defense of its very existence, New Haven appealed to the Articles of Confederation as proof of its autonomy. The leaders of New Haven urged their brethren at the River "not to suffer any mine to spring for subverting that ancient wall of New Englands safety" which God has

[27] Thomas Willett to John Winthrop, Jr., July 26, 1664, John Pynchon to John Winthrop, Jr., March 2, 1664[/65], John Winthrop, Jr. to Richard Nicolls, July 11, 1665, Winthrop Mss., IV, 143, XVI, 141, V, 50; "The noat drawne up by one of the magistrates presented to the [Connecticut General] Court," April 22, 1665, Winthrop-Davenport Mss., New York Public Library.
[28] General Court of Massachusetts Bay to the King's Commissioners, May 1665, printed in *Recs. of Mass. Bay*, IV, Part II, 231.
[29] For a discussion of the Puritan missionary activities under the Confederation, see Vaughan, *New England Frontier*, Chapters X–XI.

"erected upon the foundation of our . . . confoederations" and they suggested that the independence of their colony would uphold "peace in this wilderness." Massachusetts and Plymouth, "foreseeing danger of ruin to all for want of union, or through divisions of some," implored the interior colonies to abandon their contention.[30] As internal discord undermined the Confederation, the colonists significantly attempted to perpetuate its existence by appealing to the walls of safety which it represented. The royal commissioners who visited New England in the mid-1660s further challenged the sanctity of the Confederation by questioning the legitimacy of the union. In criticizing the behavior of the king's agents, the General Court of Massachusetts regretted that "the unity of the English colonyes (which is the wall and bulworke, under God, against the heathen) [is] discountenanced, reproached, and undermined." [31]

Gradually, New Englanders became more conscious of the importance they ascribed to the United Colonies. As an institution for intercolonial cooperation, the Confederation stood as a crumbling facade of the Puritan ideal of the organic society and linked New Englanders of a later generation to the collective endeavors of their parents. In the summer of 1665, Samuel Willis of Hartford urged John Winthrop, Jr. to attend the unofficial session of the Confederation at Boston. If a delegate does not represent this colony, he advised, "it is feared [that] the odium of breakinge the Confederation may be Cast upon us." But

---

[30] Hull, "Diary of Public Occurrences," 211; "Remonstrance of the General Court of New Haven to the General Court of Connecticut," May 6, 1663; New Haven Committee to the General Court of Connecticut, October 6, 1663, both printed in *N.H. Recs.*, II, 480, 500–501. The Connecticut Charter of 1662 provided for the incorporation of New Haven into that colony.

[31] Hull, "Diary of Public Occurrences," 216; Massachusetts General Court to King Charles II, August 1, 1665, printed in *Recs. of Mass. Bay.*, IV, Part II, 274.

in September, John Hull noted that "The Commissioners of the United Colonies kept not their wonted yearly meeting." "The Lord grant it be not portentious"! he added with dejection.[32] Two years later, the delegates of the Confederation convened at Hartford and consented to perpetuate the union. The dissolution of the confederacy, they agreed, would be "of noe lesse tendency then the breaking downe [of] that wall which . . . is the meanes of our owne safety . . . against foraigne and domesticke enimies." And in 1670, the colonies reaffirmed the Articles of Confederation to account for the union of New Haven and Connecticut.[33] The new compact, however, failed to revitalize the Confederation.

Although the New England Confederation died with a whimper, its existence had not been entirely futile. The remoteness of New England from the traditional sources of security and the dispersal of the settlements about the wilderness compelled the Puritans to fabricate a system of social solidarity. The union of the four colonies provided a logical solution to two of the most pressing problems which confronted the settlers: frontier expansion and distrust of the Indians. By extending the limits of the Hedge, the Puritans reconciled the polar forces of cohesion and disruption and thereby facilitated inland expansion. At the same time, the colonists created an institutional framework to deal with the natives. And though the Puritans remained fearful of the Indians, the Confederation provided some indefinable assistance for the frightened people in the wilderness. This psychological support, however, was recognized only after the Confederation had declined in importance. "Possibly it might

[32] Samuel Willis to John Winthrop, Jr., August 14, 1665, Winthrop-Davenport Mss.; Hull, "Diary of Public Occurrences," 219.
[33] *Acts of the Commissioners*, II, 326; *Recs. of Mass. Bay*, IV, Part II, 471.

have been as well for the whole," if Massachusetts Bay and Connecticut "could have been included in one jurisdiction," wrote William Hubbard in retrospect, "for by that means their union together, by an incorporation," would have been "much firmer and stronger, than by a confederation, as afterwards it came to pass." [34]

[34] Hubbard, "A General History," VI, 306.

CHAPTER IX

"The Further Improvement
of the Wildernes"

THE transit of European civilization to the New World in the seventeenth century inevitably affected both the transplanted culture and the wilderness environment of America. While the forest influenced New England thought in covert ways, the Puritans radically altered the appearance of the untamed continent which confronted them. Despite the implicit threats to an organic society, the settlers of New England stressed the importance of subjugating the wilderness, and, in the course of the century, Puritan commentators extolled the process of transforming the virgin forest into habitable areas. Within one generation of the founding of Massachusetts, however, the physical changes wrought by the colonists challenged the Puritans' self-image and compelled them to adjust their attitudes toward their wilderness settlements.

Supporters of the Winthrop expedition of 1630 had emphasized the value of subduing the earth in justification of the migration to New England. Francis Higginson, to promote the settlement of Massachusetts, lamented the sparsity of good Christians "to make use of this fruitful land." It is sad, he informed his friends in England, "to see so much good ground . . . lie altogether unoccupied." "Colonies," asserted John White, "have their warrant from

God's direction and command . . . to replenish the earth, and to subdue it." [1] New Englanders rationalized their claims to the Indian lands with similar rhetoric. "The Indians are not able to make use of the one fourth part of the land," observed Higginson, "neither have they any settled places, . . . but change their habitation from place to place." John Cotton assured the departing Winthrop group that whoever "taketh possession of [vacant soil], and bestoweth culture and husbandry upon it" has an inviolable right to the land. In subsequent years, the colonists issued similar appeals to justify the acquisition of wilderness territories. William Pynchon erected the town of Springfield on the east side of the Connecticut River because the local Indians occupied the best ground on the west bank and Pynchon wished to avoid needless encroachment. John Winthrop later argued that the Indians possessed "only a natural right to so much land as they had or could improve," and "the rest of the country lay open to any that could and would improve it." [2]

The Puritan colonists resolved from the beginning to transform the wilderness into settled estates. Prior to the departure of the advance-guard settlers in 1629, the leaders of the New England Company drafted a list of items that they believed would be necessary in the New World. This catalog included "Vyne Planters" and "Stones of all sorts of fruites," and indicates an early desire to make New England productive. Early in 1632, the Massachusetts Court of Assistants granted an island to John Win-

---

[1] Higginson, "New-Englands Plantation," pp. 254–56; White, "Planter's Plea," 371–72. For a fuller discussion of these ideas, see Chapter I.

[2] Higginson, "New-Englands Plantation," pp. 256–57; Cotton, "Gods Promise," 6; William Pynchon to John Winthrop, Jr., June 2, 1636, John Winthrop to [John Wheelwright?] [c. March 1638/39], *Winthrop Papers*, III, 267, IV, 101–102; Winthrop, *Journal*, I, 294. For a complete analysis of the Puritans' claim to the lands, see Chester E. Eisinger, "The Puritans' Justification for Taking the Land," *Essex Institute Historical Collections*, LXXXIV (1948), 131–43.

throp, "with all the liberties and privilidges of fishing and fowleing." Winthrop covenanted "to plant a vineyard and an orchard" there, provided that the Court permitted his heirs to inherit the territory, later known as Governor's Island. The Court warned, however, that if "att any time" these heirs "suffer the said ileland to lye wast, and not improve the same, then this present demise [is] to be voide." Such caveats proved unnecessary, for by 1634 William Wood reported that an orchard and a vineyard flourished on Winthrop's Island, and in 1638 John Josselyn, a visitor to New England, maintained that there was "not one Apple-tree, nor Pear planted . . . [in] the Countrey, but upon that Island." [3]

To achieve the ideal of a closely-knit society, the Puritan authorities, unlike colonials elsewhere in America, endeavored to prevent the acquisition of large and diffuse estates. The leaders of New England therefore attempted to base their policy of land distribution upon the ability of people to subdue the earth.[4] In 1634 the General Court of Massachusets Bay ordered "that if any man hath any great quan[tity] of land . . . and doeth not builde upon it or imp[rove it] within three yeares," the Court may "disp[ense] of it to whome they please." Although New Englanders, like all seventeenth-century Europeans, believed that certain men of quality deserved greater wealth than the masses of society, they nevertheless stressed the

[3] *Recs. of Mass. Bay,* I, 24, 94; Wood, *New Englands Prospect,* p. 45; Josselyn, "An Account of Two Voyages," 232; Herbert Pelham to John Winthrop, February 23, 1635[/36], *Winthrop Papers,* III, 228.
[4] Melville Egleston, "The Land Tenure System of the New England Colonies," *Johns Hopkins University Studies in Historical and Political Science,* IV (Baltimore, 1886), Parts XI–XII, 5–56; Marshall Harris, *Origins of the Land Tenure System in the United States* (Ames, Iowa, 1953), p. 286; Leach, *Northern Colonial Frontier,* pp. 44, 171. William Penn also attempted, with little success, to enforce similar restrictions on land tenure; see Leach, *Northern Colonial Frontier,* p. 68.

necessity of improving the soil before parceling out the land. In a series of proposed statutes, John Cotton recommended that the land should be divided according to a person's estate, the size of his family, "and partly by the number of beasts" he owns in order "to occupy the land assigned to him to subdue it." With similar qualifications, the town of Springfield resolved to grant more land to "persons who are most apt to use such ground." [5]

Recognizing that geographic dispersal threatened the collective society, the authorities of the Bay colony urged the settlers to improve the nearby lands before engaging in frontier expansion. John Winthrop advocated the equitable division of the lands because "it would be very prejudicial to the commonwealth, if men should be forced to go far off for land, while others had much, and could make no use of it." Edward Johnson later urged New Englanders to sell their land to newcomers at a just price, "for so soone as you shall seeke to ingrosse the Lords wast into your hands," he warned, the Almighty "will ease you of your burden" by diminishing the migration of new settlers "and then be sure you shall have wast Land enough." Shortly after the Hooker congregation consented to remain in the Bay colony in 1634, the townsmen of Cambridge attempted to alleviate the problem of overcrowding by requiring all the residents to improve their lots within six months or forfeit their holdings back to the town. "Our purpose is to have no great bands," insisted Nathaniel Ward in opposition to the extensive land claims of the town of Rowley. "Our neighbour Townes are much greived to see the lavish liberality of the Court," he exclaimed, "in giving away the Countrye," and he urged Governor Winthrop to prevent the spoilation of "many plantations . . . by the extreme largeness of those

---

[5] *Recs. of Mass. Bay*, I, 114; Cotton, "An Abstract," pp. 167–68; Burt, *First Century of . . . Springfield*, I, 158.

that are already given." Ezekiel Rogers, founder of Row-ley, appropriately replied to Ward's objections by denying that the additional land would be unoccupied. "Neither doe we purpose to keepe this lande unimployed," he informed Winthrop, "if God prosper us." [6]

Because of the commitment among Puritans to improve waste lands, New Englanders frequently appealed to the value of physically transforming the wilderness in support of inland expansion. The Massachusetts General Court approved the extension of the town of Linn in 1639, provided that the settlers "make some good proceeding in planting" within two years, "so as it may bee a village fit to conteine a convenient number of inhabitants." In 1643 six residents of the town of Concord requested the General Court to grant them "some reasonable quantitie of land" because the area about Concord was "very barren, and the meadows very wet and unuseful." They supported their petition by reminding the authorities that "it is your desire [that] the lands might be subdued" and persuaded the General Court to offer them a plantation "provided that within two years they make some good improvement of it." In response to a petition from several inhabitants of Hartford in 1650, the Connecticut General Court authorized the founding of Norwalk and announced its approval "of the indeavors of men for the further improvement of the wildernes, by the beginning and carrying on of new plantations in an orderly way." [7]

As the government of Massachusetts became reconciled

[6] Winthrop, *Journal*, I, 144; Johnson, *Wonder-working Providence*, p. 35; *The Records of the Town of Cambridge (Formerly Newtowne) Massachusetts: 1630–1703* (Cambridge, 1901,) p. 10; Nathaniel Ward to John Winthrop [c. April 1640], Ezekiel Rogers to John Winthrop, October 5, 1640, *Winthrop Papers,* IV, 222, 290.

[7] *Recs. of Mass. Bay,* I, 272; Petition of the Inhabitants of Concord to the General Court of Massachusetts Bay, September 7, 1643, quoted in Lemuel Shattuck, *History of the Town of Concord* (Boston, 1835), pp. 14–15; *Pub. Recs. Conn.,* I, 210.

to increased inland extension, would-be frontiersmen justified their desire to remove by reiterating the need to subjugate the wilderness. The founders of Northampton, for example, advised the General Court that their proposed plantation would provide surplus agricultural products for the benefit of the entire colony. Similarly, in 1659 the General Court approved the erection of the town of Hadley in order "that this wildernes may be populated and the maine ends of our coming into these parts may be promoted." Several inhabitants of Newbury," beinge senseable of the need of multiplyinge of towneshippes for the inlargement of the countrey and accommodateinge of such as want opportunity to improve themselves," urged the Bay colony to endorse a plantation at Pennecooke which, they felt, would meet their requirements.[8]

In addition to these ordinary appeals, New Englanders often cited the desirability of subduing the wilderness to support expansionist endeavors beyond the traditional limits of their settlements. In 1659, the Bay colony challenged the Dutch claims to certain portions of the Hudson River valley, particularly those areas "not being actually possessed" by that nation. "Wee conceive [that] no reason can be imagined," the General Court notified Peter Stuyvesant, "why we should not improve and make use of our just rightes in all the Landes granted us." Stuyvesant, of course, ignored the Puritans' questionable logic. But the Duke of York had other plans for the Dutch settlements and, by September 1664, the English navy had hoisted the Union Jack above the colony of New Netherland. Shortly after the surrender of New Amsterdam, John Winthrop, Jr., a witness to the proceedings on Man-

---

[8] Petition to the General Court of Massachusetts Bay [c. 1653], in Trumbull, *History of Northampton*, I, 5–6; *Recs. of Mass. Bay*, IV, Part I, 368; Petition from the Inhabitants of Newbury to the General Court of Massachusetts Bay [1659], quoted in John J. Currier, *History of Newbury, Mass., 1635–1902* (Boston, 1902), p. 169.

hattan Island, praised the take-over "wherby there is [a] way made for inlargement of [the English] dominions, by filling that vacant wildernesse in tyme with plantations of his Majesties subjects." And in 1672, John Paine explored the Albany region for the Bay colony in search of land that was "cleer for the Plough." [9]

With similar metaphors, John Winthrop, Jr. later defended the transplantation of several New Haven men to Newark, New Jersey. Responding to a request from Abraham Pierson, a former leader at New Haven, the magistrates of Connecticut assured Sir George Carteret, proprietor of New Jersey, that the New Englanders would be worthy additions to his colony. The leaders of Connecticut confessed that they preferred these settlers to return to their original habitations, but they also acknowledged their desire to "promote in your Honours Colony that good worke of subdueing the Earth, and replenishing of it." It "is A very diffecult worke, [which] requires much hard Labour, to subdue so Ruff and woody A wildernesse," they declared, because "this remote, desert part of the world [was] never Formerly inhabitted nor Cultivated." To John Berry, Deputy Governor of New Jersey, Winthrop insisted that he did not desire "to incourage or invite any one to a removall thence." But, he added, "I have often . . . incouraged that good publicke designe of planting that place, and am alwaies desirous to promote the prosperous increase of those plantations." In this manner, New Englanders rationalized the advantages of expansion along the frontier.[10]

[9] General Court of Massachusetts Bay to Peter Stuyvesant, November 12, 1659, printed in *Acts of the Commissioners,* II, 445; John Winthrop, Jr. to Lord Clarendon, September 25, 1664, Photostat, Winthrop Mss.; "John Paine's Journal," *Publications of the Colonial Society of Massachusetts,* XVIII (1917), 188–89.

[10] Abraham Pierson to John Winthrop, Jr., May 14, 1673, Samuel Willis and John Winthrop, Jr. to Sir George Carteret, July 2, 1673, Winthrop

"As the earth bred us," preached John Cotton, "so it feedeth us till we return to it." And he encouraged the settlers of New England to undertake "all labour about the earth," because "it breedeth sufficient profit." [11] In pursuit of their callings, the Puritan colonists committed themselves to replenishing the American soil and, within one generation, they had transformed large portions of the wilderness into cultivated fields. But before the settlers recognized the significance of these changes and celebrated the process of physical transformation, they concentrated their attention upon the more visible products of their labors.

The Lord "hath brought us into a plentifull land," observed Thomas Shepard, and although the "country is great waste . . . plenty [is] ordinary." In the course of the seventeenth century, New Englanders frequently praised God for providing His people with "plenty and abonndance of the blessings of the earth." In 1647 a serious drought in the West Indies depleted the crop and forced the ships which usually obtained supplies there to seek assistance in Massachusetts. John Winthrop viewed these events as "an observable providence," because "many of the London seamen were wont to despise New England as a poor, barren country," but now were "relieved by our plenty." In response to Oliver Cromwell's scheme to transplant the Puritans in Ireland, the Massachusetts General Court assured the Protector that "God hath blessed the countrey with plentie of food of all kindes" and poverty therefore could not be "a ground of removall." The Lord "beyond expectation made this poore barren Wildernesse become a fruitfull Land," maintained

Mss., XVI, 113, V, 108; John Winthrop, Jr. to John Berry, July 29, 1673, Photostat, Winthrop Mss.

[11] Cotton, "A Brief Exposition Upon Ecclesiastes," 51–52.

historian Edward Johnson, and fed His children "with the flower of Wheat." [12]

In advocating the proper use of the land, the Puritans also endeavored to exploit the natural resources of the wilderness. But although they encouraged the judicious employment of the Lord's blessings, the authorities opposed the reckless abuse of the land. The ideal of the organic state determined the economic policy of the New England colonies and led the Puritans to support the idea of a regulated economy. To protect the general welfare from the onslaughts of selfish individuals, the leaders of Massachusetts Bay resolved to control the development of the public domain. In 1631 the Court of Assistants ordered "that noe person whatsoever shall make any use" of the nearby islands, "by putting on cattell, felling wood, raiseing slate, etc., without" official permission.[13]

Despite the popular myth of the abundance of natural resources during the seventeenth century, the colonies of New England frequently complained of shortages of wood and enacted legislation to regulate the destruction of trees. The lack of timber was especially acute at the Bay, and in the winter of 1637–38 John Winthrop reported that the inhabitants of Boston "were almost readye to breake up for want of wood." The inland settlements at Springfield, Connecticut, and New Haven also suffered from a paucity of wood and provided laws "for the better preserving of Tymber." The individual town governments controlled the use of common woods and established penalties for violations of these laws. In 1635 the selectmen of Boston regretted the destruction of some nearby

[12] Thomas Shepard, Sermon [c. 1637–38], Shepard Mss., Houghton Library; *Recs. of Mass. Bay*, I, 109, IV, Part I, 279; Winthrop, *Journal*, II, 328; "Copy of a Letter to Oliver Cromwell in 1651," in Hutchinson, *History of Massachusetts-Bay*, I, 431–32; Johnson, *Wonder-working Providence*, p. 108.

[13] *Recs. of Mass. Bay*, I, 89.

wood and provided relief for the poor people who would have benefited from the use of this timber. Such legislation ordinarily reflected the pragmatic concern of a wilderness people for preventing the needless destruction of a valuable commodity. In at least one exceptional case, however, New Englanders employed conservationist rhetoric to enjoin the felling of timber. Early in 1658, the town of Dorchester asserted that "timber and fire wood is of great use to the present and alsoe future generations and therefore [should] be prudently preserved from wracke" and destruction.[14] But short-term practicality offers a more typical explanation of these restrictive measures.

Such prohibitions, of course, did not retard the subjugation of the New England forest. Since the economic controls usually lacked conservationist impulses, the authorities did not oppose the purposeful exploitation of the wilderness. In response to the economic depression of the early 1640s, the colonial governments, exercising their powers to regulate the economic affairs of their jurisdictions, repealed some of the legislation which proscribed the exportation of pipe staves and other types of wrought timber. The Massachusetts General Court also recommended that the settlers compensate for the lack of cotton by substituting "a kind of wild hempe groweing plentifully all over the countrey." And in subsequent years, the colonies of Massachusetts and Connecticut permitted certain resourceful inhabitants to supply their saw mills with timber from the public waste lands.[15]

[14] John Winthrop to John Winthrop, Jr., January 22, 1637[/38], *Winthrop Papers*, IV, 10; *Pub. Recs. Conn.*, I, 60; Burt, *First Century of . . . Springfield*, I, 158, 162, 164, 167; *N.H. Recs.*, I, 25; *Boston Town Records, 1634–1660 (Second Report of the [Boston] Record Commissioners)* (Boston, 1877), p. 4; *Dorchester Town Records (Fourth Report of the [Boston] Record Commissioners)*, second ed. (Boston, 1883), pp. 91–92.

[15] *Pub. Recs. Conn.*, I, 67, 243, 262; *Recs. of Mass. Bay*, I, 292, 322, IV, Part I, 65–75.

The New England legislatures also expressed interest in appropriating the mineral wealth of the wilderness and urged the settlers to locate "mynes of mettalls and miner-ralls." Although the General Courts of Massachusetts and Connecticut retained the ultimate control of all mining operations in order to protect the general welfare, the colonial governments nevertheless offered bounties and partial monopolies "for the discovery of any mine." Periodically the New England colonies awarded land or other inducements to enterprising colonists for the extraction of mineral deposits. More than anyone else, however, the younger John Winthrop attempted to tap the natural wealth of the wilderness. He assured the Massachusetts General Court that the rocky hills about New England were "the nurceries of mynes and mineralls" and believed that they contained iron, lead, tin, copper, "and other mettalls noe lesse profitable to the Countrye." Encouraged by the Bay colony and supported by English investors, Winthrop enthusiastically assisted in the establishment of an ironworks near Linn in the mid-1640s. But this venture, like many subsequent ones initiated by Winthrop, proved to be only partially successful. "It may be God reserves such of his bounties to future generations," concluded Winthrop after a long career of abortive, though imaginative, enterprises.[16]

The settlers of New England diligently exploited the maritime wealth of their region. In the early years of settlement, the General Court permitted every house-

[16] *Recs. of Mass. Bay,* I, 106, 206, 327, II, 11, III, 256; *Pub. Recs. Conn.,* I, 223, 420; "Petition of John Winthrop, Jr. to the Massachusetts General Court" [c. 1644], *Winthrop Papers,* IV, 422–23; John Winthrop, Jr. to Henry Oldenburg, November 12, 1668, Photostat, Winthrop Mss. For a discussion of one mining endeavor, see Edward Neal Hartley, *Ironworks on the Saugus: the Lynn and Braintree ventures of the Company of Undertakers of the Ironworks in New England* (Norman, Okla., 1957); for Winthrop's mining activities, see Robert C. Black, III, *The Younger John Winthrop* (New York, 1966).

holder to "have free fishing and fowling" provided that the separate towns had not established special restrictions. But within three decades of the founding of Massachusetts, the New England authorities responded to the pleas of the fishermen and prohibited the catching of certain fish during their spawning seasons. The destruction of these fish "at unseasonable times," they stated, "will in the issue tend to" spoil the trade.[17] Economic motives, above all, determined the passage of such legislation, because the colonists generally overlooked the advantages of conservation. Governor Winthrop considered the migration of pigeons in 1648 "a great blessing, it being incredible what multitudes of them were killed daily." New Englanders also attempted to exterminate such common nuisances as wolves and foxes. And at mid-century, several towns offered bounties for black birds, jays, woodpeckers, and crows in order to protect the growing crops.[18] Such measures reveal the colonists' short-sighted pragmatism in their endeavor to subjugate the wilderness.

As the settlers of New England successfully replenished the earth and exploited the natural resources of America, they commenced to praise not only the immediate products of their work, but also the transformation process itself. "What shall we say of the singular Providences of God," exclaimed Thomas Shepard and John Allin in the mid-1640s, "what shall wee say of the . . . Commonwealth erected in a Wildernesse, and in so few yeares brought" to such a state "that scarce the like can bee

[17] *The Body of Liberties* [1641], reprinted in Whitmore, ed. *The Colonial Laws of Massachusetts*, p. 37; *Acts of the Commissioners*, II, 251; *Recs. of Mass Bay*, IV, Part II, 400, 450.

[18] Winthrop, *Journal*, II, 348; *Recs. of Mass. Bay*, I, 81, 102, 156; Records of the Town of Newbury, quoted in Currier, *History of Newbury*, pp. 125–26; Town Records of Sudbury, quoted in Hudson, *History of Sudbury*, p. 130.

seen in any of our English Colonies in the richest places of this America, after many more yeares standing"? Writing a decade later, Edward Johnson extolled the transformation of "the close, clouded woods into goodly corn-fields." "Wolves and Beares nurst up their young from the eyes of all behoulders," he declared, "in those very places where the streets are full of Girles and Boys sporting up and downe, with a continued concourse of people." In describing this metamorphosis, Johnson glorified the ceaseless task of subduing the earth. "[T]his remote, rocky, barren, bushy, wild-woody wilderness," he wrote, has "becom a second England for fertilness in so short a space, that it is indeed the wonder of the world." Although Johnson did not always endorse frontier expansion, he nevertheless recognized that such dispersal accelerated the transformation of the wilderness. "The constant penetrating farther into this Wilderness," he suggested, "hath caused the wild and uncouth woods to be fil'd with frequented wayes, and the large rivers to be over-laid with Bridges."[19]

In subsequent years, New Englanders continued to praise the ongoing subjugation of the wilderness. John Norton admonished his congregation not to succumb to worldliness, but nevertheless declared with pride and wonder that "A spot of this vast *Jeshimon* [i.e., wilderness]" has been "converted into *Corn-fields, Orchards, streets inhabited,* and a place of *Merchandize.*" John Hig-

[19] Shepard [and Allin], "Preface," *A Defence of the Answer,* pp. 7–8; Johnson, *Wonder-working Providence,* pp. 180, 71, 210, 234. Alan Heimert, in "Puritanism, the Wilderness, and the Frontier," *New England Quarterly,* XXVI (1953), 361–82, mistakenly asserts that Johnson made a positive virtue of frontier expansion. Johnson did not, however, support the migration to Connecticut (pp. 105–106). It would seem therefore that he regarded inland extension simply as a means to a higher purpose: the physical transformation of the wilderness. For a discussion of the philosophical ramifications of the subjugation of the wilderness, see O'Gorman, *Invention of America,* Part III.

ginson, in the Massachusetts Bay election sermon of 1663, similarly lauded the physical transformation in New England. "Look upon your townes and fields, look upon your habitations and shops and ships," he preached, "and behold your numerous posterity, and great encrease in the blessings of the Land and Sea." Michael Wigglesworth assured New Englanders that the Lord had turned "an howling wildernes . . . into a fruitfull paradeis." And Nathaniel Saltonstall later explained the outbreak of the Indian War of 1675 in these terms. He maintained that King Philip, chief of the Wampanoag tribe, resented the occupation of his lands by the colonists, particularly after "seeing what Product the English have made of a Wilderness, through their Labour, and the Blessing of God thereon." Describing the forest in unsentimental language, these commentators applauded the constructive results of the cultivation of the wild lands of America.[20]

As the settlers placed more and more land under the plough, they gradually perceived that New England and the wilderness were separate entities. To be sure, the idea of the Hedge suggested a distinction between the wilderness and the settlements from the beginning of colonization. But in the earlier period, the ambiguities within Puritan thought concealed the significance of this dichotomy. To the men of John Winthrop's generation, New England society in itself was a wilderness community. But as a result of physically transforming certain portions of the American forest, the colonists distinguished the cultivated acres from the remaining untrammeled areas

[20] Norton, *The Heart of N-England rent*, p. 58; Higginson, *The Cause of God*, pp. 10–11; Wigglesworth, "Gods Controversy," 87; N[athaniel] S[altonstall], "The Present State of New-England With Respect to the Indian War" [1675], reprinted in *Narratives of the Indian Wars: 1679–1699*, ed. by Charles H. Lincoln (New York, 1913), p. 26; see also, Shepard, Jr., *Eye-Salve*, p. 11.

with greater clarity. While they regarded the wilderness as the antithesis of civilization, the Puritans recognized that the emergence of habitable settlements constituted a permanent alteration of the American forest. Since they could now view New England as a distinct and unique place instead of as a vast wilderness with various theological attributes, the transformation of the forest accelerated the process of provincialization. For although the Puritans could reconcile the coexistence of wildness and civilization, they were clearly committed to civilization. The appearance of maturing towns thereby enabled New Englanders to focus their attention upon home lands instead of waste places.

These changes emerged in land surveys, travel reports, and natural descriptions. In the mid-1650s, several Massachusetts surveyors began to distinguish the wilderness lands from the virgin tracts they laid out. Thomas Danforth and Andrew Belchar surveyed a plot "surrounded with wildernes land," and other New Englanders often delineated boundaries with reference to "the wilderness land." In search of a suitable location for a plantation near Albany in 1672, John Paine implied that "the wildernes up the Rivor" varied measurably from the "valuable Landes" in the vicinity. Such descriptions reveal that New England and the wilderness were no longer synonymous terms and that the settlers qualitatively differentiated between the habitable areas and the unsubdued territories.[21]

At this time, New Englanders portrayed intercolonial journeys with similar rhetorical distinctions. In 1659 several members of the church at Hartford requested the elders of the Bay colony to travel to Connecticut in order to resolve a theological debate there. The younger Thomas

---

[21] *Recs. of Mass. Bay*, IV, Part I, 295, 335, 370–71; "John Paine's Journal," 190. See also, the Petition from Hadley to the General Court, May 3, 1667, quoted in Judd, *History of Hadley*, pp. 79–80.

Shepard pointed out that he had undertaken a similar mission two years earlier and now was reluctant "once againe to take a journey through the vast howling wilderness, to compose againe some new differences . . . in that church." Several months later, as the winter snows began to impede traffic between the colonies, John Winthrop, Jr., reported that he found someone who "will adventure through the wilderness" to deliver his correspondence. "We are not only separated by soe vast an Ocean from our deare English Brethren," maintained the Connecticut General Court in 1661, "but alsoe, by a lone tract of a dismall wilderness[, we] are very remote from our other English Americans." [22] From these statements, it would appear that second-generation colonials viewed the wilderness as uninhabited regions which separated the isolated plantations of New England.

John Hull of Boston also differentiated the wilderness from the settled areas in depicting several natural phenomena. During the autumn of 1663, he noted that "there came very many bears out of the wilderness." And two years later, Hull reported that "multitudes of flying caterpillars arose out of the ground . . . ; yet," he added, "they only seized upon the trees in the wilderness." [23] To Hull, the wilderness constituted border areas beyond the limits of the New England settlements.

Thirty years after the founding of Massachusetts, the physical transformation of the wilderness began to modify the Puritans' self-image. No longer exiles in an amorphously-defined wilderness, the colonists dwelled in the settled regions of New England. The younger John Woodbridge revealed this transition in a letter to Richard Bax-

[22] Thomas Shepard, Jr. to John Winthrop, Jr. and the General Court of Connecticut, July 4, 1659, John Winthrop, Jr. to John Richards, December 12, 1659, Winthrop Mss., IV, 138, V, 22; The Connecticut General Court to King Charles II [1661], printed in *Pub. Recs. Conn.*, I, 582.

[23] Hull, "Diary of Public Occurrences," 210, 218.

ter in which he referred to "our Controversyes in the (*I may call it an*) Howling wilderness." [24] For Woodbridge, the wilderness differed greatly from his home, and in his parenthetical statement he self-consciously labeled New England a wilderness, but only for rhetorical purposes. The settlers who had tamed the wilds of America found that their towns were more inviting than the virgin forests which surrounded them.

Many Puritan commentators, to be sure, continued to ascribe wilderness attributes to the settled sections of New England. As a refuge, as the site of temptation, as the place of religious insight, the wilderness of America retained its meaning for the colonists. But rhetorical devices seldom keep pace with experiential changes. The transformation of the wilderness gradually undermined these older ideas and hastened the settlers' adaptation to the New World. By committing the colonists to the subdued portions of America, the physical regeneration of the soil facilitated the provincialization of New England. The settlers now concentrated upon the process, as well as the products, of their toil.

[24] John Woodbridge, Jr. to Richard Baxter, October 14, 1669, "Correspondence of Woodbridge and Baxter," 565 (itals. added).

CHAPTER X

"A Smart Rod and Severe Scourge"

NEVER was any plantation brought unto such a considerableness, in a space of time so inconsiderable"! exclaimed Cotton Mather at the end of the seventeenth century, for "an *howling wilderness* in a few years became a *pleasant land,* accomodated with the *necessaries*—yea, and the *conveniences* of humane life." [1] As New Englanders replenished and transformed the earth, they readily adjusted to life in America and grew increasingly self-confident in their wilderness communities. Within three decades of the founding of Massachusetts, the settlers betrayed their security by disregarding the underlying threats to the colonies of New England. But paradoxically this superficial stability concealed a deeply rooted malaise, an abiding sense of distrust for the wilderness environment. The outbreak of King Philip's War in 1675 brought these counterforces into conflict. Thereafter, the Puritan colonists grappled with the tensions between security and insecurity, cohesion and expansion.

By 1660 the settlers of New England manifested their self-assurance in America by abating their cautious Indian policy. The Bay colony first revealed signs of a thaw in their attitude toward the natives when the authorities

---

[1] Mather, *Magnalia,* I, 80.

declined to chastise the Indians for their insolent behavior in Connecticut. The inhabitants of the River colony, exposed to frequent Indian depredations, vainly protested the relaxation of Massachusetts' Indian policy. "We intreat you to consider how incongruous and cross it would have bin 20 yeares agoe to an English spirit," affirmed the General Court of Connecticut in 1660, "to beare such things as now we are forct to beare." And they urged their fellow New Englanders "to renew upon the memory of these Pagans the obliterate memorials of the English." [2] Unmoved by these pleas, the settlers of Massachusetts ignored their more martial brethren of Connecticut.

Besides neglecting the militant appeals of the Connecticut people, the Bay colony also eased the prohibition of the arms trade with the natives. As William Hubbard later recalled, the commissioners of the United Colonies "for a long time carefully and seriously endeavored" to prevent the Indians from acquiring weapons. But "the continued Solicitation of some of our own People . . . who alleadged the Example of the French and Dutch" forced the colonies to repeal the ban on the arms traffic. With a sudden reversal of priorities, the Massachusetts General Court in 1661 ordered the colony's treasurer to compensate with shot and powder, as well as with bounties, any Indian who brought in wolves' heads. Seven years later, the Court permitted the inhabitants to trade guns and ammunition with Indians "not in hostillity with us or any of the English in New England" in return for animal skins. The authorities of Massachusetts apparently valued their prosperity more than their safety. Although the General Court of Connecticut criticized the revocation of the arms embargo by Massachusetts, it nevertheless desired to compete effec-

[2] The General Court of Connecticut to the Commissioners of the United Colonies, June 9, 1660, printed in *Pub. Recs. Conn.*, I, 576–77.

tively with its sister colonies for the Indian trade. In 1669 Connecticut reluctantly rescinded its prohibition of the arms traffic with the natives.[3]

As the settlers of New England became increasingly complacent about the dangers of wilderness life, they penetrated deeper and deeper into the unknown continent. The colonists had inaugurated inland expansion primarily to satisfy the needs of a growing population, and the authorities of New England usually insisted that the settlers occupy the new plantations immediately. But in 1659, the Bay colony endorsed the establishment of a new settlement "forty or fifty miles from Springfield to the westward," a considerable distance from the existing towns, ostensibly for the purpose of extending the fur trade. Unlike the traditional forms of inland expansion, this remote outpost was not designed for immediate occupation. The General Court of Massachusetts did not require the proprietors to settle families or to acquire a ministry, but merely advised them "to plant and possesse the said land and setle the . . . [Indian] trade."[4]

The Bay colony, recognizing the difficulty of reaching such an isolated area, requested permission from the Dutch to sail ships up the Hudson River to facilitate the planting of this region near Albany. The plea to Governor Peter Stuyvesant reveals the close relation between this endeavor and the development of security in Massachusetts. Because of the "opportunity of planting nearer together whilest our numbers were fewer," the Bay colony informed Stuyvesant, we "have made no use of our rights" upon the Hudson River. "Yet being now increased and wanting convenient places to settle our people," added the New

[3] Hubbard, *A Narrative of the Troubles,* II, 252–53; *Recs. of Mass. Bay,* IV, Part II, 2, 365; *Pub. Recs. Conn.,* II, 119.
[4] *Recs. of Mass. Bay,* IV, Part I, 374, 438–39.

Englanders, "wee conceive no reason" for not asserting "our just rightes." [5] During the formative stages of colonization, the authorities of Massachusets believed that they were ill-equipped to undertake such ventures; by 1660 they had acquired sufficient self-confidence and numbers to challenge the Dutch claims to these regions. In 1672 John Paine petitioned the Bay colony for permission to erect a plantation in this area, arguing that "it will be a defence against forain Intrusones, And an Accomodation to the Settleing [of] other Plantations." In response to this appeal, the General Court approved Paine's scheme and granted him a temporary monopoly of the Indian trade there. The Court also implied that this adventure, though primarily an economic enterprise, would result in a settled plantation.[6] A sense of security, however superficial, encouraged New Englanders to expand outward beyond the traditional limits of the Hedge.

Beneath this self-assured exterior, however, the Puritans were deeply concerned about the health of their wilderness society. The conservative orthodoxy distrusted the implications of this self-confidence and warned, with theological metaphors, of the dangers of oversecurity. The late Perry Miller appropriately characterized these caveats as jeremiads, or prophetical admonitions against self-destruction. As New Englanders seemed to be growing increasingly worldly and secure, the Puritan ministry repeatedly advised their congregations to renew their faith

[5] Commissioners of the United Colonies to Peter Stuyvesant, September 7, 1659, General Court of Massachusetts Bay to Peter Stuyvesant, November 12, 1659, printed in *Acts of the Commissioners*, II, 220–21, 445.

[6] "John Paine's Petition, 1672," *Publications of the Colonial Society of Massachusetts*, XVIII (1917), 191–92; *Recs. of Mass. Bay*, IV, Part II, 548. In 1674 Daniel Gookin drafted an elaborate plan for the exploration and tentative plantation of the "vast lake" to the west (Lake Champlain). See Gookin, "Historical Collections of the Indians in New England," 158–59.

in the Lord and to return to the pristine godliness of the founding fathers. As Miller stated it, the jeremiads "were the voice of a community bespeaking its apprehensions about itself."[7]

In a manner similar to their English ancestors of the 1620s, the Puritan clergy warned that the sins of the age would try the patience of the Lord, and He would chastise New England with His wrath. They cautioned that the Almighty would dismantle His Hedge of grace and expose the colonies of New England to the vicious onslaughts of the world. Earlier settlers, to be sure, had suggested that the wilderness would be a secure refuge only as long as the inhabitants remained faithful to the Lord. God "can reach us at what distance soever," maintained John Humfrey in 1631, and He "can easilie find out his enemies where ever they thinke vainely to shrowde themselves under anie false refuges." Thomas Shepard, a decade later, advised the colonists that "the wall of magistracy [would] be broken down" if the people questioned the political wisdom of their leaders.[8]

Such forebodings reached a crescendo by the mid-1660s. The Massachusetts General Court reminded the settlers that "wee have binn a people singularly exempted" from the "sharpened stroakes" of the Lord, "wherein so many abroad have had so deepe and piersing a sense." But, the Court added with trepidation, "of late it pleaseth him righteously . . . to chainge his way" and threaten the sanctuary blessings of New England. John Oxenbridge urged the people to protect their civil and religious liberties from the dangers of oversecurity. "If ye shall break down the hedge of your Churches and Commonwealth,"

[7] Miller, *The New England Mind: From Colony to Province,* p. 47 and *passim.*

[8] John Humfrey to John Winthrop, Jr., November 4 [1631], *Winthrop Papers,* III, 52; Shepard, *Parable,* 259–60. See also, Shepard, Sermon of October 4, 1648, Seaborne Cotton Mss.

he preached in the Massachusetts election sermon of 1671, "you will lay the field open to such as watch to make spoile of you." "God hath walled his outward host," declared Peter Thacher in 1674, and "great is the concernment to improve it least you let in destroying judgments." [9]

Other New England preachers admonished the colonists to reform their ways to prevent the destruction of the protective Hedge. Only a mad man, averred Urian Oakes, "will hope for the Continuation of our Spiritual Liberties, If the Wall of our Civil Government be once broken down." Bad magistrates, he suggested, jeopardize the church as well as the state. The "Beasts that break down the Hedge of our Civil Government . . . do it [not] merely because they are angry with the Hedge," maintained Oakes, "but because they would break in and devour all that is precious and dear to us." Although "god hath hedged about his vineyard with Pious magistrates," argued Oakes, "many [would] have these stakes Plucked out of the hedge." He therefore urged New Englanders "to get into the Gap, and make up the Hedge" when the Lord "seems to be going from us." In the Connecticut election sermon of 1674, James Fitch similarly warned the settlers of the River colony that sin would cause the Lord to depart from New England and urged the people to return to the purity of their fathers. [10]

In criticizing the decline of religious zeal in New England, the Puritan clergy also expressed concern for the state of religion upon the frontier and argued that the in-

[9] *Recs. of Mass. Bay,* IV, Part II, 44; John Oxenbridge, *New-England Freemen Warned and Warmed* . . . ([Boston], 1673), p. 26; [Peter] Thacher, Sermon of December 10, 1674, in John Hull, Commonplace Books, III, Boston Public Library.

[10] Oakes, *New-England Pleaded with,* pp. 49, 62; [Urian] Oakes, Sermon of February 19, 1672[/73], in Hull, Commonplace Books, II; Urian Oakes, "To the Christian Reader," in Mather, *The Day of Trouble;* James Fitch, *An Holy Connexion* . . . (Cambridge [Mass.], 1674), *passim.* See also, Danforth, *A Brief Recognition,* p. 19.

land towns which lacked the Lord's ordinances lay beyond the protection of the Hedge. John Cotton had earlier stressed the importance of residing near an established meeting house and had urged the settlers "to be more slow of removal from liberty [and] purity of Ordinance." Edward Johnson, writing at mid-century, interpreted a plague of caterpillars which devoured the New England crop as a divine chastisement against those people "whose over eager pursuit of the fruits of the earth made some of them many times run so far in the Wilderness" that they could not hear "the sweet sound of the silver Trumpets blown by the laborious Ministers of Christ." When colonies are "erected in [a] Wilderness, or any uninhabited places in the world," declared John Eliot, "It is a singular point of wisdom and love, to manage such a design religiously, so . . . that God may go with them, and dwell in the midst of them." Thus, he concluded, "it is necessary that they have the Ministry of Gods Word, and some other godly persons with them, who may carry on Church-work among them." [11]

The colonial governments of New England responded to these proposals by attempting to insure the religiosity of the frontier settlements. In 1653 the General Court of Massachusetts noted that while the number of settlements increased, many of them, "especially in theire beginning, are destitute of persons fitly quallified to undertake the worke of the ministrie." Thereafter, the Bay colony endeavored to provide "a godly ministry" in all its new plantations, so that the inland settlers "may not live like lambs in a large place." The colony of Connecticut similarly required its frontier towns to possess godly churches. In

[11] Cotton, *A Brief Exposition with Practical Observations upon the Whole Book of Canticles*, p. 48; Johnson, *Wonder-working Providence*, p. 253; John Eliot, *Communion of Churches: Or, the Divine Management of Gospel Churches By the Ordinance of Councils* . . . (Cambridge [Mass.], 1665), p. 26.

1671 the General Court approved the founding of Derby, provided that the people "mayntayne an orthodox ministry amongst them there." [12] In this manner, the New England colonies strived to extend their ecclesiastical institutions along the frontier to strengthen the protective Hedge.

Despite the underlying uncertainty which the Puritans revealed by the jeremiads and by their concern for doctrinal purity upon the frontier, the eruption of King Philip's War in 1675 stunned the colonists and shocked them out of their complacency. [13] Although this Indian war lasted less than two years, its impact upon Puritan society was more enduring. As the Indians rampaged through the countryside and destroyed numerous towns, the immense dangers of the war reminded second-generation New Englanders that the wilderness continued to be a hostile environment. And the contingencies of wartime underscored the importance of social collectivity.

As a battleground, the New England wilderness offered a decided advantage to the Indians. Accustomed to the secrets of the forest, the natives could assault the isolated English towns and then retreat into the woods before the Puritan troops could confront them. One inhabitant of Sudbury reported that "our woods are pestered with Indians." The hazards are great, asserted John Pynchon of Springfield, "if we do but stir out for wood, to be shot down by some skulking Indians." Daniel Gookin later recalled that the colonists "at first thought easily to chastise the insolent doings and murderous practices of the heathen." But, he remembered, Indian fighting proved to be

[12] *Recs. of Mass. Bay*, IV, Part I, 122, 139–40, 235, 264, 368, 417, 421, 423–24, 445, Part II, 15, 409, 557; *Pub. Recs. Conn.*, II, 24, 148.
[13] For a complete discussion of the Indian war of 1675, see Douglas Edward Leach, *Flintlock and Tomahawk: New England in King Philip's War* (New York, 1958).

more difficult, because "our men could see no enemy to shoot at." Besides lying in "ambushments," the natives would "apparel themselves from the waist upwards with green boughs," so that the pursuing armies "could not readily discern them . . . from the natural bushes." [14]

The problem of tracking the Indians in the wilderness convinced many New Englanders that the war would be long and difficult. Shortly after the commencement of hostilities, one observer noted the significance of "the Leaves in the wilderness" in concealing the enemy and recommended that the Puritan troops wait until the underbrush was "dried and burnt and the swampes frozen hard." "When it will be over[,] wee cannot as yet see," remarked John Hull several months later, because the natives "are like wild Deare in the Wilderness . . . [so] that our souldiers can rarely find any of them." William Hubbard later described several episodes in which the dense wilderness enabled King Philip to evade the Puritan armies. Experience taught the English "how dangerous it is to fight in such dismal Woods," stated Hubbard, "when their Eyes were muffled with the Leaves, and their Arms pinioned with the thick Boughs of the Trees, [and] their Feet were continually shackled with the Roots." "It is," concluded Hubbard, "ill fighting with a wild Beast in his own Den." Increase Mather subsequently urged the settlers to be grateful for the abrupt conclusion of the war. "For we expected," Mather suggested, "that when the summer was come on, and the bushes and leaves come forth, the enemy would do ten times more mischief then

[14] Edmund Browne to Gov. John Leverett, September 26 [1675], printed in *N.E.H.G.R.*, VII (1853), 268; John Pynchon to Gov. Leverett, October 8, 1675, quoted in Judd, *History of Hadley*, p. 145; Daniel Gookin, "An Historical Account of the Doings and Sufferings of the Christian Indians in New England in the years 1675, 1676, 1677," printed in *Transactions and Collections of the American Antiquarian Society*, II (1836), 441.

in the winter season." Since the dense underbrush played such a prominent role in this war, the colonists undoubtedly resented the wilderness as much as their enemies. Major John Talcott, a leader of the Connecticut troops, for example, depicted stalking the Indians as "wilderness work." Such metaphors suggest that many New Englanders probably projected their antipathy for the natives onto the wilderness about them. For besides being an inhospitable environment, the wilderness now actively imperiled the settlers of New England.[15]

Above all, the Indian War of 1675 constituted a social crisis for the Puritan colonists. Not since the early years of settlement did the wilderness condition so threaten the existence of New England colonies. "Wee Are in A very sad Condition," reported the inhabitants of Stonington at the outbreak of hostilities. As the war progressed, fear spread throughout the English settlements. "Many people in these parts are like soules distracted," wrote Samuel Gorton from Rhode Island, "running hither and thither for shelter and no where at ease." The General Court of Connecticut ordered each plantation "to make . . . suitable places of defence" into refuges "for their women and children and others that are not able to help themselves." The Indian outburst terrified the settlers in Massachusetts Bay, and towns as remote from the frontier as Cambridge approved defensive preparations. "These are perillous times which we now live in," preached Increase Mather, "when men are getting their Bread with the peril of their lives, because of the Sword of the Wilderness." People

---

[15] Thomas Stanton to Wait Winthrop, July 11, 1675, Winthrop Mss., XVIII, 138; John Hull to Philip French, September 2, 1675, John Hull's Letter Book, Transcription, I, 271, American Antiquarian Society; Hubbard, *A Narrative of the Troubles*, I, 85, 87; Increase Mather, *A Brief History of the Warr With the Indians in New-England* (Boston, 1676), p. 50; John Talcott to Deputy Governor Treat and the Council of Connecticut, June 8, 1676, quoted in Judd, *History of Hadley*, p. 170.

"can scarce look out of [their] doors," he maintained, "but they are in danger of being seized upon by ravening Wolves, who lye in wait to shed blood, . . . and fear is on every side." [16]

In response to these terrors, the New England colonies urged the settlers to collaborate to protect their plantations from external assault. "Wee are calling in all our out Livers and shall by Gods Assistance doe our best for our Defenc," declared one resident of New London shortly after the outbreak of war. Stressing the need for collective efforts against the common foe, the Connecticut Council ordered the inhabitants to cooperate in gathering the harvest and storing the crops in places of safety. The Connecticut General Court advised the inhabitants of the newly planted town of Derby either to remove to a larger settlement for defense or to "well fortify themselves and stand upon their guarde"; the Court presented similar requests to the residents of Simsbury and Haddum. At this time, the Bay colony recommended that the towns along the Connecticut River consolidate for mutual protection. "To remain in such a scattered state," wrote Secretary Edward Rawson in behalf of the Massachusetts Council, "is to expose lives and estates to the merciless cruelty of the enemy, and is no less than tempting Divine Providence." [17]

Although fear engulfed all the settlements of New Eng-

[16] Thomas Stanton and Thomas Minor to the Governor and Council of Connecticut, June 1, 1675, Samuel Gorton to John Winthrop, Jr., September 11, 1675, Winthrop Mss., XVIII, 137, III, 184; *Pub. Recs. Conn.*, II, 268–69; *Records of the Town of Cambridge*, p. 227; Increase Mather, *An Earnest Exhortation to the Inhabitants of New-England, To hearken to the voice of God in his late and present Dispensations* (Boston, 1676), p. 9.

[17] Daniel Witherell to John Winthrop, Jr., June 30, 1675, Winthrop Mss., XIX, 120; *Pub. Recs. Conn.*, II, 373, 266–67, 412, 425; Edward Rawson to Major Thomas Savage, March 26, 1676, quoted in Trumbull, *History of Northampton*, I, 315–16. The Council of Connecticut disputed Rawson's advice to the town of Hadley; see, *Pub. Recs. Conn.*, II, 438.

land, the war particularly menaced the isolated plantations upon the frontier. "It is hardly imaginable," declared
Daniel Dennison, a leader of the Puritan forces, "the pan-
nick fear that is upon the upland plantations and scattered
places." The uncertainties which Dennison described were
not unfounded rumors, for these remote settlers suffered
immensely during the war as they endeavored to defend
their homes. Woodbury requested assistance from the
Connecticut government because "we have bin Nackid
from any help of man" and feared an Indian attack. The
inhabitants of Northampton rejected the advice of the
Massachusetts Council to merge with Hadley and announced their intention to defend their town. "The Lord
has wonderfully appeared of late for our preservation,"
they argued, "and we fear it would be displeasing unto
him, if we should" surrender to "our enemies, that which
the Lord so eminently delivered out of their hands." The
desertion of so strong a town, they concluded, "may so
animate the enemy, and discourage other plantations, as
may prove no small prejudice unto the country." [18] Despite such determination, however, the Indians destroyed
several towns upon the frontier and threatened the existence of the New England settlements.

Although the colonial governments sympathized with
the embattled frontiersmen, the authorities nevertheless
recognized the importance of preserving the frontier towns
as defensive outposts for the densely populated areas. In
urging the settlers upon the Connecticut River to join
forces, Edward Rawson confessed that "our present work"
is to "secure the principal towns upon the sea coast." In
October 1675, the Massachusetts General Court author-

[18] Daniel Dennison to———, October 28, 1675, printed in *N.E.H.G.R.*,
XXIII (1869), 327; Samuel Sherman to the Council of Connecticut, February 9, 1675[/76], "Wyllys Papers," 231–32; Inhabitants of Northampton to the Council of Massachusetts Bay, March 28, 1676, quoted in Judd,
History of Hadley, p. 159.

ized Thomas Hinchman "to garrison his house upon Mer-
rimacke River," because it "is a very apt place to secure
that frontier." The Bay colony, to be sure, advised the
women and children to withdraw from the more exposed
plantations. But the authorities were determined to retard
the abandonment of the inland settlements by able-bodied
men. In the autumn of 1675, the General Court ordered
that all persons who departed from their habitations without official permission would "forfeite theire interest in
that place." The following spring, the Court reiterated
the need to preserve the inland plantations since the weak-
ening of the frontier would undermine the entire commonwealth. The Court prohibited anyone with military responsibilities from removing from these towns, and enacted various defensive measures.[19] The New England
leaders thereby endeavored to solidify the frontier plantations as a means of safeguarding the colonies as a whole.
By appealing to the need for collectivity and by stressing
the importance of cohesion, the Puritan leaders hoped to
preserve the shaken settlements from utter extinction.

The terrors of King Philip's War shattered the self-confidence of the New England colonies and confirmed the
accuracy of the prophets of woe. "Why are our hedges
broken down." William Hubbard asked rhetorically in the
Massachusetts election sermon of 1676. To most New Englanders, the reply was self-evident. Three years earlier,
Samuel Willard had advised the congregation of Groton
that "Afflictions and Calamities are . . . Gods Judgements, ordered and fore-determined by him." And Increase
Mather had concurred that "War is the greatest of all outward Judgements."[20]

[19] Edward Rawson to Major Thomas Savage, March 26, 1676, quoted
in Trumbull, *History of Northampton*, I, 315–16; *Recs. of Mass. Bay*, V,
54, 48, 51, 65, 81, 79.
[20] William Hubbard, *The Happiness of a People* (Boston, 1676), p.
49; Samuel Willard, *Useful Instructions for a Professing People in times*

In assessing King Philip's War, the Puritan colonists viewed the holocaust as a divine punishment for unrepented sins. We have ignored earlier warnings and lesser judgments, declared the General Court of Massachusetts in November 1675, and hence "God hath heightened our calamity, and given commission to the barbarous heathen to rise up against us, and to become a smart rod and severe scourge to us." Increase Mather, citing the destruction of plantations and the deaths of prominent soldiers, agreed that God had brought the war as a just punishment for His backsliding people. John Eliot suggested that the sin of oversecurity compelled the Lord to chastise New England to remind the people of His ultimate power. "We were too ready to think that we could easyly suppresse that flea," he wrote shortly after the beginning of the war, "but now we find that all the craft is in catching of them, and that in the meane while they give us many a soare nip." Eliot's son, Joseph, compared this war to the catastrophes which had humbled the sinful nations of Europe earlier in the century. "In this our calam[a]tous times," he remarked, "we can the better sympathize with the European stories of the sad effects of these wars." [21]

For more than a decade, the Puritan clergy had warned their congregations of the dangers of worldliness and irreligion. But although the ministers forecasted divine chastisements for these sins, the jeremiads remained an abstract rhetorical device. The Indian war of 1675, however, added new meaning to these prophetical cries. As the natives swarmed through the wilderness and devastated remote

of Great Security and Degeneracy (Cambridge [Mass.], 1673), p. 28; Increase Mather, *The Day of Trouble*, p. 6.

[21] *Recs. of Mass. Bay*, V, 59; Increase Mather, Sermon of February 24, 1675[/76], Mather Mss., American Antiquarian Society; John Eliot to John Winthrop, Jr., July 24, 1675, Photostat, Winthrop Mss.; Joseph Eliot to John Winthrop, Jr., August 16, 1675, Winthrop Mss., IV, 153.

frontier settlements, the colonists became aware of the fragility of their society. The wilderness crisis of 1675 thereby grounded the jeremiads in experience and dramatized the warnings of the Puritan ministry. King Philip's War generated immense fear in New England and forced the settlers to reassess their attitudes toward themselves and the wilderness about them. Drawn together by the collective terrors of the war, the colonists reexamined the relevance of their social theory and attempted to adjust their ideas to satisfy the needs of a wilderness community.

As an immediate effect, of course, the war revitalized the Puritans' distrust of the Indians. Unwilling to distinguish between friends and foes, many New Englanders wished to extirpate all the natives. According to Daniel Gookin, "the common people" opposed not only the Christianized Indians, "but also all such English as were judged to be charitable to them." The defection of the friendly (but non-praying) Indians near Springfield, Gookin confessed, "had a tendency to exasperate the English against all Indians, that they would admit no distinction between one Indian and another." At the height of the crisis, Increase Mather criticized the people of New England for their blind hatred of the Indians. In his subsequent narrative of the war, however, Mather suggested that the natives were untrustworthy. "No man that is an inhabitant of any considerable standing," maintained Mather, can doubt that the Indians "have at sundry times been plotting mischievous devices against" the colonies of New England.[22]

These ideas aggravated the sense of insecurity in the aftermath of the war. In the autumn of 1677, numerous Indians attacked the settlers at Hatfield, "who were a little

---

[22] Gookin, "An Historical Account," 452–53, 454; Increase Mather, "Diary of Increase Mather," *Proc. M.H.S.*, second ser., XIII (1899–1900), 359; Mather, *A Brief History*, pp. 1, 27.

too secure, and too ready to say the bitterness of death was past," and captured several inhabitants. At this time, Increase Mather noted that the residents of Cambridge and Watertown were needlessly alarmed at rumors of an Indian attack. The following spring, one inhabitant of Connecticut reported that the settlers there feared "new trouble from the Indians." "This year begins awfully," declared Increase Mather in 1681. "The latter end of last year was attended with a fearful blazing star whereby the whole earth hath been alarmed," he remarked, and "Tis reported that at Wallingford an Indian appeared in the star." There are "Rumors and great fears," he concluded, "lest N[ew] E[ngland] should be involved in another War with the Indians." And to avoid any misunderstandings, the Massachusetts General Court reenacted the prohibition of trading guns and ammunition to the natives. In subsequent years, similar fears of an Indian conspiracy coursed through the Puritan settlements.[23]

This long series of alarms, as in the earlier years of colonization, betrays an underlying unease among the New England settlers. But significantly the colonists did not advocate the extermination of the Indians. In the years immediately after King Philip's War, the commissioners of the United Colonies recommended that the English erect schools for the natives "as being most probable to Reduce them to Civillity; and capassitate them to be Religiously Instructed." Increase Mather later praised the missionary activities among New Englanders and implied the absence of any genocidal interests. His son, Cotton Mather, tended

---

[23] Hubbard, "A General History," VI, 636–37; Mather, "Diary," 406, 409; Joseph Eliot to Increase Mather, May 3, 1678, John Russell to Increase Mather, March 28, 1681, Samuel Sewall to Increase Mather, October 8, 1688, Joshua Moodey to Increase Mather, January 8, 1688[/89], "Mather Papers," 375, 82–83, 519, 370; *Recs. of Mass. Bay*, V, 136, 304–305, 500; Samuel Sewall, "Diary of Samuel Sewall: 1674–1729," *Colls. M.H.S.*, fifth ser., V–VII (1878–1882), V, 95.

to be vitriolic, but distinguished justly between Indian allies and Indian foes.[24] In Indian affairs, King Philip's War effectively reminded the colonists of the hostility of their environment in the New World. For the remainder of the century, New Englanders cautiously observed the movements of the Indians and repressed any feelings of oversecurity.

The war of 1675, by threatening the very existence of the New England settlements, stimulated a renewed concern for social cohesion. On the eve of conflict, the jeremiads had criticized the breaches within Puritan society and had urged the people to coalesce. "Division hath been one great cause of our defection, and will be a total obstruction unto Reformation, if it continue," preached Samuel Torrey. "It concerns us and becomes us, now that trouble is near, to be a United people," exhorted Increase Mather, for "These are not times for us to be contending one against another." King Philip's War vividly underscored the dangers of social disintegration, for the Indians wrought the greatest havoc upon the isolated settlements along the frontier. In the midst of the crisis, the Massachusetts General Court regretted that "our inhabitants in the severall townes [are] in so scattering and remote a condition." [25]

Since the natives destroyed many of the inland plantations, New England commentators often blamed the war upon overexpansion and suggested that the frontiersmen had tempted the Lord by removing beyond the confines of the Hedge. The founders of Massachusetts "could not well tell what to doe with more Land than a small number

[24] *Acts of the Commissioners,* II, 368; [Increase Mather], *A Brief Relation of the State of New England From the Beginning of that Plantation* . . . (London, 1689), pp. 15–18; Mather, *Magnalia,* I, 215, II, 400, 434.

[25] Torrey, *An Exhortation unto Reformation,* p. 38; Mather, *The Day of Trouble,* pp. 29–30; *Recs. of Mass. Bay,* V, 66.

of acres," intoned William Hubbard, "yet now men more easily swallow down so many hundreds and are not satisfied." Hubbard especially criticized those people who departed from "a good neighbourhood, and the beautiful heritage of Church communion" simply because they hungered for land. "God is knocking the hands of New-England people off from the world, and from new Plantations," he asserted, "till they get them new hearts, resolved to reform this great evill." [26]

Increase Mather echoed these statements and argued that the engrossment of thousands of acres of land simply revealed the increased worldliness of the settlers. In 1679 Mather drafted the report of the Boston synod which condemned unnecessary expansion. "There hath been in many professors an insatiable desire after Land, and worldly Accomodations," lamented the elders of the Bay colony, "yea, so as to forsake Churches and Ordinances, and to live like the Heathen, only that so they might have Elbow-room enough in the world." In describing the course of the Indian war, William Hubbard emphasized that "those Parts of a Country that lye next bordering upon the Coast of the common Enemy" suffered greater hardships than the older plantations. Furthermore, Hubbard noted, many of these settlements "were contented to live without, yea, desirous to shake off all Yoake of Government, both sacred and civil." New Englanders then drew the logical conclusion that these ungodly dispersals provoked the Lord to punish His people. The Almighty "hath let loose the heathen upon us," averred Increase Mather, to cure us of this disease. "And," he concluded ominously, "wo to this land" if it neglect His warnings.[27]

---

[26] Hubbard, *The Happiness of a People*, pp. 58–59.

[27] Mather, *An Earnest Exhortation*, pp. 9–10, 23–24; [Boston Synod], *The Necessity of Reformation With the Expedients subservient thereunto asserted* . . . (Boston, 1679), p. 7; Hubbard, *A Narrative of the Troubles*, II, 267, 256–57.

The authorities of New England resolved to prevent a recurrence of this dispersal by regulating the resettlement of the colonies. In 1676 the Council of the Bay colony ordered the selectmen of the coastal towns "to take effectual care" that the refugees from the frontier "settle themselves . . . in some orderly and diligent way of Imployment and Government." Despite the chaos of war, the Council determined to uphold the traditional social order. In 1677 the General Court of Connecticut declared that the "woefull experiance in the late warr" revealed that "liveing in a single and scattering way, remoate from townships and neighbourhood" weakened the commonwealth and tempted posterity "to degenerate to heathenish ignorance and barbarisme." To prevent such evils and to promote "common safety," the Court ordered that all future town-planters "shall settle themselves in such neerness together" so that "they may be a help, defence and succour each to [the] other against any surpriz, onset or attempt or any comon enemie." The Bay colony similarly provided safeguards for the western towns upon the Connecticut River. In 1677 the General Court ordered each of these settlements to "endeavor the new modelling . . . of their houses, so as to be more compact . . . for theire better deffence against the Indians." And two years later, the inhabitants of Westfield consented to relocate their town for reasons of safety.[28]

The colonial governments also endorsed the resettlement of the inland plantations which had been abandoned during the war. Usually the refugees from the frontier provided the impetus for rebuilding the gutted settlements. The former inhabitants of Deerfield regretted that "our Plantation has become a wilderness, a dwelling for owls

---

[28] *At A Council Held at Boston*, April 4, 1676 [Boston, 1676] [broadside]; *Pub. Recs. Conn.*, II, 328; *Recs. of Mass. Bay*, V, 170, 171, 238–39.

and a pasture for flocks" and expressed sorrow "that a plantation soe circumstanced should lie desolate." The General Court of the Bay colony responded by passing several laws regarding land tenure for "promoting the planting, and speedy setling" of Deerfield. Massachusetts and Connecticut subsequently encouraged the reconstruction and resettlement of the other deserted plantations along the frontier.[29]

The Deerfield petition, which advocated resurrecting that town out of the wilderness, underscored a renewed interest in the postwar years to physically transform the virgin forest. Although New Englanders had praised the metamorphosis of the wilderness prior to King Philip's War, the role of the forest as an ally to the Indians probably stimulated these tendencies by revealing the essential brutality of the American environment. Furthermore, the burdens of rebuilding the settlements compelled New Englanders to stress the transformation of the wilderness. "The English go . . . now to their Old Habitation[s]," observed one colonist in 1677, "and Mow down their Ground, and make Hay, and do other Occasions necessary for their resettling." In a petition to the Massachusetts General Court, the uprooted inhabitants of Groton stressed the importance of rebuilding "waste places" so that they might "see this desolation a quiet habitation." To encourage "the good people in this Colony in cleareing land," the Connecticut General Court ordered that "whosoever shall henceforth inclose land" will be exempted from taxation for this land for four years.[30] The efforts of the

---

[29] The Inhabitants of Deerfield to the General Court of Massachusetts Bay, April 30, 1678, quoted in George Sheldon, *A History of Deerfield, Massachusetts* . . . , 2 vols. (Deerfield, 1895–96), I, 189–90; *Recs. of Mass. Bay*, V, 209, 360–61, 145–46, 345; *Pub. Recs. Conn.*, II, 491, III, 10.

[30] R[ichard] H[utchinson], "The Warr in New-England Visibly

New England authorities to reclaim the wilderness land led logically to the affirmation of the subjugation of additional virgin territories.

In the years after King Philip's War, Puritan commentators continued to extol the transformation of the wilderness. In his history of New England, William Hubbard applauded the changes wrought by a half-century of colonization. Writing of the arrival of the Higginson group in 1629, Hubbard suggested that "New England . . . at that time [did] more resemble a wilderness, then a country whose fields were white unto the harvest." Hubbard praised the transition of New England from a refuge outpost to a settled land. "When God first made man," declared Hubbard, "he gave him a command . . . to increase and multiply, and replenish the earth; of which," Hubbard added, "it is no question but America was intended as a part." Although our "fore-runners were made to fly into the wilderness from the dragon," he maintained that New England was more than a spiritual sanctuary. It is, he concluded, "a country capable with good improvement to maintain a nation of people, after once it comes to be subdued." A decade later, Increase Mather echoed Hubbard's apotheosis of the transformation process. In a few years time, stated Mather, "that which was . . . a howling Wilderness . . . became a pleasant Land, wherein was abundance of all things meet for Soul and Body." Cotton Mather later devoted large portions of his *Magnalia Christi Americana* to lauding the subjugation of the New England wilderness. Mather expressed little love for "the dismal thickets of America" prior to colonization and reserved his strong-

Ended . . ." [1677], printed in Lincoln, *Narratives of the Indian Wars,* pp. 105–106; Petition of the Inhabitants of Groton to the General Court of Massachusetts Bay, May 20, 1679, quoted in Caleb Butler, *History of Groton* (Boston, 1848), p. 88; *Pub. Recs. Conn.,* II, 327–28. See also, Hubbard, "The Epistle Dedicatory," *The Happiness of a People.*

est accolades for the "immense toyl and charge [which] made a wilderness habitable." [31]

The desire among New Englanders to rebuild their colonies after the defeat of King Philip and the renewed interest in transforming the wilderness accelerated the process of frontier expansion in the last quarter of the seventeenth century. In regulating the resettlement of the inland communities, the Massachusetts General Court acknowledged its acceptance of frontier extension. Although the General Court intended to promote social cohesion, it ordered that "no deserted towne or *new plantation* shallbe inhabitted" without permission of the magistrates.[32] Whether or not the authorities recognized the full implications of their decision, this order betrayed the difficulty of restraining the disruptive forces of the wilderness. Despite their disclaimers to the contrary, the leaders of New England conceded that they could not impede the dispersal of plantations. In subsequent years, both Massachusetts and Connecticut approved the establishment of numerous plantations, usually with the requirement that the settlers transplant "an able orthodox minister." Thus King Philip's War merely delayed the growth of New England, for the colonies continued to expand, though perhaps unevenly, in the ensuing years.[33]

The acceptance of dispersal, however, merely highlighted the basic problem of Puritan society in the wilderness: the need to reconcile expansion and collectivity. During the last decade of the seventeenth century, New England commentators deplored the tendency to transplant beyond the Lord's Hedge without the holy ordi-

[31] Hubbard, "A General History," V, 112, 26, 22; [I. Mather], *A Brief Relation,* pp. 4–5; Mather, *Magnalia,* I, 552, 85, 214, II, 526–27, 583.

[32] *Recs. of Mass. Bay,* V, 213–14 (itals. added).

[33] *Recs. of Mass. Bay,* V, 360, 408–409, 410–11, 426, 467, 482, 486, 487; *Pub. Recs. Conn.,* III, 83, Mather, *Magnalia,* I, 88.

nances. In a lecture preached in 1690, Cotton Mather argued that "those places which the [Indian] Devastations of the last year fell upon, were the more pagan skirts of New-England, where no Minister of God was countenanced." In the Massachusetts election sermon of 1698, Nicholas Noyes urged the General Court to protect "the Frontiers and Out-Plantations" from the Indians. Cotton Mather responded to this concern for the inland settlements by admonishing the frontiersmen to provide for their own safety by seeking the Lord. Mather stressed the protective benefits of true religion and urged the "scattered plantations" to reform. In 1707, while lauding the settlers "in the Exposed Frontiers" of New England as "the best People in the Land," he implored them to establish godly institutions. During the recent wars, he reminded them, those plantations "that have had Churches regularly formed in them, have generally been under a more sensible Protection of Heaven" while "the Unchurched Villages" have been "utterly broken up."[34]

The paradox which plagued Puritan society in the wilderness thereby persisted beyond the seventeenth century. The commitment among New Englanders to replenish the soil and transform the wilderness contradicted the desires of the Puritan establishment to maintain a modicum of social cohesion. Cotton Mather summarized this dilemma in the Massachusetts election sermon of 1690, *The Serviceable Man* . . . , in which he lamented the decline of religion and education in the remote inland plantations. "Doubtless, men of ingenuity, might instruct

[34] Mather, *The Present State of New-England* . . . , p. 32; Nicholas Noyes, *New Englands Duty and Interest to Be a Habitation of Justice and Mountain of Holiness* . . . (Boston, 1698), pp. 83–84; Mather, *Magnalia*, II, 572, 675, 678; Cotton Mather, *Frontiers Well-Defended: An Essay to Direct the Frontiers of a Countrey Exposed unto the Incursions of a Barbarous Enemy* . . . (Boston, 1707), pp. 3, 7, 28, 31. For additional discussion of this problem, see Clifford K. Shipton, "The New England Frontier," *New England Quarterly*, X (1937), 25–36.

us how at once we may Advance our Husbandry," he preached, "and yet Forbear our Disperson; and moreover at the same time fill the Countrey with a Liberal Education." [35] There was, of course, no solution to this problem. Social security engendered confidence which, in turn, fostered a disregard for social stability. The terror of King Philip's War posed as a chilling reminder of the uncertainties of the wilderness condition. But the defeat of the Indians and, more important, the ongoing transformation of the forest convinced New Englanders that such menaces were both transitory and surmountable. With renewed confidence, the settlers turned their backs upon the warnings of their ministers and returned to their tasks of subjugating the wilderness.

[35] Cotton Mather, *The Serviceable Man* . . . (Boston, 1690), p. 51.

Epilogue

IN retrospect, the pleas of Cotton Mather and his col-
leagues indeed sound like voices crying in the wilderness. Their inability to understand the changes occurring
in their society, nevertheless, reveals the importance of
the American environment in the development of New
England thought. The complex ideas transported to America underwent significant changes in the New World. To
be sure, most of the symbolic views of the wilderness
persisted and, in slightly variant form, enabled the Puritan colonists to better interpret their experiences in New
England. The tenacity of these perspectives reflects the
common inadequacy of language to keep pace with new
experiences. Yet the ongoing transformation of the wilderness into settled habitations and continued frontier expansion altered considerably the original meaning of the
old rhetoric. The absence of self-consciousness of change
did not mean that the modifications within Puritan
thought were unimportant. For as the Puritans defined
their existence, they were compelled to reconcile the
vision with the reality.

Their solutions to this problem revealed the essential
ambiguities of their original position. Though the paradoxes remained to the end of the seventeenth century, it
is apparent that the Puritan colonists were less than satisfied with their answers. As a transplanted people, they

attempted to draw upon familiar forms of expression. Thus their subsequent endeavors to make these metaphors meaningful in the New England situation illuminates the delicate balance between continuity and novelty in the evolution of Puritan attitudes toward the wilderness. As one commonwealth split into many, as new lands were brought under the plough, the Puritans examined their society from new vantage points and with new insights. The wilderness experience thereby influenced in fundamental ways the self-image of seventeenth-century New England society.

Selected Bibliography

IN preparing this study, the author examined every available printed primary source relating to the topic. The existence of several excellent bibliographies, however, proscribes the necessity of reproducing a complete listing here. Interested readers should consult Perry Miller and Thomas Johnson, eds., *The Puritans*, 2 vols., with revised bibliographies by George McCandlish (New York, 1963). These compilations should be supplemented with the bibliographies in Babette May Levy, *Preaching in the First Half Century of New England History* (Hartford, 1945) and Alden T. Vaughan, *New England Frontier: Puritans and Indians, 1620–1675* (Boston, 1965). The selected bibliography which follows consists of those works which have been most helpful in exploring the relationship between Puritanism and the wilderness.

I. Manuscript Sources

John Cotton Mss., Prince Collection, Boston Public Library.
Seaborne Cotton Mss., New-York Historical Society.
John Davenport Mss., American Antiquarian Society.
John Davenport Mss. Sermons, 1649–52, Shepard Historical Society of the First Church of Cambridge [Massachusetts], Congregational.
John Hull Mss. Commonplace Books, Boston Public Library.
John Hull Letter Books (Transcriptions), American Antiquarian Society.
Mather Mss., American Antiquarian Society.
Miscellaneous Bound Mss., I–II, Massachusetts Historical Society.
Miscellaneous Mss. Sermons, Massachusetts Historical Society.

Shepard Mss., American Antiquarian Society.

Thomas Shepard Mss. Sermons, Houghton Library (Harvard College Library).

Sloane Mss. (Transcriptions), Library of Congress.

Winthrop Mss., Massachusetts Historical Society.

Winthrop-Davenport Mss., New York Public Library.

II. *Public Records*

Boston Town Records, 1634–1660 (*Second Report of the Record Commissioners of the City of Boston*). Boston, 1877.

Burt, Henry M., ed. *The First Century of the History of Springfield: The Official Records from 1636 to 1736.* 2 vols. Springfield, Mass., 1898.

Dorchester Town Records (*Fourth Report of the Record Commissioners of the City of Boston*). 2nd ed. Boston, 1883.

Hoadly, Charles J., ed. *Records of the Colony or Jurisdiction of New Haven, from May, 1653, to the Union.* Hartford, 1858.

——. *Records of the Colony and Plantation of New Haven, from 1638–1649.* Hartford, 1857.

Pulsifer, David, ed. *Acts of the Commissioners of the United Colonies.* 2 vols. Boston, 1859.

The Records of the Town of Cambridge (*Formerly Newtowne*) *Massachusetts: 1630–1703.* Cambridge, 1901.

Shurtleff, Nathaniel B., ed. *Records of the Governor and Company of the Massachusetts Bay in New England.* 5 vols. Boston, 1853–54.

Trumbull, J. Hammond, ed. *Public Records of the Colony of Connecticut.* 15 vols. Hartford, 1850–90.

III. *Printed Primary Sources*

Adams, Charles Francis, ed. *Antinomianism in the Colony of Massachusetts Bay, 1636–1638.* Boston, 1894.

Allin, John. *The Spouse of Christ Coming out of affliction, leaning upon Her Beloved.* Cambridge, 1672.

Alsop, George. "A Character of the Province of Maryland . . . , 1666," in Hall, *Narratives of Early Maryland*, pp. 337–87.

Ames, William. *Conscience with the Power And Cases thereof . . . .* London, 1643.

[Anonymous]. "Narrative [addressed to Secretary Cooke?] concerning the settlement of New England—1630," in *Pro-*

ceedings of the Massachusetts Historical Society, 1st. ser.,
V (1862), 129–31.

At A Council Held at Boston. [Boston, 1676].

Bradford, William. *Of Plymouth Plantation: 1620–1647.* Edited
by Samuel Eliot Morison. New York, 1967.

[Bradstreet, Anne]. *The Works of Anne Bradstreet in Prose
and Verse.* Edited by John Harvard Ellis. New York, 1932.

[Boston Synod]. *The Necessity of Reformation With the Expedients subservient thereunto, asserted . . . .* Boston,
1679.

Bulkeley, Peter. *The Gospel Covenant: Or the Covenant of
Grace Opened.* London, 1646.

Carlton, William R., ed. "Overland to Connecticut in 1645: A
Travel Diary of John Winthrop, Jr.," in *New England Quarterly,* XIII (1940), 494–510.

Charlevoix, Pierre de. *Journal of a Voyage to North-America.*
2 vols. Ann Arbor, 1966.

Chauncy, Charles. *Gods Mercy, shewed to his people in giving
them a faithful Ministry and schooles of Learning for the
continual supplyes thereof.* Cambridge, 1655.

[Clap, Roger]. *Memoirs of Capt. Roger Clap.* Boston, 1731.

Cobbet, Thomas. *The Civil Magistrates Power In matters of
Religion Modesty Debated . . . .* London, 1653.

Cotton, John. "An Abstract of the Laws of New England," in
Hutchinson, comp., *A Collection of Original Papers,* pp. 161–
79.

——. *The Bloudy Tenent, washed, And made white in the
bloud of the Lambe.* London, 1647.

——. *A Brief Exposition with Practical Observations upon the
Whole Book of Canticles.* London, 1655.

——. "A Brief Exposition Upon Ecclesiastes," in *Nichol's Series
of Commentaries,* II. Edinburgh, 1868.

——. *A Brief Exposition of the whole Book of Canticles, or,
Song of Solomon . . . .* London, 1642.

——. *The Churches Resurrection, or the Opening of the fift
and sixt verses of the 20th. Chap. of the Revelation.* London,
1642.

——. *An Exposition upon the Thirteenth Chapter of the Revelation.* London, 1655.

——. *Gods Mercie Mixed with his Justice.* Edited by Everett
H. Emerson. Gainesville, Florida, 1958.

——. "Gods Promise To His Plantations," in *Old South Leaflets,* III. Boston, n.d.

——. *The Powring Out of the Seven Vials: Or, An Exposition of the Sixteenth Chapter of the Revelation* . . . . London, 1645.

——. *The Way of the Congregational Churches Cleared,* in Hooker, *Survey of the Summe of Church-Discipline.*

Danforth, Samuel. *A Brief Recognition of New-Englands Errand into the Wilderness.* Cambridge, 1671.

——. *MDCXLVIII An Almanack for the Year of our Lord 1648* . . . . Cambridge, 1648.

Davenport, John. *Another essay for the Investigation of the Truth in Answer to two Questions* . . . . Cambridge, 1663.

[D'Ewes, Sir Simonds]. *Autobiography and Correspondence of Sir Simonds D'Ewes.* Edited by James Orchard Halliwell. 2 vols. London, 1845.

Dudley, Thomas. "Letter to the Countess of Lincoln," in Young, *Chronicles of the First Planters,* pp. 303–341.

"The Early Records of Charlestown," in Young, *Chronicles of the First Planters,* pp. 369–87.

Eliot, John. "The Christian Commonwealth: or, The Civil Policy of The Rising Kingdom of Jesus Christ," in *Collections of the Massachusetts Historical Society,* 3rd ser., IX (1846), 127–64.

——. *Communion of Churches: Or, the Divine Management of Gospel Churches By the Ordinance of Councils* . . . . Cambridge, 1665.

——. "A Late and Further Manifestation of the Progress of the Gospel amongst the Indians in New-England," in *Collections of the Massachusetts Historical Society,* 3rd. ser., IV (1834), 261–88.

——. "The Learned Conjectures touching the Americas," in Thomas Thorowgood, *Jews in America, or, Probabilities That the Americans are of that Race.* London, 1660.

Fitch, James. *An Holy Connexion; Or a true Agreement Between Jehovahs being a Wall of Fire to his People, and the Glory in the midst thereof.* Cambridge, 1674.

Force, Peter, ed. *Tracts and Other Papers Relating Principally to the Origin, Settlement, and Progress of the Colonies in North America* . . . . 4 vols. Washington, 1838–46.

[Gookin, Daniel]. "An Historical Account of the Doings and Sufferings of the Christian Indians in New England in the years 1675, 1676, 1677," in *Transactions and Collections of the American Antiquarian Society,* II ((1836), 423–534.

Gookin, Daniel. "Historical Collections of the Indians in New England," in *Collections of the Massachusetts Historical Society,* 1st. ser., I (1792), 141–226.

Graves, Thomas. "A Letter sent from New-England by Master Graves, Engineer, now there resident," in Young, *Chronicles of the First Planters,* pp. 264–66.

[Hakluyt, Richard]. *The Original Writings & Correspondence of the two Richard Hakluyts.* Edited by E. G. R. Taylor. 2 vols. London, 1935.

Hall, Clayton Colman, ed. *Narratives of Early Maryland: 1633–1684.* New York, 1910.

[Herbert, George]. *The Works of George Herbert.* Edited by F. E. Hutchinson. Oxford, 1941.

Higginson, Francis. "New-Englands Plantation. Or a Short and True Description of the Commodities and Discommodities of that Countrey," in Young, *Chronicles of the First Planters,* pp. 240–59.

——. "Some brief Collections out of a Letter that Mr. Higginson sent to his friends at Leicester," in Young, *Chronicles of the First Planters,* pp. 260–64.

——. "A True Relation of the last Voyage to New-England," in Young, *Chronicles of the First Planters,* pp. 215–38.

Higginson, John. *The Cause of God and his people in New-England.* Cambridg[e], 1663.

[Horne, Robert?] "A Brief Description of the Province of Carolina . . . , 1666," in Salley, *Narratives of Early Carolina,* pp. 66–73.

Hooke, William. *New-Englands Sence, of Old-England and Irelands Sorrowes,* in Emery, *The Ministry of Taunton,* I, 99–129.

——. *New Englands Teares, for Old Englands Feares. Preached in a Sermon on July 23, 1640 . . . .* London, 1641.

Hooker, Thomas. *The Application of Redemption.* London, 1657.

——. *A Comment upon Christ's Last Prayer In the Seventeenth of John . . . .* London, 1656.

———. *The Covenant of Grace opened* . . . . London, 1649.

———. *The Danger of Desertion or A Farewell Sermon of Mr. Thomas Hooker* . . . . London, 1641.

———. *The Saints Dignitie and Dutie. Together with the Danger of Ignorance and Hardnesse* . . . . London, 1651.

———. *A Survey of the Summe of Church-Discipline.* London, 1648.

Hubbard, William. "A General History of New-England from the Discovery to 1680," in *Collections of the Massachusetts Historical Society,* 2nd. ser., V–VI (1848).

———. *The Happiness of a People.* Boston, 1676.

———. *A Narrative of the Troubles with the Indians In New-England.* Edited by Samuel G. Drake under the title *The History of the Indian Wars in New England.* 2 vols. Roxbury, Massachusetts, 1865.

Hull, John. "Diary of Public Occurrences," in *Transactions and Collections of the American Antiquarian Society,* III (1857), 167–265.

———. "Some Passages of God's Providence," in *Transactions and Collections of the American Antiquarian Society,* III (1857), 141–64.

H[utchinson], R[ichard]. "The Warr in New-England Visibly Ended . . . , 1677," in Lincoln, *Narratives of the Indian Wars,* pp. 101–106.

[Hutchinson, Thomas, comp.]. *A Collection of Original Papers Relative to the History of the Colony of Massachusetts-Bay.* Boston, 1769.

Jantz, Harold S., ed. "The First Century of New England Verse," in *Proceedings of the American Antiquarian Society,* LIII (1943), 219–58.

Johnson, Edward. *Johnson's Wonder-working Providence, 1628–1651.* Edited by J. Franklin Jameson. New York, 1910.

Josselyn, John. "An Account of Two Voyages to New-England," in *Collections of the Massachusetts Historical Society,* 3rd. ser., III (1833), 211–354.

Kennedy, P. A., ed. "Verses on the Puritan Settlement of America, 1631," in Thoroton Society, *Record Series,* XXI (Nottingham, 1962), 37–39.

[Laud, William]. *The Works of . . . William Laud.* 7 vols. Oxford, 1848–60.

Le Page du Pratz. *The History of Louisiana, or of the Western Parts of Virginia and Carolina* . . . . London, 1774.

Lescarbot, Marc. *The History of New France.* Translated by W. L. Grant. 3 vols. Toronto, 1907–14.

"Letter of Emanuel Downing," in *Proceedings of the Massachusetts Historical Society,* 2nd. ser., VIII (1894), 383–85.

"Letter of John Wiswall," in Historical Manuscripts Commission, *Fourteenth Report* (London, 1894), appendix, part IV, 56.

"Letters written by Rev. Ezekiel Rogers of Rowley, Rev. Daniel Rogers of Wethersfield, and Samuel Shepard of Cambridge, 1626–1647," in *Essex Institute Historical Collections,* LIII (1917), 215–27.

Lincoln, Charles H., ed. *Narratives of the Indian Wars: 1679–1699.* New York, 1913.

Mason, John. "A Brief History of the Pequot War," in *Collections of the Massachusetts Historical Society,* 2nd. ser., VIII (1819), 120–53.

Masters, John. "Letter to Lady Barrington and Others, March 14, 1630/1," in *New England Historical and Genealogical Register,* XCI (1937), 68–71.

"The Mather Papers," in *Collections of the Massachusetts Historical Society,* 4th ser., VIII (1868).

Mather, Cotton. *Frontiers Well-Defended: An Essay to Direct the Frontiers of a Countrey Exposed unto the Incursions of a Barbarous Enemy* . . . . Boston, 1707.

——. *Magnalia Christi Americana; Or, The Ecclesiastical History of New-England.* 2 vols. Hartford, 1855.

——. *The Present State of New-England* . . . . Boston, 1690.

——. *The Serviceable Man* . . . . Boston, 1690.

——. *The Wonders of the Invisible World* . . . . Boston, 1693.

Mather, Increase. *A Brief History of the Warr With the Indians in New-England.* Boston, 1676.

[——]. *A Brief Relation of the State of New England From the Beginning of that Plantation* . . . . London, 1689.

——. *The Day of Trouble is Near* . . . . Cambridge, 1674.

——. "Diary of Increase Mather," in *Proceedings of the Massachusetts Historical Society,* 2nd. ser., XIII (1899–1900), 340–74, 398–411.

——. *An Earnest Exhortation to the Inhabitants of New-*

England, *To hearken to the voice of God in his late and present Dispensations* . . . . Boston, 1676.

——. *Essay for the Recording of Illustrious Providences* . . . . Boston, 1684.

[——]. *The Life and Death of* . . . *Richard Mather.* Cambridge, 1670.

——. *The Mystery of Israel's Salvation Explained and Applyed, Or a Discourse Concerning the General Conversion of the Israelitish Nation.* Cambridge, 1669.

——. *A Relation Of the Troubles which have hapned in New-England, By reason of the Indians there.* Boston, 1677.

——. *Wo to Drunkards* . . . . Cambridge, 1673.

[Mather, Richard, and John Davenport]. *Church-Government and Church-Covenant discussed in an answer of the elders of the several churches in New England to two and thirty questions* . . . . London, 1643.

Mather, Richard. "Richard Mather's Journal," in Young, *Chronicles of the First Planters,* pp. 445–81.

Metcalfe, Michael. "To all the true professors of Christs gospel within the city of Norwich," in *New England Historical and Genealogical Register,* XVI (1862), 279–84.

Mitchel, Jonathan. *A Discourse of the Glory To which God hath called Believers By Jesus Christ.* 2nd ed. Boston, 1721.

——. *Nehemiah on the Wall in Troublesom Times.* Cambridge, 1671.

Morton Thomas. *New English Canaan.* Edited by Charles Francis Adams, Jr. Boston, 1883.

New Englands First Fruits, in Morison, *Founding of Harvard College,* Appendix D.

Norton, John. *Abel being Dead yet Speaketh* . . . . London, 1658.

——. *The Answer To* . . . *Appolonius* . . . . Edited and translated by Douglas Horton. Cambridge, 1958.

——. *The Heart of N-England rent at the Blasphemies of the Present Generation.* Cambridg[e], 1659.

——. *Three choice and profitable sermons.* Cambridge, 1664.

Noyes, Nicholas. *New Englands Duty and Interest to Be a Habitation of Justice and Mountain of Holiness* . . . . Boston, 1698.

Oakes, Urian. *New-England Pleaded with, And pressed to*

consider things which concern her Peace, at least in this her Day. Cambridge, 1673.

Oxenbridge, John. *New-England Freemen Warned and Warmed; To be Free indeed having an Eye to God in their Elections.* [Boston], 1673.

——. *A Quickening Word for the Hastening a Sluggish Soul to a Seasonable Answer to the Divine Call . . . .* Cambridge, 1670.

[Paine, John]. "John Paine's Journal," in *Publications of the Colonial Society of Massachusetts,* XVIII (1917), 188–91.

[——]. "John Paine's Petition, 1672," in *Publications of the Colonial Society of Massachusetts,* XVIII (1917), 191–92.

"Pincheon Papers," in *Collections of the Massachusetts Historical Society,* 2nd ser., VIII (1826), 227–49.

Preston, John. *Life Eternall . . . .* 4th ed. London, 1634.

——. *The New Covenant, or the Saints Portion . . . .* London, 1629.

Quinn, David Beers, ed. *The Roanoke Voyages: 1584–1590.* 2 vols. London, 1955.

"Relation of the Plott—Indian," in *Collections of the Massachusetts Historical Society,* 3rd. ser., III (1833), 161–64.

"Report of Edmund Browne [to Sir Simonds D'Ewes]," in *Publications of the Colonial Society of Massachusetts,* VII (1905), 76–80.

Salley, Alexander S., Jr., ed. *Narratives of Early Carolina: 1650–1708.* New York, 1911.

S[altonstall], N[athaniel]. "The Present State of New-England With Respect to the Indian War," in Lincoln, *Narratives of the Indian Wars,* pp. 19–50.

Sewall, Samuel. "Diary of Samuel Sewall. 1674–1729," in *Collections of the Massachusetts Historical Society,* 5th ser., V–VII (1878–82).

——. "Letter-Book of Samuel Sewall," in *Collections of the Massachusetts Historical Society,* 6th ser., I–II (1886–88).

Shepard, Thomas. "The Autobiography of Thomas Shepard," in *Publications of the Colonial Society of Massachusetts,* XXVII (1932), 343–400.

——. "Meditations and Experiences," in *Three Valuable Pieces* (Boston, 1747), Part III.

——. *New Englands Lamentation for Old Englands present*

errours, and divisions, and their feared future desolations if not timely prevented . . . . London, 1645.

——. *The Parable of the Ten Virgins* . . . , in *Works of Thomas Shepard,* II.

——. *A Short Catechism Familiarly Teaching the Knowledg of God and of our Selves.* Cambridg[e], 1654.

——. *The Sincere Convert, Discovering the Paucity of True Beleevers; and the great difficulty of Saving Conversion.* London, 1642.

——. "Some Select Cases Resolved," in *Three Valuable Pieces* (Boston, 1747).

——. *The Sound Beleever. Or A Treatise of Evangelicall Conversion.* London, 1653.

——. *Subjection to Christ in all his Ordinances, and Appointments, The best means to preserve our Liberty* . . . , in *Works of Thomas Shepard,* III, 273–384.

——. *Theses Sabbaticae. Or, The Doctrine of the Sabbath.* London, 1649.

——. "Thomas Shepard's Election Sermon, in 1638," in *New England Historical and Genealogical Register,* XXIV (1870), 361–66.

——. *Wine for Gospel Wantons.* Cambridge, 1668.

——. *The Works of Thomas Shepard.* Edited by John A. Albro. 3 vols. Boston, 1853.

Shepard, Thomas [and John Allin]. *A Defence of the Answer made unto the Nine Questions or Positions sent from New-England.* 3rd ed. titled *A Treatise of Liturgies, Power of the Keyes, And of Matter of the Visible Church* . . . . London, 1653.

Shepard, Thomas, Jr. *Eye-Salve; Or, A Watch-Word From our Lord Jesus Christ unto his Churches.* Cambridge, 1673.

Shipton, Clifford K., ed. "The autobiographical Memoranda of John Brock, 1636–1659," in *Proceedings of the American Antiquarian Society,* LIII (1943), 96–105.

Smith, John. "Advertisements For the unexperienced Planters of New-England, or any where," in *Collections of the Massachusetts Historical Society,* 3rd. ser., III (1833), 1–53.

——. "A Description of New-England," in *Collections of the Massachusetts Historical Society,* 3rd. ser., VI (1837), 95–140.

——. "A Map of Virginia. With a Description of the Countrey . . . ," in *Travels and Works,* I.

——. *Travels and Works of Captain John Smith: President of
Virginia, and Admiral of New England, 1580–1631.* Edited
by Edward Arber. 2 vols. Edinburgh, 1910.

Stearns, Raymond Phineas, ed. "Correspondence of John
Woodbridge, Jr., and Richard Baxter," in *New England
Quarterly,* X (1937), 557–83.

Stoughton, William. *New-Englands True Interest; Not to Lie.*
Cambridge, 1670.

Taylor, Edward. "Diary," in *Proceedings of the Massachusetts
Historical Society,* 1st. ser., XVIII (1880–81), 5–18.

Torrey, Samuel. *An Exhortation unto Reformation . . . .*
Cambridge, 1674.

"A [True] Relation Concernynge the Estate of New-England,"
in *New England Historical and Genealogical Register,* XL
(1886), 68–73.

Underhill, John. "News from America," in *Collections of the
Massachusetts Historical Society,* 3rd. ser., VI (1837), 1–28.

[Ward Nathaniel]. *The Simple Cobler of Aggawam in America,* in Force, *Tracts and Other Papers,* III.

White, Father Andrew. "A Briefe Relation of the Voyage unto
Maryland . . . , 1634," in Hall, *Narratives of Early Maryland,* pp. 27–45.

White, John. "The Planter's Plea or the grounds of plantations
examined and usuall objections answered," in *Proceedings
of the Massachusetts Historical Society,* LXII (1929), 367–
425.

Whitfield, Henry. "The Light appearing more and more towards the perfect Day. Or, A Farther Discovery of the
present state of the Indians in New-England . . . ," in *Collections of the Massachusetts Historical Society,* 3rd. ser.,
IV (1834), 100–47.

Whitmore, William H., ed. *The Colonial Laws of Massachusetts.* Boston, 1889.

Wigglesworth, Michael. "Autobiography," in *New England
Historical and Genealogical Register,* XVII (1863), 137–39.

——. "Gods Controversy with New England," in *Proceedings
of the Massachusetts Historical Society,* XII (1873), 83–93.

——. *Meat out of the Eater.* Cambridge, 1670.

Willard, Samuel. *Useful Instructions for a Professing People in Times of Great Security and Degeneracy.* Cambridge, 1673.

Williams, Roger. *The Complete Writings of Roger Williams.* Edited by Perry Miller. 7 vols. New York, 1963.

———. "A Key into the Language of America: Or, An help to the Language of the Natives in that part of America, called New-England," in *Complete Writings,* I, 77–282.

———. "Letters of Roger Williams, 1632–1682," in *Complete Writings,* VI.

[Wilson, John?]. "The Day-Breaking, if not the Sun-Rising of the Gospell with the Indians in New-England," in *Collections of the Massachusetts Historical Society,* 3rd. ser., IV (1834), 1–23.

W[inslow], E[dward]. *Good Newes From New-England* . . . . London, 1624.

———. "New Englands Salamander," in *Collections of the Massachusetts Historical Society,* 3rd ser., II (1830), 110–45.

Winthrop Papers, 5 vols. Boston, 1929—.

[Winthrop, John]. *A Short Story of the Rise, Reign, and Ruine of the Antinomians* . . . , in Adams, *Antinomianiam in-Massachusetts,* pp. 67–233.

Winthrop, John. *Winthrop's Journal, "History of New England" 1630–1649.* Edited by James Kendall Hosmer. 2 vols. New York, 1908.

———. "A Modell of Christian Charity. Written on Board the Arbella, on the Atlantic Ocean," in *Collections of the Massachusetts Historical Society,* 3rd. ser., VII (1838), 31–48.

Wright, Franklin M., ed. "A College First Proposed, 1633: Unpublished Letters of Apostles Eliot and William Hammond to Sir Simonds D'Ewes," in *Harvard Library Bulletin,* VIII (1954), 255–82.

Wood, William. *New Englands Prospect.* Edited by C. Deane. Boston, 1865.

"Wyllys Papers," in *Collections of the Connecticut Historical Society,* XXI (1924).

Young, Alexander, comp. *Chronicles of the First Planters of the Colony of Massachusetts Bay, From 1623 to 1636.* Boston, 1846.

IV. Secondary Sources

Adams, Sherman W., and Henry R. Stiles. *The History of Ancient Wethersfield, Connecticut.* 2 vols. New York, 1904.

Albro, John A. *The Life of Thomas Shepard.* Boston, 1847.

Andrews, Charles M. *The Colonial Period of American History.* 4 vols. New Haven, 1934–40.

Baritz, Loren. "The Idea of the West," *American Historical Review,* LXVI (1961), 618–40.

Bridenbaugh, Carl. *Vexed and Troubled Englishmen: 1590–1642.* New York, 1968.

Black, Robert C., III. *The Younger John Winthrop.* New York, 1966.

Butler, Caleb. *History of Groton* . . . . Boston, 1848.

Calder, Isabel M. *The New Haven Colony.* New Haven, 1934.

——. "John Cotton and the New Haven Colony," *New England Quarterly,* III (1930), 82–94.

Cawley, Robert Ralston. *Unpathed Waters: Studies in the Influence of the Voyagers on Elizabethan Literature.* Princeton, 1940.

——. *The Voyagers and Elizabethan Drama.* Boston, 1938.

Currier, John J. *History of Newbury, Mass., 1635–1902.* Boston, 1902.

Dunn, Richard S. *Puritans and Yankees: The Winthrop Dynasty of New England, 1630–1717.* Princeton, 1962.

East, Robert A. "Puritanism and New Settlement," *New England Quarterly,* XVII (1944), 255–64.

Egleston, Melville. "The Land System of the New England Colonies." *Johns Hopkins University Studies in Historical and Political Science,* IV (Baltimore, 1886), Parts XI–XII, 5–56.

Eisinger, Chester E. "The Puritans' Justification for Taking the Land," *Essex Institute Historical Collections,* LXXXIV (1948), 131–43.

Emery, Samuel Hopkins. *The Ministry of Taunton,* 2 vols. Boston, 1853.

French, Allen. *Charles I and the Puritan Upheaval: A Study of the Causes of the Great Migration.* London, [1955].

Haller, William Jr. *The Puritan Frontier: Town-Planting in New England colonial development, 1630–1660.* New York, 1951.

Harris, Marshall. *Origin of the Land Tenure System in the United States.* Ames, Iowa, 1953.

Hartley, Edward Neal. *Ironworks on the Saugus: the Lynn and Braintree ventures of the Company of Undertakers of the Ironworks in New England.* Norman, Okla., 1957.

Heimert, Alan. "Puritanism, the Wilderness, and the Frontier," *New England Quarterly,* XXVI (1935), 361–82.

Howard, Leon. *Literature and the American Tradition.* New York, 1960.

Hudson, Alfred Sereno. *The History of Sudbury, Mass.* Sudbury, 1889.

Hutchinson, Thomas. *The History of the Colony and Province of Massachusetts-Bay.* Edited by Lawrence Shaw Mayo. 3 vols. Cambridge, 1936.

Jones, Howard Mumford. *O Strange New World: American Culture, the Formative Years.* New York, 1964.

Judd, Sylvester. *History of Hadley . . . .* 2nd. ed. Springfield, Mass., 1905.

Kellaway, William. *The New England Company: 1649–1776.* London, 1961.

Laslett, Peter. *The World We Have Lost.* New York, 1965.

Leach, Douglas Edward. *Flintlock and Tomahawk: New England in King Philip's War.* New York, 1958.

——. *The Northern Colonial Frontier: 1607–1763.* New York, 1966.

Le Guin, Charles A. "Sea Life in Seventeenth-Century England," *American Neptune,* XXVII (1967), 111–34.

Levy, Babette May. *Preaching in the First Half Century of New England History.* Hartford, 1945.

Lockridge, Kenneth A. "The History of a Puritan Church: 1637–1736," *New England Quarterly,* XL (1967), 399–424.

Miller, Perry. *Errand Into the Wilderness.* Cambridge, 1956.

——. *The New England Mind: From Colony to Province.* Cambridge, 1953.

——. *The New England Mind: The Seventeenth Century.* New York, 1939.

——. *Orthodoxy in Massachusetts, 1630–1650.* Cambridge, 1933.

Morgan, Edmund S. *The Puritan Dilemma: The Story of John Winthrop.* Boston, 1958.

Morison, Samuel Eliot. *Builders of the Bay Colony.* Boston, 1930.

——. *The Founding of Harvard College.* Cambridge, 1935.

——. "The Plantation of Nashaway—an Industrial Experiment," *Publications of the Colonial Society of Massachusetts,* XXVII (1932), 204–22.

Nash, Roderick. *Wilderness and the American Mind.* New Haven, 1967.

O'Gorman, Edmundo. *The Invention of America: An inquiry into the historical nature of the New World and the meaning of its history.* Bloomington, 1961.

Paige, Lucius R. *History of Cambridge, Massachusetts, 1630–1877.* Boston, 1877.

Parry, J. H. *The Age of Reconnaissance.* New York, 1963.

Pearce, Roy Harvey. "The 'Ruines of Mankind': The Indian and the Puritan Mind," *Journal of the History of Ideas,* XIII (1952), 200–17.

Powell, Sumner Chilton. *Puritan Village: The Formation of a New England Town.* Middletown, Conn., 1963.

Rutman, Darrett B. *Winthrop's Boston: Portrait of a Puritan Town, 1630–1649.* Chapel Hill, 1965.

Sachse, William L. "The Migration of New Englanders to England, 1640–1660," *American Historical Review,* LIII (1948), 251–78.

Shattuck, Lemuel. *History of the Town of Concord.* Boston, 1835.

Sheldon, George. *A History of Deerfield, Massachusetts . . . .* 2 vols. Deerfield, 1895–96.

Shipton, Clifford K. "The New England Frontier," *New England Quarterly,* X (1937), 25–36.

Sprunger, Keith L. "William Ames and the Settlement of Massachusetts Bay," *New England Quarterly,* XXXIX (1966), 66–79.

Tillyard, E. M. *The Elizabethan World Picture.* London, 1943.

Trumbull, James Russell. *History of Northampton Massachusetts . . . .* 2 vols. Northampton, 1898.

Turner, Frederick Jackson. "The First Official Frontier of the Massachusetts Bay," in *The Frontier in American History.* New York, 1920.

Vaughan, Alden T. *New England Frontier: Puritans and Indians, 1620–1675.* Boston, 1965.

Walzer, Michael. *The Revolution of the Saints: A Study in the Origins of Radical Politics.* Cambridge, 1965.

Ward, Harry M. *The United Colonies of New England, 1643–1690.* New York, 1961.

Willey, Basil. *The Seventeenth Century Background: Studies in the Thought of the Age in Relation to Poetry and Religion.* New York, 1955.

Williams, George Huntston. *Wilderness and Paradise in Christian Thought: The Biblical Experience of the Desert in the History of Christianity and the Paradise Theme in the Theological Idea of the University.* New York, 1962.

Wright, Louis B. *Religion and Empire: The Alliance between Piety and Commerce in English Expansion, 1558–1625.* Chapel Hill, 1943.

Ziff, Larzer. "The Social Bond of the Church Covenant," *American Quarterly,* X (1958), 454–62.

V. *Unpublished Dissertations*

Denholm, Andrew Thomas. "Thomas Hooker: Puritan Teacher, 1586–1647," Ph.D. dissertation, The Hartford Seminary Foundation, 1961.

Gilsdorf, Joy Bourne. "The Puritan Apocalypse: New England Eschatology in the Seventeenth Century," Ph.D. dissertation, Yale University, 1965.

Index